Drawn from Life

Edinburgh Studies in Film and Intermediality

Series editors: Martine Beugnet and Kriss Ravetto
Founding editor: John Orr

A series of scholarly research intended to challenge and expand on the various approaches to film studies, bringing together film theory and film aesthetics with the emerging intermedial aspects of the field. The volumes combine critical theoretical interventions with a consideration of specific contexts, aesthetic qualities, and a strong sense of the medium's ability to appropriate current technological developments in its practice and form as well as in its distribution.

Advisory board
Duncan Petrie (University of York)
John Caughie (University of Glasgow)
Dina Iordanova (University of St Andrews)
Elizabeth Ezra (University of Stirling)
Gina Marchetti (University of Hong Kong)
Jolyon Mitchell (University of Edinburgh)
Judith Mayne (The Ohio State University)
Dominique Bluher (Harvard University)

Titles in the series include:

Romantics and Modernists in British Cinema
John Orr

Framing Pictures: Film and the Visual Arts
Steven Jacobs

The Sense of Film Narration
Ian Garwood

The Feel-Bad Film
Nikolaj Lübecker

American Independent Cinema: Rites of Passage and the Crisis Image
Anna Backman Rogers

The Incurable-Image: Curating Post-Mexican Film and Media Arts
Tarek Elhaik

Screen Presence: Cinema Culture and the Art of Warhol, Rauschenberg, Hatoum and Gordon
Stephen Monteiro

Indefinite Visions: Cinema and the Attractions of Uncertainty
Martine Beugnet, Allan Cameron and Arild Fetveit (eds)

Screening Statues: Sculpture and Cinema
Steven Jacobs, Susan Felleman, Vito Adriaensens and Lisa Colpaert (eds)

Drawn From Life: Issues and Themes in Animated Documentary Cinema
Jonathan Murray and Nea Ehrlich (eds)

edinburghuniversitypress.com/series/esif

Drawn from Life
Issues and Themes in Animated Documentary Cinema

Edited by Jonathan Murray and Nea Ehrlich

EDINBURGH
University Press

Edinburgh University Press is one of the leading university presses in the UK. We publish academic books and journals in our selected subject areas across the humanities and social sciences, combining cutting-edge scholarship with high editorial and production values to produce academic works of lasting importance. For more information visit our website: edinburghuniversitypress.com

© editorial matter and organisation Jonathan Murray and Nea Ehrlich, 2019, 2020
© the chapters their several authors, 2019, 2020

Edinburgh University Press Ltd
The Tun – Holyrood Road
12 (2f) Jackson's Entry
Edinburgh EH8 8PJ

First published in hardback by Edinburgh University Press 2019

Typeset in Garamond MT Pro by
Servis Filmsetting Ltd, Stockport, Cheshire

A CIP record for this book is available from the British Library

ISBN 978 0 7486 9411 2 (hardback)
ISBN 978 1 4744 3182 8 (paperback)
ISBN 978 0 7486 9412 9 (webready PDF)
ISBN 978 1 4744 1400 5 (epub)

The right of the contributors to be identified as authors of this work has been asserted in accordance with the Copyright, Designs and Patents Act 1988 and the Copyright and Related Rights Regulations 2003 (SI No. 2498).

Contents

List of Figures	vii
The Contributors	viii
Editors' Introduction *Nea Ehrlich and Jonathan Murray*	1

Part 1 Past and Present

1. From Contextualisation to Categorisation of Animated Documentaries — 15
   Pascal Lefèvre

2. Before Sound, there was Soul: The Role of Animation in Silent Nonfiction Cinema — 31
   Mihaela Mihailova

3. Indeterminate and Intermediate or Animated Nonfiction: Why Now? — 47
   Nea Ehrlich

Part 2 Defining Terms and Contexts

4. Animated Documentary, Recollection, 'Re-enactment' and Temporality — 69
   Paul Ward

5. The Documentary Attraction: Animation, Simulation and the Rhetoric of Expertise — 84
   Leon Gurevitch

6. Never Mind the Bollackers: Here's the Repositories, Sites and Archives in Nonfiction Animation — 106
   Paul Wells

Part 3 Films and Filmmakers

7   Drawings to Remember 129
    Nanette Kraaikamp

8   Adorno, Lewis Klahr and the Shuddering Image 143
    Andrew Warstat

9   The Reasons for Animating Reality: Animated Documentary and
    Re-enactment in the Work of Jonas Odell 158
    Lawrence Thomas Martinelli

10 Memory Drawn into the Present: *Waltz with Bashir* and
    Animated Documentary 172
    Jonathan Murray

Part 4 Practice-based Perspectives

11 Making *The Trouble with Love and Sex* 191
    Jonathan Hodgson

12 'Does this look right?' Working Inside the Collaborative
    Frame 206
    Samantha Moore

13 Creative Challenges in the Production of Documentary
    Animation 221
    Sheila M. Sofian

Index 235

unproductive' (2010: 79). As a compensatory alternative, the scene also, in Hetrick's view, 'introduces the film's concern with memory, trauma, and responsibility' (ibid.: 85). More supportively, however, Ohad Landesman and Roy Bendor propose that *Waltz with Bashir*'s opening scene:

> establishes right from the onset the basic thematic contradictions that epitomize Folman's film: the unresolved tension between dream and reality, the absurdly short distance between sanity and psychosis, and the need to bridge cinematically between what must be shown and what cannot be represented. (2011: 354)

It is worth following these critics' general lead in seeing the visualisation of Rein-Buskila's story as a possible synecdoche for other aspects of *Waltz with Bashir*. Consideration of the way in which Folman depicts, and accords a structurally privileged narrative position to, this part of film offers a useful basis on which to explain and assess the film's deliberate assumption of animated documentary form and the ideological consequences of that creative decision.

Firstly, the visual treatment of Rein-Buskila's torment swiftly establishes the affective power of Folman's choice to employ Flash animation software (amongst other production tools) in order to make his film (Cheng 2009). Conventional live-action documentary interviews were shot initially, with an animated feature then storyboarded and produced from this raw material (Dawson 2008: 94). This directorial decision has a visceral emotional impact. From *Waltz with Bashir*'s outset, the viewer is immersed in a lengthy series of animated reconstructions of private nightmares and memories related to the 1982 Lebanon War. In this sense, how and what Rein-Buskila shares with Folman (and how and what Folman subsequently shares with the viewer) work to support the director's emphatic contention in many promotional interviews that:

> Animation is the only way to tell this story, with memories, lost memories, dreams and the subconscious. If you want to feel any freedom as a filmmaker to go from one dimension to another . . . the best way to do it was animation. (Erikson 2008)

Given the bewilderingly surrealistic contents of many of the memories and oneiric fantasies depicted throughout *Waltz with Bashir*, whether Rein-Buskila's or those of other protagonists, it is difficult to imagine a more logistically simple way (relatively speaking) in which the narrative content of the former could have been recreated other than via animated re-enactment. At various narrative junctures, the viewer witnesses Folman's eerily ambiguous recurring dream about coming upon the catastrophe of Sabra and Shatila;

only initial memory fragment from Lebanon – one as surreally displaced as Rein-Buskila's nightmare – links him to Sabra and Shatila. Depicted in slightly varying audiovisual forms three times as *Waltz with Bashir* proceeds, a naked teenage Folman emerges from the sea outside Beirut as dawn breaks. He then stumbles, somnambulant, into the ruined city and upon an onrushing crowd of grief-stricken Palestinian women. The process of recording the testimony of former comrades and other Israeli observers eventually prompts Folman to remember that he was one of the soldiers who fired flares to aid the Phalangists. The intrinsic private and public meanings of his initial dream-memory purportedly revealed, *Waltz with Bashir* then switches from animated recreation to contemporaneous live-action news footage in its final moments. Television reportage displays the objective horror of Sabra and Shatila's immediate aftermath: piles of massacred corpses and survivors' inconsolable grief. But despite this intensely memorable narrative climax, one of the most critically controversial aspects of *Waltz with Bashir* relates to the extent to which it may (or may not) be viewed as 'a historically nuanced film' (Hetrick 2010: 78). Nicholas Hetrick, for example, complains that *Waltz with Bashir* is severely compromised by several glaring historiographical lacunae:

> Neither Folman nor his interview subjects provides an explanation of the conflict in Lebanon or the reasoning behind the Israeli military presence there. Consequently, viewers know only the surreal experience of armed conflict . . . apart from significant understanding of what occasioned it. (ibid.: 84)

Thus, while *Waltz with Bashir* may be viewed as a courageous, compassionate and/or formally innovative film, it is hardly without controversial or equivocal aspects, aesthetically, conceptually and ideologically speaking.

To reconnoitre this complex creative and critical territory it is helpful to start at the beginning. Rein-Buskila's recurring nightmare represents a logical place for Folman to open his film – 'a very conscious decision' (Dawson 2008: 93) in the director's words – given that this event represented the project's autobiographical catalyst. Additionally, however, *Waltz with Bashir*'s opening scene also constitutes an equally apposite place at which to commence evaluation of the resultant finished film. This is because the sequence in question possesses an overdetermined status within its host text in multiple ways. Rein-Buskila's recurring nightmare establishes many of *Waltz with Bashir*'s key formal and historiographical strategies and parameters; it also lays the ground for a significant number of the critical conclusions, both positive and negative, that can be drawn about these. For Nicholas Hetrick, the film's opening scene is a consciously self-justifying, even self-exculpating, act. It 'establishes [the work's] rhetorical purpose of working out largely private psychological issues [thus] mak[ing] objections to its relative [historical] decontextualization

Rein-Buskila is haunted by the memory of the twenty-six dogs he shot during Israeli Army night raids on Lebanese villages. Decades later, the canine revenants reverse the roles of hunter and hunted within their traumatised executioner's mind.

An animated recreation/revelation of Rein-Buskila's recurring private torment constitutes *Waltz with Bashir*'s opening because the same disclosure helped to initiate the film in real life. Hearing the anguish of Rein-Buskila's memories of the 1982 war provoked Ari Folman to confront the highly limited nature of his own memories of participating in the same historical event (Dawson 2008). *Waltz with Bashir* therefore narrates the process of its own gestation as a highly personal documentary narrative (Corbett 2016; Yosef 2010: 316). His initial conversation with Rein-Buskila leads Folman to seek out other former comrades – Carmi Cna'an, Ronny Dayag, Shmuel Frenkel, Dror Harazi – from early-1980s Lebanon. Interviews with the men recount eviscerating and evasive memories of war, and are complemented by animated visualisations of those recollections. Such testimonies are complemented by more scientific insights into the workings of human memory from a psychologist friend of Folman's and an expert on post-traumatic stress disorder. These various conversations allow the director to gradually recover – and to some extent, perhaps recreate – his own story from and of the Lebanon conflict. Some critics have therefore seen *Waltz with Bashir*'s animated documentary aesthetic as a conceptual analogue for the quasi-therapeutic process of individual memory work that Folman undertakes within the film's narrative. What use of animation within a documentary context shares with individual human attempts to recuperate traumatic experience is a pronounced investment in the possibility and potential of 'extended reenactment' (Kraemer 2015: 60). Robert Moses Peaslee, for instance, argues that animated documentary as a cinematic mode possesses deep affinities with any substantive formal or quasi-formal process of memory work. Both modes of enquiry share a structuring aspiration to 'represent reality as experienced – in constantly present, simultaneously visible layers of time, place, and consciousness' (2011: 230).

Most crucial of all in this regard is Folman's attempt to clarify his stubborn (and at first apparently insurmountable) subjective confusion as to his physical and moral proximity to the notorious massacre of Palestinian civilians in the Sabra and Shatila refugee camps in Beirut. This atrocity was perpetrated by Lebanese Christian Phalangist militia (allies of the invading Israeli forces) between 16 and 18 September 1982. Israeli troops stationed immediately outside the camps made no attempt to stop the killing and even lit the night sky with flares so that the Phalangists might execute their actions more easily (Naylor 1983; Shahid 2002; Llewellyn 2013). Folman's image practice. Some observers emphasise allegedly problematic and/or paradoxical aspects of the animated documentary phenomenon: 'the documentary's moving pictures are filtered through the distorting lens of hand-drawn images ... an apparent contradiction' (Aoun 2009: 150). From this position, animation's escalating visibility within documentary contexts can look often like an artistic strategy geared towards 'implying reality, rather than demanding it, and potentially risking the possibility of denying or undermining it' (Burgin 2010: 72). Others adopt a more neutral observational stance, concluding simply that the early-twenty-first-century growth of aesthetically hybrid animated documentary works like Folman's indicates 'growing acceptance within the [global film] industry of wilful blurring of once-strict borders between genres and techniques' (Kraemer 2015: 57). Lastly, however, many commentators make ambitious claims for both *Waltz with Bashir* specifically and animated documentary more generally. Folman's film has been widely understood as a particularly suggestive individual instance of postmodern filmmaking practice (Peaslee 2011: 228). This is because of its perceived 'ability to articulate through its [animated documentary] presentation the very impossibility of authentic representation' (Burgin 2010: 72). Consequently, the film's purported 'rejection of the metanarrative of documentary realism ... represents a new way of thinking about reality and/vs. representation' (Corbett 2016: 56). Ohad Landesman and Roy Bendor, for example, argue that:

> *Waltz with Bashir* exemplifies the ways in which the animated documentary ... serve[s] as a vehicle for fostering a new relationship between the viewer and the documentary text ... one that moves away from faith in [the truth status of] photographic indexicality ... [and instead] trust[s] the documentary text to be making truth claims that reflect the world in sophisticated ways. (2011: 354)

In what follows here, textual analysis of *Waltz with Bashir* aims to further identify and explore some of the film's defining characteristics that make it such an object of ongoing critical fascination and contention.

The surreal animated pursuit sequence that starts *Waltz with Bashir* flags Folman's audacious attempt to use animation as a documentary tool, one capable of pursuing the most uncomfortable and half-repressed of private and public historical truths. As opening titles roll, a pack of feral, yellow-eyed dogs hurtles towards the rapidly retreating camera's viewpoint. The hounds wreak havoc in present-day central Tel Aviv before surrounding the home of their intended quarry, a nondescript middle-aged Israeli man. The scene's form and content suggest it is too nightmarish to be true; all the more disturbing, then, when it is revealed as the stuff of true nightmare, the recurring dream of Boaz Rein-Buskila, an Israeli veteran of the 1982 Lebanon War.

CHAPTER 10

Memory Drawn into the Present: Waltz with Bashir *and Animated Documentary*
Jonathan Murray

The current volume and many recent studies (see, for example, Honess Roe 2013; Formenti 2014) demonstrate just how much creative and critical interest in animated documentary filmmaking has grown over the past decade. This essay discusses perhaps the most widely debated individual film associated with that phenomenon, Israeli director Ari Folman's *Waltz with Bashir* (2008). The notably complex narrative and thematic subject matter of Folman's feature has provoked scholarly responses ranging across many disciplines, including trauma studies (Ashuri 2010; Morag 2013; Rastegar 2013) and memory studies (Stewart 2010; Yosef 2010). Most prominently of all, though, *Waltz with Bashir* has been widely seen as a pioneering and potentially paradigmatic reference point within ongoing attempts to establish animated documentary cinema's potential and aesthetic, conceptual and ethical parameters. Granted, there exist analyses of Folman's film that take the idea of 'animated documentary' as a relatively neutral descriptive label (see, for example, Yosef 2010: 311). Much more common, however, is the idea of *Waltz with Bashir* as an intriguing taxonomical test case. Indeed, Folman himself already drew attention to this notion at the time of *Waltz with Bashir*'s original theatrical release. He complained then that he had:

> been hassled so much about the animated documentary idea. It was so much trouble raising the budget because I declared [my film] 'an animated documentary.' . . . [Some potential funders] said it can't be a documentary because it's animated. So I went to animation and fiction funds and they said they couldn't support it because it's a documentary. (Esther 2009)

The sense of *Waltz with Bashir* as a work that calls received critical and cultural categories and conventions into question has only deepened in the years since.

In part this is because, as well as spanning multiple disciplinary fields, critical debate around *Waltz with Bashir* also displays heterogeneity in terms of the assessments that the film has provoked of animated documentary's possible strengths and weaknesses as a contemporarily emergent mode of moving especially valuable contemporary artistic attempt to think through and beyond such comforting, but perhaps now unsustainable, received axioms.

BIBLIOGRAPHY

Bendazzi, Giannalberto (2015), *Animation: A World History, Volume III: Contemporary Times*, Waltham, MA: Focal Press.

Canemaker, John (1988), *Storytelling in Animation: The Art of the Animated Image*, Los Angeles: American Film Institute.

Dobroiu, Stefan (2015), 'ptThe Magic Mountain*: an exploration of an exemplary destiny', *Cineuropa*, 6 July, <http://www.cineuropa.org/nw.aspx?t=newsdetail&l=en&did=295122> (last accessed 20 October 2016).

Glynne, Andy (2012), *Documentaries . . . and How to Make Them, Revised Edition*, Harpenden: Creative Essentials.

I Was a Winner, film, directed by Jonas Odell. Sweden: Apparat, 2016.

Kriger Judith (2012), *Animated Realism: A Behind-the-Scenes Look at the Animated Documentary Genre*, Waltham, MA: Focal Press.

Kroustallis, Vassilis (2014), '*Truth has Fallen* review: animating miscarriages of justice', *ZippyFrames.com*, 8 June, <http://www.zippyframes.com/index.php?option=com_content&view=article&id=2048%3Atruth-has-fallen-review-animating-miscarriages-of-justice&catid=191%3Aindie-features&Itemid=100101> (last accessed 20 October 2016).

Land, Ellie (2014), '"Tussilago" by Jonas Odell', *Animated Documentary.com*, 15 February, <https://animateddocs.wordpress.com/2014/02/15/tussilago-by-jonas-odell/> (last accessed 20 October 2016).

Lies, film, directed by Jonas Odell. Sweden: Filmtecknarna, 2008.

Martinelli, Lawrence Thomas (2012), *Il Documentario animato*, Rome: Tunué.

Nasta, Dominique (2013), *Contemporary Romanian Cinema: the History of an Unexpected Miracle*, London: Wallflower Press.

Never Like the First Time!, film, directed by Jonas Odell. Sweden: Filmtecknarna, 2006.

Robertson, Barbara (2004), 'Psychorealism: animator Chris Landreth creates a new form of documentary filmmaking', *Computer Graphics World*, 27: 7, <http://www.cgw.com/Publications/CGW/2004/Volume-27-Issue-7-July-2004-/Psychorealism.aspx> (last accessed 20 October 2016).

Ryan, film, directed by Chris Landreth. Canada: Copperheart Entertainment and National Film Board of Canada, 2004.

Sapovídeos (2010), 'Jonas Odell – interview about "Lies"', 29 April, <http://videos.sapo.pt/CpzFgm9NL5dKYFQBZ8fd> (last accessed 20 October 2016).

Singer, Gregory (2004), 'Landreth on "Ryan"', *Animation World Network*, 4 June, <http://www.awn.com/vfxworld/landreth-ryan> (last accessed 20 October 2016).

Sjöberg, Patrik (2015), 'Face blind: documentary media and subversion of surveillance', in Alexandra Juhasz and Alisa Lebow (eds), *A Companion to Contemporary Documentary Film*, Hoboken, NJ: John Wiley and Sons, pp. 629–46.

Sondhi, Jason (2010), '*Lies* by Jonas Odell', <https://www.shortoftheweek.com/2010/11/21/lies/> (last accessed 20 October 2016).

Tussilago, film, directed by Jonas Odell. Sweden: Filmtecknarna and Film Väst, 2010.

subjective perspective, necessary to give a fuller view of the wider documentary reality that her voice-over narration explicates, is explicitly declared by Odell. Effective communication of the emotional sphere of his characters, and in particular of 'A', is central to the viewer's more complete understanding of the story that she and Odell tell in collaboration. While the expression of emotional subjectivity is communicated by the verbal content and tone of 'A''s voice-over, it is also undoubtedly intensified by Odell's accompanying animated imagery. Towards the film's end, a drawn colour image of 'A' huddled up rotates in front of a huge 1978, the date then gradually changing, year after year, as the camera slowly dollies out. 'A' explains how 'I've lost my life. They didn't give me any medication between 1977 and 2003. I got no help . . . I almost feel like I was kidnapped instead. I'm the one who's been kidnapped for thirty years.' *Tussilago*'s fade out and end credits, accompanied by a few articulated electric piano notes, stresses an overarching feeling of solitude, emptiness and loss.

Conclusion

This chapter has tried to demonstrate the extent to which Jonas Odell's animated documentary cinema is one in which a variety of graphic styles, editing strategies and distinctive forms of visual layout respond not only to the filmmaker's personal aesthetic needs and preferences, but also to the at least equally pressing need to integrate and interrogate the specific historical, social and cultural contexts and requirements of his interviewees' personal stories and histories. Odell's extensive and enterprising recourse to animation within various documentary contexts allows him to condense and communicate the content of complex historical events (whether private or public), and protagonists' equally multifaceted descriptions and recollections of these. This is so in ways that are not always readily possible within live-action documentary film. His cinematic practice demonstrates the notable extent to which use of animation opens up an exciting and thought-provoking range of symbolic, metaphoric and visual strategies for documentary filmmakers, even (or perhaps, especially) when such artists attempt to bring to the screen human stories that are logistically difficult to tell in one or more regards. Odell's explicit acceptance and foregrounding of the fact that, even in documentary cinema, artists and audiences alike are always unavoidably dealing with manipulated, rather than unmediated, images and narratives is a valuable act of creative honesty and integrity. If the increasingly visible concept of animated documentary cinema per se problematises certain notions of truth and reality that have long influenced live-action traditions of documentary filmmaking, Jonas Odell's work represents one re-mediated into fully animated form: images of the gunman's fidgeting fingers and the cowboy raising his gun to shoot are created via animated movement, rather than through the kind of logical inference practised by a comic book reader as they move between one illustrated panel and another.

Moreover, the comic strip Odell animates here is a fictitious one, created purely for *Tussilago*'s specific purposes: there is no such comic story or series titled *Texas Hardy*. As the viewer looks more closely, they realise that the depicted strip is multilingual in nature: captions between one panel and another repeat the same sentence in English, but speech balloons within panels contain phrases and film titles in Italian, referencing canonical works such as Sergio Leone's *Duck, You Sucker!* (1971) and *Once Upon a Time in the West* (1968). The integrated multimedia approach that characterises Odell's filmmaking more generally is especially well-synthesised within this short sequence. He invents a comic strip that represents an ingenious homage to *fumetto nero* (an Italian tradition of adult comic books) and the Spaghetti Western and then animates it, all the while remembering to channel this exuberant creative invention and quotation in the service of the subjective content of 'A"s verbally narrated recollections ('He was mad about Charles Bronson too. He said he'd love to be an actor and I think that he was actually playing a part. But what part? Was he playing the role of a terrorist?'). The gunman starring in the fictitious comic strip looks like both Kröcher and Bronson, a pointed conflation that succinctly expresses the former's delusional, self-aggrandising mentality.

Other sequences within *Tussilago* display a similarly effective development of animated visuals that respond to different elements of 'A"s voice-over narration, a de facto extended flashback that is at once both subjective and documentary in its character and content. For example, at one point 'A' expresses personal discomfort as viewers see her (in computer-processed live-action footage) passing by a range of typographic characters that represent an unbearable flow of abstract ideological sloganeering while simultaneously shaping a physical wall that is visible in the background. An apple-green colour palette, manifested through the visible shapes of a huge sun, grass and plants, provides an ironic chromatic accompaniment to 'A' and Kröcher's walks around Stockholm, as the couple pursue a decidedly unfruitful search for government minister Leijon's home. 'A"s uneasiness is only resolved when she stops to pick some flowers, which for her mean colour and life: 'We never found her house, but came home with coltsfoots and anemones.' The plants in question provide yellow visual detail that breaks up the sad and strict black-and-white setting for the film at this point: 'That's how dangerous I was . . . I found it uncomfortable and thought: "I'm just a normal girl".' Here, the need to comprehensively express 'A"s at this point is composed of black-and-white triangles that, as the camera's viewpoint moves back towards long shot and away from the two onscreen protagonists, gradually turn into matchstick triangles. The precarious matchstick-made structures that occupy Kröcher's idle time are metaphorical of the actual fragility of his apparently solid terrorist projects. In terms of implied meaning, this scene can be related to the film's opening shots of the street that 'A' walks along. In addition to their descriptive narrative function, both scenes also deliberately foreground subjective viewpoints characterised by an implied sense of instability, groundlessness and inevitable collapse. The shot in question then ends with Kröcher's terrorist group watching on TV, 'the incident' (in 'A''s words) 'that was the reason why they wanted to kidnap Leijon'. On an orange background, a new shot shows at its centre a vintage portable television screening black-and-white live news coverage of the event in question. Captions explain how two terrorists and one hostage lost their lives during an April 1975 embassy siege provoked by that building's forcible occupation by RAF supporters. After the siege was over, Anna-Greta Leijon was the Swedish government minister in charge of deporting the terrorists responsible from the country. The camera then zooms back to the television set and viewers see archive footage of Leijon speaking. Kröcher immediately resolves to hijack an airplane in order to free the RAF prisoners. But 'A', in an attempt to hold her bombastic lover back from an impossible mission and also to gain time, suggests that he instead kidnaps the minister. Having accepted that suggestion, Kröcher uses matchboxes to explain to his followers what he now has in mind. Yet instead of being physically manoeuvred by hand (as they would be in real life), the matches appear to move on their own by animated means. The whole operation is explained in voice-over and illustrated by animated matchsticks that represent the various characters in projected action; the sequence then ends with a matchbox in Kröcher's hands as he lights a cigarette.

Tussilago's consequent inference that Kröcher's plan is a tragicomically flimsy one is confirmed by 'A''s voice-over: 'It sounded crazy – their talk about shooting guards and using violence. It was like the Wild West. He was crazy about the Wild West.' The governing aesthetic of the film's images then quickly adapts in response to that suggestion, producing images of black-and-white Western comic strips and quoting from the Spaghetti Western filmic canon. A range of classic Western stereotypes and icons can be found within this comic-strip sequence: the duel, the nervous trigger hand on the holster, the gunfighter's splayed legs, the gun firing. Odell's virtual camera does not follow the prescribed reading order of the comic panels, however, but instead crosses the page diagonally, browsing certain panels that are especially emblematic in their illustration of the story that 'A' narrates. The panels in question are manner of late-1960s and early-1970s psychedelic iconography. When 'A''s voice-over changes in tone or moves on to another fragment of memory, the visual look of *Tussilago* shifts in tandem: not in a flat illustrative way, but in a manner that enhances each scene by means of strongly connotative images. Maps, animation on packaging cardboard, typed characters, cut-out pictures, Indian-ink-drawn flowers and plants that recall the late nineteenth-century art nouveau style of Aubrey Beardsley: the inventory of *Tussilago*'s visual quotations and interventionist solutions is remarkably copious and various in character for a short film work.

Odell's free use of the extensive variety of cinematic techniques and visual languages facilitated by his decision to work within an animated filmmaking mode allows *Tussilago* to underscore the above-noted expressive value that animation can bring to filmmakers' attempts to document some form or aspect of lived historical reality within their work. 'A''s autobiographical voice-over narration recalls a period of bank robberies, getaways and illicit trade in weapons with a casual, and at times amused, tone: that of someone who looks back with ironical disenchantment at a time in her life characterised by personal naivety, illusion and lack of awareness. However, this aspect of her story alternates with more affectionate memories of romantic moments and relationships. Both 'A''s voice-over and Odell's accompanying images take time to scrutinise this hitherto private and subjective side of her human experience. Retrospective self-awareness ('A' has served a prison term for her juvenile errors) leads her to re-read Kröcher's identity and actions in a more critical light. Remembering certain events of 1974, she comments that when 'he built that ship out of matches, it was a warship'. At this point, an animated sequence devised around wooden matches and their boxes begins to articulate a deconstruction of Kröcher's self-fashioned strong-man persona. The male terrorist is portrayed as restless and macho ('He wasn't doing anything. I was doing everything. I worked and I cooked.') while a tracking shot links together a structure of serial triangles made of wooden matches (the material results of Kröcher's empty boredom), a black pan with two sausages, copies of the *Frankfurter Allgemeine* newspaper flung on a table, piled books, stacked beer cans and yet more triangular patterns of matches. Kröcher's hands quickly handle the matches, which also appear – in a metaphorically loaded visual gesture – in vertical formation at his shoulders. Everything collapses miserably, however – at which point viewers see 'A' sweeping the matches from the table with her arm and into the dustbin.

This signature theme, namely, of the fragile and precarious structures that Kröcher typically constructs, is then intensified as *Tussilago* continues. For example, he is seen from above, busy talking to a black-hooded person holding a sign with an anarchist circle-A. The floor filling the entire frame

To give a more specific sense of this method at work, we might consider *Tussilago*'s opening shot, which follows 'A' from behind as she walks along a street. A sequence of five suspended electric piano notes is repeated on the soundtrack, helping to build suspense preceding the first decisive event in the film's narrative. A green caption on a black background establishes place and time: Stockholm, 1977. The surrounding diegetic setting – a cobblestone street, urban pavements – is visibly destabilised by Odell's use of digital effects. As patches of the total image move and wobble, a feeling of precarious steadiness is suggested from the outset, an inference which anticipates symbolically *Tussilago*'s overarching connotation of its central protagonist's experience. Meanwhile, subtitles explain the backstory that leads to 'A''s arrest, concluding, as they fade out, that 'this is her story'. From here on, 'A''s voice-over testimony begins. *Tussilago*'s visual imagery becomes more coloured and mutable as the film flashes back to 1972, presenting the city (and within it, the specific house party at which 'A' first meets Kröcher). The visual design of this latter scene visually evokes the exuberant popular cultural iconography and aesthetics of the early 1970s: abundant white circles on a black wall, orange-, violet- and purple-coloured shirts and sweaters, and regular, visually punctuating dotting of frames in a manner that recalls halftone screens or extremely low-resolution analogue newsprint reproductions of photographs. This notably precise aesthetic touch vividly conveys a sense of the free, lively and easy-going elements of avowedly non-conformist lifestyles of the period, and thus effectively and evocatively connotes key elements of the historic sociocultural setting within which *Tussilago* develops.

Tussilago's live-action actors are also digitally retouched with the same visual effects described above. In a single narrative sequence, 'A' and Kröcher have coffee in a shop and then drink wine at her home. In the meantime, the background layout is enriched by floral and Indian motifs that characterise period setting and narrative atmosphere; 'A''s simultaneous voice-over narration recounts the progress of the characters' romantic encounters up to the point at which Kröcher starts lodging at her flat. The multimedia nature of both Odell's preferred visual aesthetic and repertoire of contemporaneous popular cultural reference points is visible in his flowing insertion into the narrative of images of black-and-white photographic proofs and a vinyl long-playing record on a turntable, as the narrating voice recalls a song from the soundtrack of *Easy Rider* (Dennis Hopper, 1969) ('He used to call it our national anthem'). Meanwhile, the wall behind the bed on which the couple happily cavort half-naked is made to appear like the sleeve art of a Steppenwolf record. Marked by an electric guitar's rock rhythm, each shot of the couple moving and of the surrounding room assumes a different bright colour (apple-green, bright violet, translucent indigo, orange-red) in the

Consideration of such issues brings the present discussion to *Tussilago*, perhaps Odell's most accomplished (and also unified) animated documentary to date. Unlike its predecessors, this film narrates a single story, that of West German terrorist Norbert Kröcher's former girlfriend, a woman known here only as 'A'. Kröcher, 'A', and a few others were arrested in Stockholm in late March and early April 1977. A member of *Die Rote Armee Fraktion* (RAF; also widely known as the Baader-Meinhof group), Kröcher was at the head of a terrorist unit that in 1976 planned the kidnapping of Swedish minister of immigration, Anne-Greta Leijon. Yet *Tussilago* is not centred on Kröcher – or at least, not in a direct way. Rather, the film focuses on his less well-known partner, a woman whose more subjective, personal (and even romantic) side emerges from her own words, collected via interview. 'A''s voice-over retraces her reckless years of juvenile irresponsibility, a period divided between mad love and bank robberies: a paradoxical sense of her ingenuous, almost innocent, side is created as a result. Odell chooses to re-enact events narrated, resorting to live-action shooting of professional actors and then treating the resulting footage with a variety of digital effects, integrating it with animation, graphics and whatever else he deems expressively useful. Above all else, this allows him to contextualise 'A''s testimony in terms of historical time, encompassing elements of 1970s Swedish fashion, way of life, collective thought and popular cultural iconography.

In this work, Odell makes consciously precise creative choices that allow disparate aesthetic, documentary, informational and cinematographic materials to converge harmoniously within a compact (though complete) short film work that combines a sense both of the historical objectivity of events narrated and the subjective feelings of individuals directly involved in those happenings, whether at the time in question or in memories of it since. In particular, a Pop Art aesthetic variously highlights dotted screen printing in the manner of Roy Lichtenstein, then-fashionable floral layouts feature in many backgrounds and textures, and a range of period movie posters and vinyl record covers are seen. Still photographs and newspaper pages come to life, through the animated mobility they are granted within individual shots, increasing narrative meaning and further defining the film's chosen aesthetics and rhythm. As in his other work, Odell avoids iconic redundancy and often leaves the background to his animated images clear, thus emphasising the most thematically interesting and significant visual elements seen in the foreground. At other times, the background imagery contributes a diverse range of ostentatiously signifying aesthetics and images, including period newspaper layouts and collages of contemporaneous press clippings and comic strips, to many of the film's scenes.

Odell does not try to evade or obscure this problem, and asks searching questions as to what a 'true story' really is, including the extent to which the participants and/or witnesses who articulate such narratives can or cannot be believed. As he notes of *Lies*,

> When you work with these allegedly true stories, you get kind of paranoid about whether people are actually telling the truth or whether they are lying. That led me to thinking that lies and deception might be a great theme for a film. (Sapovídeos 2010)

Since *Never Like the First Time!*, Odell has asked himself to what extent that which he (and we) understand and accept as 'truth' is really inherent in (and/ or is actively invented by) the documentary interviews given by his subjects. Odell appears to conclude that this vexed issue is one that remains as open as it is complex. In a 2010 interview with the present author, for example, he says of his animated documentary process and projects that:

> There is always manipulation and you are never totally objective as a film-maker, so I think in a way that openly showing that this is manipulated or staged actually is more honest. All films are partly about film itself, just like all books are partly about literature. A medium is more honest openly dealing with its own nature. (Martinelli 2012: 131–4)

Odell's concerns in this regard are ones shared by other animated documentary filmmakers dealing thoughtfully with issues relating to the reproduction and mediation of reality through film, with ethically loaded, influential concepts of authenticity and truth, and with the traditionally purported honesty of documentary narration. For example, in a 2010 interview (also with the present author), Chris Landreth noted that 'honesty' was 'the word I would use' to describe the most desirable forms of intent behind, and ultimate impact of, judiciously used animated techniques and aesthetics within documentary filmmaking contexts:

> In that imagery there is something very personal that you cannot do with live action. Live action would be subtracting, while in the case of *Ryan* [, for example,] I think [the use of animation] was really important in telling that story and being able to show that on a visual level makes the film more real, not less real. (ibid.: 124–30)

Thus, one way of explaining the pronounced interest of contemporary documentarians such as Odell and Landreth in animated filmmaking styles and techniques relates to those artists' belief that animation manifests the subjective and manipulated character of any film work in ways and to extents that are arguably more consistent and insistent than those typically achieved by live-action cinema.

also the viewing audience's experience of them). In doing so, he actively and enthusiastically applies his own subjective point of view, both as an artist and as a private individual, to the cinematic treatment and expression of the real-life issues that his films explore:

> Thinking about all the three films we've made, based on interviews, it's really become a project where you find stories that you think are strong in themselves and worth retelling and packaging them to make them accessible to a larger audience. I guess my contribution is packaging these stories that are strong already from the beginning. (Sapovídeos 2010)

The fact that Odell refers to his own directorial action as 'packaging' does not belittle the type of work he does. He is simply highlighting one of the animated documentary's central functions more generally, that is, to make a real-life story more accessible to and immediate for an audience in cinematic, emotional and social terms.

In an illustrative example of a similar way of thinking about and making contemporary animated documentary work, Chris Landreth (the Academy Award-winning director of the animated documentary short *Ryan* [2004]), comments of this distinctive filmmaking mode that:

> One of the [characteristic and distinguishing] elements is that you can add a subjective point of view that you can't do with live action. I mean, it happens with live action, but it happens in a way that is still very literal, because you're dealing with the real subjects at hand. But some of the creativity and passion of the story comes when you can change the visuals to reflect in a metaphorical or symbolic way, how the filmmaker, or the author, sees the subject matter. (Singer 2004)

Odell's modest description of his creative role as that of a mere 'packager' of stories and images barely hides the active interpretative function that his authorial input in fact possesses. As Landreth's comments above suggest, the relative extent, appropriateness and effectiveness of an animated documentary filmmaker's deliberate insertion of their subjective point of view (expressed and exposed through choice and utilisation of specific animated styles and techniques) into the possible truth content of their documentary interview sources is an issue that preoccupies many other prominent contemporary filmmakers and/or film theorists besides Odell. Illustrative examples might include Landreth himself (see Robertson 2004), Ari Folman (see Bendazzi 2015: 252), John Canemaker (see Canemaker 1988; Kriger 2012), Andy Glynne (see Glynne 2012; Martinelli 2012: 53-59), Sheila M. Sofian (see Bendazzi 2015; Kroustallis 2014), and Anca Damian (see Nasta 2013; Dobroiu 2015), to name but a few.

money from his mother, I felt a more naïve-looking style would be more appropriate. Whereas for the other two I felt we needed to work with characters based on live actors that we shot because they were much more serious in tone. There are also differences in how the different segments are edited and told cinematically, like the first story about the burglar where we tried to match his energy and restlessness in the way we worked with the camera as well. (Sapovídeos 2010)

The markedly flexible way of working that Odell describes here is one within which a varied assortment of graphic, cinematographic, narrative and editing styles are utilised and switched between, in order to engage with the specificity of each interviewee's story and also with the specificity of how the interviewer-cum-filmmaker perceives and interprets those narratives. Such calculated cinematic differentiations and mutations can unfold from one film to another, from one episode to another within the same film (as in *Lies*), and/or from one moment to another within the same episode (a phenomenon quite obvious in *Lies*' final episode, for example). These different approaches or treatments are not arranged and employed by Odell in the pursuit of one single aesthetic or didactic goal. Rather, they are the result of conscious authorial choices that integrate and synthesise the human content and identity of interviewees' testimony in ways that fully exploit the expressive flexibility and added value that animation can allow within documentary filmmaking contexts.

In short, there is a direct and intimate relationship in Odell's work between the documentary material he collects and the consequent uses of animated film techniques and languages that he deploys in response to that material. With specific reference to *Lies*, Odell stresses the importance, within this way of working, of careful pre-production identification of just which interviews (and/or interview sections) represent the most interesting and suitable material to translate into visual form:

We did quite a lot of interviews for the film. I think we made about thirty interviews with different people and during the process I listened to the interviews, I started editing some of them to see how they worked as a narrative and I had then to go back and ask some more questions to try to work the stories into film narrative. Out of those thirty, we chose in the end three stories. Really, I think all thirty stories deserved telling, but I think in the end the choice had to be which ones I thought I could do justice on film. (Sapovídeos 2010)

Odell's central concern, therefore, is to effect a complex, transformative mediation between original oral source materials (documentary interviews) and an ultimate cinematic result (not simply the films that he makes, but discreetly suggests, but does not explicitly show, that character's first sexual experience.

Lies is also a composite work, made up of what we might term, with a deliberate sense of paradox, three 'perfectly true' stories about lies. As in *Never Like the First Time!*, each of the film's episodes is based on a documentary interview. Once again, Odell turns each of these real-life social encounters into stylised animated moving image sequences through recourse to a diverse range of cinematic techniques and styles. For example, *Lies* displays a marked use of live-action video footage that is electronically treated in order to enhance its already-existing graphic and animated qualities. This is especially so in the case of the film's first episode, which presents a live-action re-enactment of the real-life event that this section narrates: the story of a burglar who, once detected in the course of a crime, declares himself to be an accountant doing overtime at the firm whose premises he is in fact robbing. The film's second story, that of a child who first lies about and then confesses to a crime never committed, deploys a more traditional cinematic style and technique: that of mainstream children's cartoons. *Lies'* final segment then presents the testimony of a woman whose whole life has been marked by a chain of untruths. The woman's final lines ('I cannot find the truth in my own story') with which the whole film concludes, could be understood as a self-conscious reflection on one of the reasons for making an animated documentary in the first place. This relates to the fact that a filmmaker's subjective perspective can make a productive contribution to the questioning, complication, completion and/or communication of seemingly objective and authentic real-life material, namely, the interview testimonies on which Odell's animated documentary works are based. Odell appears to argue that exclusive reliance on objectively measurable and observable facts and data in any attempt to describe reality in a comprehensive and sensitive way is but a partial documentary method. This is so especially when any given documentary investigation involves an introspective delving into people's private life histories and perspectives. In such cases, the documentary 'reality' from which a film is constructed encompasses not only the subjective utterances and experiences of the interviewed protagonist-witness, but also those of the filmmaker(s) who collect that material and subsequently explore and express it in moving image form.

Odell himself comments on issues and ideas like these when he notes of *Lies* that:

> I felt that each story needed its own style, both in terms of graphics but also in terms of the cinematic storytelling, editing and so on, because they are very different stories ... In the case of the middle story about the kid who steals

technique used is that of digital cut-out, initially in a dominant turquoise colour palette, a style recalling popular illustrations of the 1950s. As the interviewee's voice-over narration proceeds, all the other partygoers are visually present only as pencil sketches on a white background. This foregrounds the interviewee and his experiences as Odell's intended centre for the viewer's attention. The character starts a slow dance with a childhood girlfriend and the situation soon develops in an erotic direction, leading to his first sexual encounter.

The film's second episode is initially set in an underground station, with the main protagonist drawn as a white-contoured, transparent silhouette while her first-person narration begins. After walking through the city, she ends up in the room of her first sexual partner. The graphics for this sequence are mostly based on an invisible silhouette style for the characters with photo-realistic (though digitally treated) backgrounds. The female narrator tells of the weeks-long build-up, from kiss to full intercourse, to her sexual initiation. Narrative settings and protagonists are presented via a visual aesthetic of transparency, and some scenes are interposed with memorandum sheets that show both the passing of time and the methodical planning, shared with the protagonist's partner, that led up to her first full sexual experience; Odell's chosen animation style and aesthetic here works to visually reconstruct and materialise the memories that his interviewee shares and describes.

In contrast, the film's third episode is based on a noticeably harder, more violent visual tonality. This section opens with high-contrast, black-and-white graphics presented on a background of chequered paper. Standing on the right-hand side of the frame, this episode's young protagonist at once announces that we are dealing with a bad first sexual experience. An anxiety-inducing soundtrack of pressing rock music becomes audible as the scene transforms into flashback narration of a rape. Tracking shots of instances of punk vandalism, sneers, tattoos, beer cans and bottles depicted in dark, low-key lighting accelerate as that traumatic situation unfolds. Odell's stylistic choices here work not only to reconstruct his interviewee's memory but also to further intensify, by animated means, that individual memory's already strong emotional impact. Finally, the film's fourth episode presents a totally different, old-fashioned and quiet atmosphere that frames an elderly couple's story. Here, vintage cut-out imagery, evocative rather than illustrative, underscores the sense of past-ness attached to an elderly narrator's account of their memories. Flashback images of and from a photographic album are counterpointed by the slow, considered, self-consciously polite voice-over narration of an audibly aged protagonist. In a deliberately respectful and sympathetic echoing of the spirit that characterises the protagonist's approach to narrating their story, Odell's accompanying animation narratives are based. The cinematic styles, techniques and languages Odell uses package the stories he tells in such a way as to make them potentially more interesting and attractive to wide audiences. A complete live-action production and presentation of these interviews without Odell's characteristic authorial treatment of them would, arguably, achieve neither the same effect nor impact on audiences. Odell's choices of filmic style and technique are closely related to the stories that he and his interviewees tell. Odell's authorial decisions are not dictated solely by his aesthetic needs or preferences, but spring also (indeed, mostly) from the sense and the meaning of his interviewees' stories themselves, thus strengthening the latter's impact.

In *Never Like the First Time!*, for example, each of the film's four episodes correspond to particular aesthetic styles that are tailored to the various protagonists interviewed, in terms of their respective ages, genders, personal experiences and discursive tones. Indeed, this meticulous and sensitive process of aesthetic and interpersonal distinction is a constant in all the Odell films examined in this chapter: I argue that the process in question represents the result of Odell's characteristic intention to render his interviewees' stories as comprehensively and complexly as he possibly can. This filmmaker's technical and stylistic choices are of interest and value because they allow him to utilise a range of other communicational codes – metaphorical, emotional, subjective and aesthetic – that have the potential to translate elusive phenomena into moving images. Such phenomena include: the specific tone or inflection of an interviewee's voice; that speaker's subjective experiences and perspective; and Odell's own equivalents, as revealed and articulated through his cinematic interpretations of and responses to the material presented to him by his interviewees.

Turning to more detailed consideration of the films themselves, *Never Like the First Time!* is made up of four different stories. Each of these is based on a documentary interview; each is rendered in moving image form by use of different filmic techniques and styles; none take the form of pure live action. The common theme that links all four narratives in *Never Like the First Time!* is interviewees' recollections of their first time making love. The film's four central characters vary in terms of age and gender and their respective narrations of erotic initiation also vary in tone: from humorous to tragic, intimate to explicit. Odell's film responds to and respects such human diversity through its development of four distinctive modes of visualisation. The film opens with an introductory caption that contextualises and authenticates the interviewees' testimonies, noting that all were recorded 'between August and October 2002'. The first episode then opens with its protagonist standing in the bathroom during a party that he is attending. He wears black-framed eyeglasses, his hair combed back in the fashion of Buddy Holly. The animation

CHAPTER 9

The Reasons for Animating Reality:
Animated Documentary and Re-enactment in the Work *of Jonas Odell*

Lawrence Thomas Martinelli

This chapter examines the work of documentary animator-filmmaker Jonas Odell. Co-founder of Swedish production company Filmtecknarna, Odell specialises in making films that blend live-action and various mixed-media animation techniques; he has also scripted, co-scripted and written the music to a number of other productions. In some of his more recent short films Odell has experimented with a mix of documentary, staged and animated elements. Among the works in question, *Never Like the First Time!* (2006) was awarded the Golden Bear for Best Short Film in the 2006 Berlin Film Festival; *Lies* (2008) was awarded the Best International Short prize at the 2009 Sundance Film Festival; *Tussilago* (2010) was widely selected for inclusion within an impressive range of international film festivals, including (significantly, for this chapter's purposes) the Amsterdam International Documentary Film Festival. Odell has also directed award-winning music videos for artists such as The Rolling Stones, Erasure, Goldfrapp, U2 and Franz Ferdinand. In 2016, he directed the animated documentary *Jag Varen Vinnare (I Was a Winner)*, a film in which three people, presented in the physical appearance of their warrior avatars, speak about their experiences with gaming addiction. To date, this most recent short has already been selected for inclusion in the Tribeca Film Festival, Uppsala International Short Film Festival, Kortfilmfestivalen, Curtas Vila do Conde and Palm Springs International Film Festival.

Never Like the First Time!, *Lies* and *Tussilago* are generally considered to be animated documentaries. Many of the interlocking formal and thematic characteristics of these films explain why a significant proportion of Odell's recent creative output is generally considered to be animated documentary (see, for example, Sondhi 2010; Land 2014; Sjöberg 2015). *Never Like the First Time!*, *Lies* and *Tussilago* each proceed from collections of documentary interviews with individuals questioned on specific issues such as sex, lies and terrorism. These audio interviews, integrated into Odell's films in the form of voice-over, represent the foundations on which his animated documentary

Marx, Karl [1867] (1982), *Capital: A Critique of Political Economy, Volume One*, Harmondsworth: Penguin.
Merrill, Guy (2014), 'The glitch aesthetic: bringing authenticity to your visual brand', *gettyimages.com*, 28 August, <http://stories.gettyimages.com/glitch-aesthetic-bring-authenticty-visual-brand> (last accessed 24 October 2016).
Nash, Mark (2004), *Experiments with Truth* [curated exhibition], Philadelphia: The Fabric Workshop and Museum.
Noland, Carrie (2013), 'Adorno and affect', in James Elkins and Harper Montgomery (eds), *Beyond the Aesthetic and the Anti-Aesthetic*, University Park, PA: Penn State University Press, pp. 179–84.
The Pettifogger, film, directed by Lewis Klahr. USA: 2011.
Pipolo, Tony (2013). 'The illustrated man: Tony Pipolo talks with filmmaker Lewis Klahr', *Artforum*, March, pp. 243–9.
Redcat (2006), 'Re-animation: an evening with Lewis Klahr', 16 October, <http://www.redcat.org/event/re-animation-evening-lewis-klahr> (last accessed 24 October 2016).
Steyerl, Hito [2007] (2011), 'Documentary uncertainty', *Re-visiones*, 1, <http://www.re-visiones.net/spip.php%3Farticle37.html> (last accessed 24 October 2016).
Studio Visit with Filmmaker Lewis Klahr, film, directed by Anon. USA: Wexner Center for the Arts 2010, <http://wexarts.org/blog/video-studio-visit-lewis-klahr> (last accessed 24 October 2016).

Bibliography

Adorno, Theodor [1966] (1981), 'Transparencies on film', *New German Critique*, 24/25, pp. 199–205.

Adorno, Theodor [1947] (1994), *Composing for the Films*, London: Athlone Press.

Adorno, Theodor [1970] (1997), *Aesthetic Theory*, London: Athlone Press.

Adorno, Theodor (2001), *The Culture Industry: Selected Essays on Mass Culture*, London: Routledge.

Adorno, Theodor and Max Horkheimer [1944] (1997), *Dialectic of Enlightenment*, London: Verso.

Adorno, Theodor, Walter Benjamin, Ernst Bloch, Bertolt Brecht and Georg Lukács (2007), *Aesthetics and Politics*, London: Verso.

Altair, film, directed by Lewis Klahr. USA: 1994.

Benjamin, Walter (1999), *The Arcades Project*, Cambridge, MA: Harvard University Press.

Chimovitz, Melissa (1998), 'Declaration of independents: independent animation is alive and well in New York', *Animation World Network*, 1 May, <http://www.awn.com/animationworld/declaration-independents-independent-animation-alive-and-well-new-york> (last accessed 24 October 2016).

Foster, Hal (1996), *The Return of the Real*, Cambridge, MA: MIT Press.

Glynne, Andy (2013), 'Drawn from life: the animated documentary', in Brian Winston (ed.), *The Documentary Film Book*, Basingstoke: Palgrave Macmillan, pp. 73–6.

Goddard, Peter (2012), '*The Pettifogger*, Lewis Klahr's criminal collage', *Toronto Star*, 5 April, <www.thestar.com/entertainment/2012/04/05/the_pettifogger_lewis_klahrs_criminal_collage.html> (last accessed 24 October 2016).

Groys, Boris (2002), 'Art in the age of biopolitics: from artwork to art documentation', in Okwui Enwezor (ed.), *Documenta 11*, Ostfildern-Ruit: Hatje Cantz, pp 108–14.

Hansen, Miriam (1993), '"With skin and hair": Kracauer's theory of film, Marseille 1940', *Critical Inquiry*, 19: 3, pp. 437–69.

Hoberman, James (2000), 'The vulgar classes', *Village Voice*, 16 May, <http://www.villagevoice.com/film/the-vulgar-classes-6394814> (last accessed 24 October 2016).

Honess Roe, Annabelle (2013), *Animated Documentary*, Basingstoke: Palgrave Macmillan.

Koch, Gertrud (2000), *Siegfried Kracauer: An Introduction*, Princeton, NJ: Princeton University Press.

Kracauer, Siegfried (1985), *The Mass Ornament: Weimar Essays*, Cambridge, MA: Harvard University Press.

Kracauer, Siegfried [1960] (1997), *Theory of Film: The Redemption of Physical Reality*, Princeton, NJ: Princeton University Press.

Kracauer, Siegfried [1941] (2012), 'Dumbo', in *Siegfried Kracauer's American Writings: Essays on Film and Popular Culture*, Berkeley: University of California Press, pp. 139–41.

Leslie, Esther (2002), *Hollywood Flatlands: Animation, Critical Theory and the Avant-Garde*, London: Verso.

Leslie, Esther (2009), 'Shudder – Shutter – Shatter', *animateprojects.org*, <http://www.animateprojects.org/writing/essay_archive/e_leslie_2> (last accessed 24 October 2016).

Lind, Maria and Hito Steyerl (eds) (2008), *The Green Room: Reconsidering the Documentary and Contemporary Art #1*, Berlin: Sternberg Press.

LUX (n.d.), 'Collection/Works/*Altair* by Lewis Klahr', *lux.org*, <http://www.lux.org.uk/collection/works/altair> (last accessed 24 October 2016).

Marder, Michael and Santiago Zabala (eds) (2014), *Being Shaken: Ontology and the Event*, Basingstoke: Palgrave Macmillan.

The result is that any contemporary form that purports to show reality without engaging with the issue of how that reality is being constructed finds itself in danger of becoming what Steyerl might call an 'unmediated documentary'. As an example of this problem, she refers to a case in which a CNN reporter, embedded with a group of American soldiers, documented the latter's arrival in Iraq in 2003. The reporter, using a mobile phone camera, recorded the scene by pointing it out of the window of the vehicle he was travelling in. He then claimed that the footage he relayed showed what was happening in the world in a way never before seen. In one sense, the resulting footage was indeed new; however, due to the constraints of the recording technology, the images were merely a series of abstract blotches and patterns, an inadvertently animated sequence of images and colours that Steyerl called 'abstract documentarism'(ibid.). The attempt to show the real in all its immediacy was too unprocessed: the images meant nothing. To attempt instead to make the documentary figure as a document – to attempt to create comprehensible meaning from the manifold strangeness of the world – requires processes of active intervention and mediation on the artistic practitioner's part. It also requires sensitivity towards the provocation of a critical 'shudder' in film viewers, producers and artworks alike. What make the contemporarily much-discussed question of animated documentary so timely and necessary, then, are the potential ways in which, as this brief examination of Lewis Klahr's work has tried to indicate, that emergent film genre might allow creators and critics to fuse those concerns.

Notes

1. The literature discussing and analysing the documentary turn is diverse, extensive and not easy to summarise. See, however, books such as *The Return of the Real* (Foster 1996) for early hints about what is at stake in the reappraisal of documentary forms and later anthologies such as *The Green Room: Reconsidering the Documentary and Contemporary Art #1* (Lind and Steyerl 2008). In relation to recent visual practice, see exhibitions such as *Documenta*, curated by Okwui Enwezor from 2002, and, in particular, Boris Groys's 2002 essay 'Art in the Age of Biopolitics: From Artwork to Art Documentation' in the catalogue that accompanied *Documenta 11*; see also the exhibition *Experiments with Truth* curated by Mark Nash (Nash 2004).
2. A link could be made here to the explanation of *chôra* – the ambiguous space outside the ordered and controlled world of the city – that Plato mentions in *Timeaus*. There are, of course, more recent definitions of the term in Derrida or Kristeva, where *chôra* is used to describe an interstitial zone of encounter (see Marder and Santiago 2014).
3. For more information on Klahr's working methods, see the 2010 Wexner Center for the Arts short film, *Studio Visit with Filmmaker Lewis Klahr*.

The overarching question, though, remains one of form and content. It might be tempting to suggest that the animated documentary is premised on an encounter with Adorno's critical shudder as a marker of difference: a doubt and uncertainty about our relationship to the world and each other.

Conclusion

In her 2007 essay 'Documentary Uncertainty', the writer and filmmaker Hito Steyerl (2011) questions how documentary film processes and frames viewers' access to the reality of the neoliberal world. Neoliberal capitalism is, in many respects, complicit with the digital world. Chronologically speaking, both phenomena have become increasingly dominant since the late 1960s. Digital technology is also the key tool in establishing and managing the process of globalised financialisation of all aspects of human experience. The contradiction this connection makes apparent is that the intensification and exponential increase in the speed and quantity of images, data and facts that flicker across the different kinds of screens with which we now surround ourselves has not led to a greater understanding of how the world operates – indeed, in many respects the opposite has proved true. This process may also have ultimately drained Adorno's shuddering image of any potential. Today, creative flaw has seemingly been reduced to superficially stylised glitch art on Instagram or a commodified aesthetic. Guy Merrill, senior art director at Getty Images, recently stated (2014), for example, that: 'In our increasingly curated world, there's a pull toward an aesthetic that feels messy and unexpected.' Fortunately enough, 'the glitch aesthetic' will, he promises, cater to such desire by bringing 'authenticity to your brand'.

Hence the contemporary crisis of form and content: perhaps there is no way of seeing that is now capable of visualising our lived reality. The absence of any adequate form to represent this crisis registers as a problem for documentation and for the documentary genre in its efforts to show the real. Steyerl (2011) comments on this quandary, noting how: 'the more immediate [documentary pictures] become, the less there is to see'. Remarking on the way in which information, facts, news and 'reality' are now available constantly and inescapably through dematerialised technological images, Steyerl's text focuses on the problem of how the immediacy of this purported reality is actually meaningless. The instantaneous image is both too close and too far away from us, both overt and constant distraction and inescapable background hum. This flow and stream also lacks any filter to aid the processes of grading or deciphering: in other words, this reality's apparent lack of mediation actually leads to a lessening of our access to *any* reality.

seamless appearances. These could all be instances of a cinematic variation of Adorno's shuddering aesthetic comportment.

These links could be applied to Lewis Klahr's work in two ways, in order to see how an Adorno-esque shudder occurs in films such as *Altair*. Initially, one can see this occurring formally within both this film's narrative and its frame (because, like its alcoholic protagonist, the film itself gets the shakes). Alcohol seems to reduce the female character to a vulnerable state – she seems erratic and discomposed by the narrative's end – and the film mirrors the character's addiction through the mechanics of its animated cut-out imagery. Despite *Altair*'s partial production with digital technology (digital post-production potentially allows the image to be 'perfect', but Klahr deliberately does not use the technology in this way), the finished work shows the cinematic mechanism as still fundamentally unsound and unpredictable.[3]

The second way of linking the thought of Adorno and others to the work of a filmmaker like Klahr concerns a wider formal issue about disruption and disjuncture. It is a familiar observation to suggest that avant-garde works from the early to mid-twentieth century used disruptive shock techniques – Eisenstein's montage, Heartfield's collage, Situationist *détournement* – to create new ways of picturing modernity and shake established sociocultural conventions and meanings. Klahr's films, however, do not use these types of technique simply to disrupt or confront a set of established signifying systems. The films are not directly provocative or challenging in terms of critical interpretation and it is not easy to identify a dialectically deduced meaning, either politically or in terms of general narrative (Pipolo 2013). Rather, Klahr's frames can be described as shuddering in the transition between surface and imagery. The disjuncture in the picture plane, the sense of disconnection between surfaces, and the unsophisticated movements within the frame that one frequently encounters within Klahr's films could all be registered as a disarticulation of a certain aesthetic regime. Klahr's work unsteadies a particular way of thinking and seeing film narrative or durational cinematic flow; his animations question the mechanics of movement and what it means to make a connection. The inability to completely decipher the story in *Altair* marks, however, a potentially liberating moment – a sense where not knowing what to think is not an uncritical juncture, but a utopian one. We recognise *something* but we can't definitively say what – and, to that degree, we need to look more. Klahr's films are marked with the potential for the viewer to see a shudder or trembling shadow of critical engagement.

More generally, a nascent contemporary tradition of animated documentary filmmaking can also perhaps be thought of in these terms. What makes the idea of animated documentary relevant here is the way in which it foregrounds the constructed, mediated and social aspects of filmmaking.

to register a moment of being touched by alterity, a touching that involves both the body and cognition (see Noland 2013). In a suggestive and strange passage, Adorno (1997: 331) proposed that 'aesthetic comportment is to be defined as the capacity to shudder'. Adorno here implies that when we shudder, we are registering an encounter with something that manages to touch us. A shudder indicates an entanglement with something unsettling and strange, and a shuddering, shaking subject is one that is responsive – perhaps unwillingly – to others, otherness and difference. As he goes on to note, 'life in the subject is nothing but what shudders' because it 'is the act of being touched by the other' (ibid.: 331). The shuddering self is, therefore, the subject becoming social.

It is in this sense of aesthetic comportment that difference marks the point of social contact via an encounter with alterity. An encounter with others, through the mediation of an aesthetic shudder, shakes us out of our reified selves. It is, says Adorno, as if:

> Goose bumps were the first aesthetic image. What later came to be called subjectivity, freeing itself from the blind anxiety of the shudder, is at the same time the shudder's own development; the reaction to the total spell that transcends the spell ... that shudder which subjectivity stirs without yet being subjectivity. Aesthetic comportment assimilates itself to that other rather than subordinating it. (ibid.: 331)

The uncertainty induced by unknown difference is, according to Adorno, one of the ways that subjectivity is seen to shudder into being. Social space is the space of uncertainty.[2] This uncertain, shuddering zone opens up or exposes us to others and other possibilities. When our assumptions or expectations are shaken, we suddenly discover that things – ourselves, other people, society, histories, and ideological apparatuses – could be different. The result of such an encounter is never a foregone conclusion: it is alarming, and even potentially horrifying. Esther Leslie (2009) suggests that this unsettling experience is today most often encountered in a synthetic form, within things like horror films. The latter represent somewhere cinema audiences go for the artificial recreation of Adorno's shudder, a place where viewers can experience themselves being 'undone' by the unknown in order to shake with fear.

With such ideas in mind, the notion of the ghost in the machine takes on a new resonance. Returning to the earlier point about the breakdown of machinery, when a machine shudders we become aware of how unpredictable and fragile it actually is. When the film projector jams, viewers have to acknowledge that the cinematic flow of images is not seamless; when the pixels burn out on a screen, audiences are shaken out of a world of not completely mastered their technique, conveying as a result something consolingly uncontrolled and accidental, have a liberating quality' (ibid: 199).

When machines or works of art become erratic and unpredictable, the final product or end result is not a foregone conclusion. Depending on what production technique and technology a given artwork employs, the potential type of resulting creative accident is always different. Filmmaking, obviously enough, has created its own (often stereotypical) vocabulary of machine breakdown: the mismatched soundtrack or the burnt-out celluloid strip caught in the projector gate. But what does such a breakdown mean, and how should the viewer interpret this critically?

Referring to Kracauer's *Theory of Film*, Adorno (1981) discussed how certain types of film and filmmaking possessed the potential to critically examine both their own status as aesthetic objects and the relationship between film, politics and society. This discussion focused in part on a subtle reworking of the terms of Kracauer's ideas about the connection between the technological aspect of cinematic form and that form's intrinsic sociological content. In part, this implied a socio-ontological claim rather like Kracauer's, in the sense that the technology of filmmaking and cinematic representation inferred a link between filmed appearances and the way the world was constructed. Adorno put matters thus: 'by virtue of the relationship to the object, the aesthetics of film is thus inherently concerned with society' (ibid.: 202). If this relationship existed – that is to say, if the form and content of the film interacted with the form and content of society – then through the breakdown of the cinematic machine, or through any creative incompetence employed in a given film's construction, certain social relations could be revealed or analysed. There would be, Adorno's analysis implies, a formal link between the erratic machine that, through malfunction, reveals its inner workings and the social content and context thus revealed. Through those moments of breakdown, viewers would experience or see how erratic capitalism alienates and destroys through the mystifying process of creating abstract exchange value – the stuttering apparatus would reveal the ghost in the machine.

One way of describing this mediating connection would be to focus on how a film or artwork fitted, moulded, adapted, or even defined itself in opposition to historical/social constraints. In *Aesthetic Theory*, Adorno called this adaptation or fit of the artwork 'aesthetic comportment' (1997: 331). The concept of aesthetic comportment describes the way in which an artwork provokes engagement; it indicates a mediated, sensuous encounter between subject and object that simultaneously jolts the viewer out of their previously petrified state. It also seems, in part, to have some similarities to what Deleuze and Guattari mean by the concept of affect, if we understand affect

Like Kracauer, Adorno also considered that the animated film could have value because of the way it foregrounded the construction of movement from stilled things. The animated film could, therefore, both put on show and mediate our relationship to the dead world of exchange value. Ultimately, however, Adorno's analysis was far more pessimistic than those of many of his critical peers and affiliates. He was much more sceptical of cinema's emancipatory potential than, say, Benjamin, as was evident in their correspondence about the latter's celebrated 1936 essay 'The Work of Art in the Age of Mechanical Reproduction'. Adorno was particularly wary of the way in which he believed animation and cartoons to be complicit in the culture industry. After raising concerns at how 'The laughter of the audience at a cinema . . . is anything but good and revolutionary; instead it is full of the worst bourgeois sadism' (Adorno et al. 2007: 123–4), Adorno goes on to refer to Disney and Mickey Mouse. However, his later analysis of film is interestingly relevant when we return to the issue of animation, the medium's distinctive relationship to concepts of the document, and, in particular, the films of Lewis Klahr.

As Esther Leslie (2002) has shown, the early history of animation appeared to promise (as discerned by Kracauer and others at the time) a form of filmmaking that allowed viewers to see the unruly strangeness of the world. Leslie suggests that watching a cartoon film in the early twentieth century could be a liberating experience, because animated films of the period were often chaotic, outrageous and barely controlled cinematic sequences within which the natural laws controlling the outcome of events could not be predicted. With the subsequent industrialisation of animation via companies like Disney, however, the potential for the animated image to show this liberated world – one less confined by the regulation of capitalist society – had (certainly for Adorno, at least) practically evaporated. This would be one way of reading the essays collected in *The Culture Industry* (Adorno 2001), which can be taken as Adorno's reaction to experiencing American (and, in particular, West Coast American) mass culture in the 1940s. The commonly assumed pessimism of Adorno's critique in essays such as 'The Schema of Mass Culture or Culture Industry Reconsidered' (ibid: 61–106) needs, however, careful consideration. This is because one can find in Adorno's analysis isolated references to the way cinema might still contain traces or fragments of an alternative vision of the world. As a result, the mediums of film and animation still offered a fragile chance to show the utopian potential hidden within the dead commodity that the culture industry offered. In his 1966 essay 'Transparencies on Film' (Adorno 1981), Adorno suggested that one of the ways in which film viewers might escape from industrialised control related to occasions when the cinematic machine broke down or when, through incompetence (deliberate or not), things seemed to go wrong. As he noted: 'works which have

> The capacity to stir up the elements of nature is one of the capacities of film. This possibility is realized whenever film combines parts and segments to create strange constructs. If the disarray of the illustrated newspapers is simply confusion, the game that film plays with the pieces of disjointed nature is reminiscent of *dreams* in which the fragments of daily life become jumbled. (ibid.: 62)

For Kracauer, film therefore contained the potential for the redemption of things, not just their photographic mortification or reification. Based on the activation of things through the medium of film via movement and time, film had a dialectical relation to reality: the world, the film, and the viewer interacted. This dialectic created momentum, and even drew attention to this process of seeing that it itself provoked. As a consequence, Kracauer proposed, film, rather than mimetically reflecting reality, instead 'look[ed] under the table' (Hansen 1993: 450) of modernity in order to show viewers the process of materialisation – how things do (or do not) enter into meaning within a contemporary world dominated by exchange value. In this way, film had the potential to critically mimic (if not, ultimately, to reverse) the process of commodification. The allusion here to core Marxist concepts should be clear: for Marx, commodification animated objects with a false vitality. Things had a deceitful power over people when the former acquired an exchange value – one aspect of what Marx called, in *Capital*, the commodity's 'theological capers' (Marx 1982: 163). Commodification created the illusion of activity in inanimate objects. What film could do was to document the effects of this process by shaking the commodified object free – if only for a moment – of the deadening weight of exchange value.

Kracauer's conception of film as a medium could readily be applied within a properly nuanced account of what we see happening in Lewis Klahr's films more specifically. The apparently fixed world of late-1940s *Cosmopolitan* magazine, laid out according to the order of the magazine's picture editor or the demands of its advertisers, is re-ordered in the collaged *Altair*. The meaning of the archival magazine imagery that Klahr utilises is found to be more indeterminate than the original capitalistic and consumerist uses to which it was originally put. Klahr re-orders the images and imagery in question so as to create new meanings: what once appeared fixed is latterly revealed to be changeable. One set of possible interpretations (the received idea that a promotional image incontrovertibly tries to sell you something) is superseded when the image in question is suddenly revealed to contain a quite different meaning. In *Altair*, for example, an advert for a pair of gloves is revealed to be a murderous object that can kill. What Kracauer describes as being generally true of film per se seems true of Klahr's films more specifically.

cartoons and the unfortunate in real life get their thrashing so that the audience can learn to take their own punishment.

The cartoon form itself – as a product manufactured to entertain – participated in the sadomasochistic exploitation of contemporary audiences who were shown how to laugh at their own servitude.

The source of these writers' interest in animation was the manner in which the animated film processed and represented reality in ways that extended beyond the naturalising technology of photography and live-action cinema. The animated image was purposefully – and obviously – constructed. This mediation, while ostensibly disqualifying animated cinema from presenting any neutral and 'pure' access to the external world (which would, obviously, be suspect), actually foregrounded what it meant to imaginatively engage and interact with reality, to the point of effecting an alteration of it. As Gertrud Koch (2000: 106) notes of film – and particularly, animated film – in her book on Kracauer: 'the mediate[d] character of images, insulate[d] [. . .] film against the suggestion of directness'. Such a suggestion points to a possibility that interested many of Critical Theory and the Frankfurt School's leading figures: namely, that the animated film had the potential to foreground the constructed nature of human experience. Animated film 'teaches us to see the world' because it allows us to 'see through the false and superficial sensuousness and conventionality of things and perceive behind them the material being of things' (ibid.: 106).

Kracauer, especially in his 1960 book *Theory of Film* (Kracauer 1997), emphasised this aspect of filmmaking. He suggested that film engages with reality precisely through its constructed material dimension. This was not a pre-given technical capacity of all cinema: rather, it required that a process of visual education and learning to see should occur in the course of making and/or viewing a film. This process implied a physical aspect: an attunement towards movement or, more generally, a somatic, bodily registration during the experience of film viewing. It also implied an awareness that came from the way the viewer saw still or stilled things come alive in film. As a result, Kracauer was very careful to differentiate film from photography. This was because he believed that photography had a tendency to fix and determine the visible world, to create a 'comprehensive catalogue' (Kracauer 1985: 61) of appearances. In an essay on photography, he commented on how: 'The disorder of the detritus reflected in photography cannot be elucidated more clearly than through the suspension of every habitual relationship among the elements of nature' (ibid.: 62). Photography, quite simply, had the power to extract and fix meaning. It was, however, one of film's special qualities to reintroduce movement to the photographically frozen world:

archaeological remnants of a now-lost culture is of significance because it allows us to think about how Klahr's work can be read as cultural autobiography and, perhaps, as a form of animation that has a relationship to wider critical and cultural concepts of the document.

Walter Benjamin, of course, was fascinated with how the detritus of the nineteenth-century shopping arcade could be retrospectively interpreted as documents linked to wider cultural and political shifts associated with that period and still influential within his own. The challenge, for Benjamin, was to show how the fragmented rubbish of consumer capitalism was linked to the development of the dreams and nightmares of modernity. Benjamin used allegory in an attempt to show how the remnants of consumption – the discarded adverts and objects – could not be interpreted in their immediacy (that is, simply as adverts and consumables), but always referred back to some further set of codes and forces. The key reference here is Benjamin's *Arcades Project* (1927–40) and, in particular, his work on Baudelaire (Benjamin 1999: 228–388). Benjamin's above-described critical insight and method can be usefully applied within a reading of Klahr's *Altair*. That film can be understood to show the reality of post-war American consumer culture. However, this is not because Klahr makes a mimetic, purely reflective documentary examining the period in question. Rather, what *Altair* provides is a creative re-assembly of a set of codes that allude to the wider framework of post-war American society. Understanding Klahr's film simply as evidence of a now-dead vernacular image culture represents only half the picture. *Altair* does not just re-present the afterlife of one specific phase in American popular culture: it does something else with that now-discarded imagery. As Klahr has commented: 'What's interesting to me about appropriation is that you are dealing with something that is received, but you are also shaping it in a way that might bring out latent meanings that are not immediately clear' (Chimovitz 1998).

The challenge is to construct a way of linking Klahr's 'shaping' or collaging with animation within *Altair* to wider cultural and critical notions of 'the document'. In order to develop that project further, productive reference can be made to the work of Siegfried Kracauer, Theodor Adorno, and mid-twentieth-century intellectual movements such as Critical Theory and the Frankfurt School. Critical Theory scholars such as Adorno (1994), Benjamin, Max Horkheimer and Kracauer (2012) were notably preoccupied by film and, in particular, by the animated film. As Adorno and Horkheimer (1997: 138) noted,

> Cartoons . . . accustom the senses to the new tempo, they hammer into every brain the old lesson that continuous friction, the breaking down of all individual resistance, is the condition of life in this society. Donald Duck in the

in 1994 on 16 mm film, using images culled from six late-1940s issues of *Cosmopolitan* magazine; it subsequently became one part of Klahr's seven-film series *Engram Sepals* (2000). One way of reading *Altair* is to understand it as the story of a female protagonist who travels through a world populated by more or less malign forces. The character is swayed by the mysterious power of money, suffers numerous forms of identity crisis, is the victim of the power of desire (both sexual and material), and falls prey to the instability of time (unable to move into the future, she regresses into the murkiness of the unresolved past). The film concludes with the character engulfed in an alcoholic daze: drifting off into a stupor, the woman is smothered by the hand of an unseen antagonist. She is trampled underfoot, the victim of uncontrollable and unpredictable forces.

Altair is peppered with references to the stars (the film's title refers to the eponymous star that is one of the closest celestial bodies visible to the naked eye); to astrology (an allusion to the process of forecasting the future, but also a reference to science fiction); and to colour symbolism and coding (blue works within this film, for example, as a cipher for transcendence or generalised notions of 'the beyond'). As Klahr comments:

> The narrative is highly smudged leaving legible only the larger signposts of the female protagonist's story. The viewer is encouraged to speculate on the nature and details of the woman's battle with large, malevolent societal forces and her descent into an alcoholic swoon. However, it is important to note that all of the above was only discovered on the editing table. What motivated me during the shooting of this film, which was largely improvisatory, was a fascination with the colour blue and some ineffable association it has for me with both California and what I imagined to be the great sense of relieved openness of the post-war 1940s. (LUX n.d.)

It might be possible, therefore, to suggest that this film simply wallows in a lost past, one made safely surreal through use of fashionably retro imagery and an artfully crafted mood. *Altair*'s ostensible content shows a fascinating, melancholic, but essentially sealed-off place to dream about a slightly sinister past.

Klahr has done nothing to dissuade viewers from thinking of *Altair* in this way, suggesting in interviews that his work is a Benjaminian fragment fixated on the outdated *Arcade* that is mid-twentieth-century American popular culture. He has noted that his filmmaking work is motivated by the urge to preserve: 'Since I was a boy I've been sensitive to what was disappearing. Once an object or image is outmoded, it is dead. So I primarily work with dead images, which makes me a *re*animator, not an animator' (Pipolo 2013: 247). But this authorial suggestion that *Altair* is constructed from the document or evidence of something – that one can begin to understand the reasons why, and ways in which, animated documentaries are contemporarily significant.

Brief consideration of this overarching contemporary critical and cultural context brings us to the work of Lewis Klahr. Klahr has been making cut-and-paste, stop-frame animated films since the late 1970s. Although originally based in New York, his work has a clear visual connection to that of West Coast American animators such as Harry Smith and Larry Jordan, although Klahr's work may also owe a debt to the 1970s Punk aesthetic of DIY cut-and-paste. Klahr is known for his unsettling work with dreamlike narratives, constructed from the remnants of 1940s, '50s and '60s American mass visual culture: the magazines, adverts and flyers left over from the so-called 'golden age' of US pop culture. In the words of James Hobermann (2000), Klahr is a filmmaker who 'traffics in both psychic scars and cultural remembrance'. According to Mark McElhatten, Klahr is 'intensely archeological [sic] in his approach to autobiography and cultural ephemera ... he is a creator of atmospheres – ontological terrains where events and emotions register with archetypal power and dreamlike intensity' (Redcat 2006). In essence, imagine the world of mid-twentieth-century-set television series *Mad Men* (2007–15) turned into a stop-frame animation. Indeed, commenting on his 2011 film *The Pettifogger*, Klahr himself connects his work to the style and mood of *Mad Men*. He suggests that the latter channels the 'optimism felt in early-'60s American culture and the kind of modernity found in *The Pettifogger*' (Goddard 2012).

Reading the secondary literature on Klahr, one invariably finds the suggestion that the sequences he constructs invite the viewer to drift off into an uncanny world, one haunted with nostalgia for the recently lost past. Given that Klahr builds his films from collected archival material, it is unsurprising to find his work described as the reanimation of a disappeared world of American popular culture. Klahr calls his dense psychosocial narratives cultural autobiographies, suggesting that his films work as 'an exploration of the parts of his identity [that Klahr] has culturally inherited' (Chimovitz 1998). Moreover, if the visual material from which Klahr constructs his films is deliberately out-dated, so too are the formal techniques of filmic construction (stop-frame and cut-out animation) that he uses in order to make those works. Klahr's use of such techniques is far more crude (in purely craft-based terms) than that of, say, Lotte Reiniger's 1926 cut-out masterpiece *The Adventures of Prince Achmed*.

To understand how the above-noted opposition between ideas of documentary and ideas of the document can be a productive one to invoke when analysing Klahr's work, we need to look in more detail at a specific film: in this instance, the stop-frame, 1950s film noir-inflected *Altair*. *Altair* was made matter; it might (or might not) be a film work that is constructed according to certain consensually recognised and respected narrative conventions; it might (or might not) conform to certain similarly agreed rules about how to represent particular real-life events or issues. But to study this supposed cinematic genre as a symptom of something broader, or as a documentary form (and/or repository) in and of itself, would also be to consider the so-called documentary turn in recent cultural production (including animation). Recent shifts in cinematic forms and genres, together with alterations in the content addressed by those forms, suggest broader movements within contemporary society: that a certain set of artistic and cultural forms links to a certain set of cultural and historical issues.

One central question within such an exploration relates, therefore, to how cultural texts (such as films) are, arguably, subject to a two-stage encoding process. Such texts' ostensible narrative and aesthetic content is supplemented by another order of content altogether. The latter is associated with historical events and processes of change witnessed and experienced within the wider world. Every film is simultaneously 'about' something while also implying something else beyond the text itself. In Theodor Adorno's terms, this problem with form and content indicates how artistic forms are always encrusted with, or enmeshed in, history. This is so regardless of any given artwork's struggle to describe, show, or even escape from the very history that informs and enfolds it. Such a formulation of the concept of 'the document' seems implicit in Adorno's claim (1997: 5) in *Aesthetic Theory* that every artistic form contains 'sedimented content'. Questions of form – and why a form is used or occurs at one historical moment rather than another – can only be answered, Adorno argues, through an analysis of how a specific form relates or connects to the wider world. The notion of sedimented content is, therefore, the artwork or film's social life, something that is built up through viewing, re-viewing, attention and forgetting, analysis and reflection (ibid.).

Of course, the suggestion that individual films and works of art are products of a specific social context might seem no more than an unremarkable statement of the obvious, an idea now automatically accepted as par for the course within scholarly disciplines such as cultural studies and film studies. But this essay argues that what the relationship between the form and content of the document and the documentary throws into relief is how, during the past twenty years, a significant proportion of contemporary art and film production has actively attempted to develop innovative strategies to engage with a diverse range of social and political issues. More specifically, it is possible to identify the reason why the documentary form has recently assumed such prominence within a range of different creative media. It is only by considering this question – in other words, by considering the documentary as itself a

CHAPTER 8

Adorno, Lewis Klahr and the Shuddering Image
Andrew Warstat

The work of animator and filmmaker Lewis Klahr is barely recognisable as documentary. His works are fragmented, surreal, stop-frame investigations hard to categorise alongside contemporary films routinely referred to as examples of animated documentary, work such as *Waltz with Bashir* (Ari Folman, 2008) or *Persepolis* (Vincent Paronnaud and Marjane Satrapi, 2007) (see, for example, Honess Roe 2013: 139–69). Klahr makes no direct attempt to engage with common-sense, conventional definitions of 'reality' through naturalistic forms of cinematic representation or storytelling. To see Klahr's films as documentary, one has to look beyond a straightforward definition of that concept. Making such an interpretative leap, however, allows for an examination of how animation itself can be understood as a visual medium that is entangled in history and politics, and that thus contains individual works that can be plausibly understood as 'documents' in certain ways.

This essay uses consideration of Klahr's work as a vehicle through which a range of questions closely related to the idea of 'animated documentary' can be explored. Is there an opposition between the documentary and the document? What are some of the ways in which the 'documentary turn'[1] in filmmaking and art practice during the last two decades might be symptomatic of contemporaneous concerns with the relationship between the factual, the social and the cultural? Is a distinction between concepts of the documentary and the document helpful when we come to consider a specific emergent filmmaking tradition such as documentary animation? And, does that attempted distinction relate to the traditional binary opposition between form and content visible within countless critical discussions and creative works drawn from a variety of aesthetic traditions, documentary film and animation included?

Recent critical suggestions that there is indeed such a genre of film as animated documentary perhaps have their roots in a conviction that it is possible to identify a more or less coherent form of film object which can be associated with that generic label (see, for example, Glynne 2013; Honess Roe 2013). An animated documentary might (or might not) address certain forms of subject

Jennings and Gary Smith (eds), *Selected Writings, Volume 2: 1931–1934*, Cambridge, MA: Harvard University Press, pp. 720–2.

Benjamin, Walter [1940] (2003a), 'On the concept of history', in Howard Eiland and Michael W. Jennings (eds) *Selected Writings, Volume 4: 1938–1940*, Cambridge, MA: Harvard University Press, pp. 389–400.

Benjamin, Walter [1940] (2003b), 'Paralipomena to "On the concept of history"', in Howard Eiland and Michael W. Jennings (eds), *Selected Writings, Volume 4: 1938–1940*, Cambridge, MA: Harvard University Press, pp. 401–11.

Berger, John (2005), *Berger on Drawing*, ed. Jim Savage, Cork: Occasional Press.

Busch, Kathrin (2006), 'The language of things and the magic of language: on Walter Benjamin's *Concept of Latent Potency*', <http://eipcp.net/transversal/0107/busch/en/base_edit> (last accessed 19 October 2016).

Christov-Bakargiev, Carolyn (1998), *William Kentridge*, Brussels: Société des expositions du Palais des beaux-arts de Bruxelles.

Christov-Bakargiev, Carolyn (1999), 'Carolyn Christov-Bakargiev in conversation with William Kentridge', in Dan Cameron et al. (eds), *William Kentridge*, London: Phaidon, pp. 8–35.

Derrida, Jacques (1993), *Memoirs of the Blind: The Self-portrait and Other Ruins*, Chicago: University of Chicago Press.

Felix in Exile, film, directed by William Kentridge. South Africa: 1994.

Fisher, Jean (2003), 'On drawing', in A. Newman and C. de Zegher (eds), *The Stage of Drawing – Gesture and Act*, New York/London: The Drawing Center/Tate Publishing, pp. 217–26.

Johannesburg – 2nd Greatest City after Paris, film, directed by William Kentridge. South Africa: 1989.

Klee, Paul (1953), *The Pedagogical Sketchbook*, New York: Frederick A. Praeger, Inc.

'Linguistic mysticism as cure of the "language myth"', *Epoché: The University of California Journal for the Study of Religion*, 24, pp. 19–48.

Newman, Michael (2003), 'The marks, traces and gestures of drawing', in A. Newman and C. De Zegher (eds), *The Stage of Drawing – Gesture and Act*, New York/London: The Drawing Center/Tate Publishing, pp. 93–108.

Seyhan, Azade (1996), 'Visual citations: Walter Benjamin's dialectic of text and image', in Beate Allert (ed.), *Languages of Visuality: Crossings between Science, Art, Politics and Literature*, Detroit: Wayne State University Press, pp. 229–41.

van Alphen, Ernst (2008), 'Looking at drawing: theoretical distinctions and their usefulness', in Steve Garner (ed.), *Writing on Drawing: Essays on Drawing Practice and Research*, Bristol: Intellect Books, pp. 59–70.

and is never seen again' (Benjamin 2003a: 390–1). When looking at *Felix in Exile*, it is as if the flashing up of history in Benjamin's sense happens before our very eyes. Both for the viewer and for Felix, this flashing up of history happens through different gazes and forms of representation in recognisable imagery: An image flashes up through a lens, images appear in the stars or through drawings, measuring instruments, or gazes exchanged between Nandi and Felix.

In this sense, history is as an ongoing presence, similar to the deluge of water that continuously floods, or the natural landscape that changes all the time. In that respect, Kentridge's drawing process is itself similar to the process of history that flows and moves within the animation. Drawing leaves a physical trace behind for our eyes; history leaves a mental trace behind in our minds. Whether this trace is formed by memory, by imagination, or by written or mediated historical narratives is not clear. Whether the events witnessed on African land are imagined, retold from written or mediated history, or personally remembered by Kentridge is equally uncertain. But this blurry and ambiguous process of remembering the past is exactly what Kentridge tries to visualise in *Felix in Exile*. Kentridge does not so much create a story as an experience. The latter makes us feel that conceiving history is based on an instant magical similarity in Benjamin's sense, one between recognisable images from the past and the memories of our own. Dealing with history in this visual form is an ever-active process that continues in the present moment. Kentridge's animated drawings make us reflect and remember in an interactive fashion, wherein the artist's and the viewer's memories mesh together to continuously constitute new meanings, new realities and new possibilities within which past and present are interrelated in complex and enabling ways.

NOTE

1. Grateful acknowledgement is made to William Kentridge for permission to reproduce material previously published elsewhere. Every effort has been made to trace the copyright holders, but if any have been inadvertently overlooked, the publisher will be pleased to make the necessary arrangements at the first opportunity.

BIBLIOGRAPHY

Benjamin, Walter [1916] (1996) 'On language as such and on the language of man', in Marcus Bullock and Michael W. Jennings (eds), *Selected Writings, Volume 1: 1913–1926*, Cambridge, MA: Harvard University Press, pp. 62–74.

Benjamin, Walter [1933] (1999), 'On the mimetic faculty', in Howard Eiland, Michael W.

in Exile, however, it is not so easy to find such a neat historical narrative. This is partly due to the style in which the whole film is drawn: Kentridge and Nandi's respective drawing styles are alike, and it is therefore not immediately evident that the film contains a story within the story, a representation within the representation. On top of this, the fact that the film's drawn images follow one upon the other in an abrupt manner makes it doubly likely that the viewer's first impression of the work will be more poetical than epical in nature. In order to read *Felix in Exile*'s images as dealing with historical events and experience, we need to invoke Walter Benjamin's concept of history, as opposed to Hayden White's.

Benjamin rejects the notion of history as a narrative, and instead thinks of it as a constructive force that is always present in the now. In his famous essay 'On the Concept of History' (often referred to as the *Theses on the Philosophy of History*), he opposes two different ways of looking – historicist and materialist – at history. Benjamin identifies his own work with the latter method, due to his belief that: 'Historicism contents itself with establishing a causal nexus among various moments in history' (Benjamin 2003a: 397). While the historicist scholar is content to make up a story from factual history, their materialist counterpart defies the fundamentally complacent idea of 'once upon a time' (ibid.: 396). The materialist historian wants instead to 'blast open' (Seyhan 1996: 237) the continuum of history. As a result, they are just as concerned with exploring the present as the past, believing that these are entangled phenomena that cannot be understood independently from one another.

History, to Benjamin, is thus not so much a story as it is a moment, and it is filled with the present as well as with the past: 'History is the subject of a construction whose site is not homogenous, empty time, but time filled by the presence of the now' (Benjamin 2003a: 395). He defies the idea of history as something that exists eternally and stably in the past and sees it instead as a phenomenon filled with possibilities and change, something that can be used as a constructive force in the present. Benjamin explains his idea of history as a moment by comparing history with the process of thinking:

> Thinking involves not only the movement of thoughts, but their arrest as well. Where thinking suddenly comes to a stop in a constellation saturated with tensions, it gives that constellation a shock, by which thinking is crystallised as a monad. The historical materialist approaches a historical object only where it confronts him as a monad. (Benjamin 2003b: 407)

As with individual thoughts, history confronts us at certain moments. Benjamin refers to these confrontations as flashes, the flashing up of history in recognisable images: 'The true image of the past flits by. The past can be seized only as an image that flashes up at the moment of its recognisability, via conscious emphasis. His animation enables the viewer to experience a similarity between the active process of remembering and the artist's similarly active gestures in trying to capture history in a visual form.

If history is something that can be preserved and/or recreated in the present through animated drawings that the viewer actively engages with, then how do we make sense of such things? How does historical evidence come to the fore in animated work like that of Kentridge? It is apparent that *Felix in Exile* does not present a clear story, but rather, a range of effective images that are offered to viewers in a non-linear manner, each image piling up on the other in no chronological order. In this way, Kentridge's animation represents the fact that it is very hard to mediate history. Billboards, newspapers, all sorts of recording instrument (the theodolite, the seismograph, the telescope) are all objects and artefacts that echo wider human attempts to mediate information and knowledge about a given society and its history.

THE FLASHING UP OF HISTORY IN *FELIX IN EXILE*

How, then, can viewers make sense of the history that Kentridge narrates, and how does the character of Felix deal with the past from his exiled situation? This is a difficult subject to tackle without having recourse to a range of other, equally complex abstractions, such as past, future, present, time and space. It could be argued that history mainly comes to us in the form of stories: narratives of past events are, for example, considered to be 'histories' of something. Histories that become collective in scope and/or impact therefore have to be constructed and communicated in understandable and logical narrative forms (think, for instance, of the expository clarity of school history textbooks). This remains so even when (as is, arguably, always the case) any given historical process, event or period can be narrated in many different ways.

As is well known, Hayden White and many other scholars subsequently considered the notion of history as a narrative discipline and form. White argues that all historical works or explanations are in fact rhetorical and poetic by nature: human beings make sense of the world by making clear connections between the scattered fragments that we perceive in our daily lives. This sense-making process is partly dependent on the forging of connections that are not always literally or logically present. Imagination is what binds disparate fragments together into seemingly coherent historical narratives, stories that frequently offer the comforting promise that past experiences somehow relate to those of the present and will in turn continue to inform future events in some essentially progressive (because linear) fashion. In Kentridge's *Felix* its very materiality, and maybe also through the things that are represented in the film. Just as Derrida has stated that drawing is in the first place an act, so Benjamin thinks an active or behavioural aspect is implicit in all our forms of language. In his essay 'On the Mimetic Faculty' Benjamin describes how, in all languages, our mimetic capacity is at work. He does not see this capacity as one primarily related to vision, but instead views it as a more overarching characteristic of various beings, human or otherwise, in the world:

> Nature creates similarities. One need only think of mimicry. The highest capacity for producing similarities, however, is man's. His gift of seeing resemblances is nothing other than a rudiment of the powerful compulsion in former times to become and behave like something else. Perhaps there is none of his higher functions in which his mimetic faculty does not play a decisive role. (Benjamin 1999: 720)

All forms of communication are, according to Benjamin, based on humankind's gift for seeing or experiencing resemblances. So it might be that seeing or experiencing a resemblance between a moving line and a historical process (as is the case when we watch Kentridge's *Drawings for Projection*), or perceiving a link between the medium of drawing and the process of thinking and remembering, is based on this idea of language's behavioural rudiments. Benjamin states that the relationships or similarities between things were very clear to us in ancient times. Back then, there was a form of immediate similarity between humankind and the world. Human beings were, for example, able to see similarities between themselves and the stars (as in astrology) and created rituals precisely in order to assert and experience a sense of similarity with a diverse range of non-human objects and phenomena. Benjamin describes how humankind's inherent mimetic gift developed through various stages into language:

> To read what was never written. Such reading is most ancient: reading prior to all languages from entrails, the stars or dances. Later the mediating link of a new kind of reading, of runes and hieroglyphs, came into use. It seems fair to suppose that these were the stages by which the mimetic gift . . . gained admittance to writing a language . . . a medium into which the earlier powers of mimetic production and comprehension have passed without residue, to the point where they have liquidated those of magic. (Benjamin 1999: 722)

Benjamin states that in modern times the perceptual world contains only minimal residues of the magical correspondences and analogies that were familiar to ancient peoples. But perhaps within drawing (which is an ancient medium) we can still sense this magical similarity. This is especially so in Kentridge's animation, where the medium of drawing's characteristics as an act and the visual remainder of drawing's material traces are both enhanced

Indeed, Kentridge himself considers drawing as a form of knowledge. He explains how, for him:

> Arriving at the image is a process, not a frozen instant. Drawing for me is about fluidity. There may be a vague sense of what you are going to draw but things occur during the process that may modify, consolidate or shed doubts on what you know. So drawing is a testing of ideas; a slow-motion version of thought. It does not arrive instantly like a photograph. The uncertain and imprecise way of constructing a drawing is sometimes a model of how to construct meaning. What ends in clarity does not begin that way. (Christov-Bakargiev 1999: 8)

The process of creation and perception through drawing that Kentridge describes here is reminiscent of Merleau-Ponty's notion of embodied seeing, our intertwined relation with the material world and our reflecting consciousness that continuously sees itself seeing. The experience of ourselves that arises while viewing a drawing is thus simultaneous with the process of formulating and responding to the work itself: looking at a drawing allows one to reflect (Newman 2003: 97). As viewers, we are simply watching charcoal lines and marks, the gestures of another conscious being, on paper. As viewers, we have to make sense of the subjective processes of another human being. Drawing in this respect can be considered as a special kind of communication or language.

Drawing as a magical language

Developing this last point further, when we look at Walter Benjamin's notion of language and mimesis we can actually consider drawing as a special form of communicating ideas – in Kentridge's case, ideas about a specific local history. Benjamin stated that language is part of everything. His spiritual view does not regard language as an arbitrary system of signs. Rather, Benjamin sees language as something that is inherent within things, including humankind itself : 'we cannot imagine a total absence of language in anything' (Benjamin 1996: 62). According to Benjamin, it is possible that there is a language of music, of sculpture, of justice, of technology, and so on. Language is more than mere communication of information through words: 'it includes any perceptible articulation which may be understood as a formative principle of expression generally' (Busch 2006).

Felix in Exile can in this respect be considered an artwork that carries a language within it. This film tries to communicate, and, more specifically, exhibits a strong tendency towards communicating Kentridge's state of mind. The artist's drawing-based language is communicated to the viewer through can read his mind directly, even though his thoughts are entangled with the viewer's own.

For Jacques Derrida, in *Memoirs of the Blind: The Self-Portrait and Other Ruins* (1993), a book that accompanied an exhibition of drawings at the Louvre, this idea of drawing as an act, as a gesture, is the key definition of the medium. According to Derrida, the act of drawing is not so much about transcribing visual observation as it is about the physical mark-making gesture itself, about the exploratory movement. For Derrida, a certain blindness is involved in drawing. Ernst van Alphen has described Derrida's definition of drawing as follows:

> He presents drawing as an intransitive activity: our attention does not focus on the image we perceive, a represented world, but on the representation of that world – as activity. We see nothing in the drawing (transitive); we see only the drawing as intransitive act. (van Alphen 2008: 60)

Drawing is thus not only about vision but also about interpretation (or, reading between the lines). This process also happens every time we look at a drawing. As viewers, we want to distil a recognisable form out of the lines that we see. But right at the moment of recognisability, we lose sight of the lines as autonomous entities. Derrida's certain blindness implicit in drawing arises because the trait (the line/mark) escapes the field of vision:

> At the instant when the point at the point of the hand ... moves forward upon making contact with the surface, the inscription of the inscribable is not seen. Whether it be improvised or not, the invention of the trait does not follow, it does not conform to what is presently visible ... even if drawing is, as they say mimetic, that is reproductive, figurative, representative, even if the model is presently facing the artist, the *trait*... escapes the field of vision. (Derrida 1993: 51)

The blindness implicit in the respective processes of making and perceiving a drawing are put into motion in *Felix in Exile* when Nandi's face appears in Felix's mirror for the first time. At first, marks appear in the mirror, not meaning anything yet; at this point, viewers see the marks. Then the marks turn into the contours of Nandi's face. As soon as her face is recognisable, the lines escape the viewer's field of vision. Only what is between the lines – the character's face – is visual. This process of recognition has, of course, a lot to do with memory, and the memory of drawn images. Moreover, the process of watching *Felix in Exile* is a very active one, involving following the gestures, and retracing the memories and thoughts, of the artist – and also of making sense of these through our own memories and imagination. Kentridge's work thus highlights the possibility that drawing could be seen as a different kind of knowledge transcription.

was extraordinary ... so I would say that although when I was drawing the bodies for *Felix in Exile* I did not have the Sharpville massacre in mind – this was only a connection I made some months or years later – I'm sure that, in a sense, it was trying to tame that horror of seeing those images. (Christov-Bakargiev 1998: 28)

In *Felix in Exile*, memory is thus entangled with imagination. Kentridge has said that one of the film's starting points was a friend's description (rather than Kentridge's direct observation) of forensic police photographs of dead bodies. When he eventually saw these photographs himself, Kentridge observed that the images did not look like how he had imagined them: the photographed bodies were lying in narrow spaces, whereas he had imagined them in an open landscape (ibid.: 28). The conception of *Felix in Exile* thus originated from memory, from things that Kentridge had seen, experienced and felt previously. He may have drawn also from observation of photographs, models, and so on, but such observations are always engaged with the memory of experiences, whether visual or non-visual.

Drawing is about observation/seeing, but also about the experience of thinking, remembering, feeling and imagining. Drawing, in both its conception and perception, is therefore more about a complete (as opposed to an exclusively visual) experience of something. Matisse, for example, remarked about drawing from nature:

> It is not a matter of drawing a tree I see. I have an object in front of me that produces an effect on my mind, not only as a tree, but in relation to all sorts of other feelings. I shan't get rid of my emotions by exactly copying the tree. (Fisher 2003: 218)

Thus, the impulse to draw is not so much about capturing an appearance as it is a demand to animate thought. In other words, drawing is an active and direct process in its conception as well as in its perception. While looking at *Felix in Exile*, the viewer experiences the active coming into form of a human thought or gesture: it is as if we see Kentridge making his gestures (and thus, articulating his thoughts) on paper. According to John Berger, this kind of perception is particularly apparent in drawing, and differs from that evident in (or evoked by) the medium of painting:

> A viewer in front of a painting or statue tends to identify himself with the subject, to interpret the images for their own sake; in front of a drawing he identifies himself with the artist, using the images to gain the conscious experience of seeing as though through the artist's own eyes. (Berger 2005: 4)

Because of the process of identification with the artist that Berger describes, it is as if Kentridge's thoughts are present in the here and now – as if viewers stages of a mark-making process that normally go by too fast (and are thus unnoticed by the viewer) are now traceable. Kentridge makes present what once was there: his images contain the physically present traces of the past. He slows the process of time by showing his audience each moment of change, thereby making visible that which the land and our memory cannot otherwise hold onto: the recording of the slight changes in between objects and moments.

Drawing as a mental trace

Apart from understanding the drawn line as a materialised, active process – that is, one in a state of ever becoming – lines and gestures can also be understood to contain a certain mental trace as well. Pliny the Elder, for example, addressed this aspect of drawing when he described the medium's origin (which was then immediately put into use by another discipline, the plastic arts, to give the latter's fugitive character a more solid existence):

> It was through the service of that same earth that modeling portraits from clay was first invented by Butades, a potter from Sicyon, at Corinth. He did this owing to his daughter, who was in love with a young man; and she, when he was going abroad, drew in outline on the wall the shadow of his face, thrown by a lamp. Her father pressed clay on this and made a relief, which he hardened by exposure to fire with the rest of his pottery; and it is said that this likeness was preserved in the Shrine of Nymphs until the destruction of Corinth by Mummius. (Newman 2003: 93)

The shadow on the wall is a direct trace of Butades' daughter's lover, and is thus a temporal phenomenon. This trace can be considered as the starting point of her need to draw. In other words, it can be argued that drawing starts with a personal need to hold onto, or remember, something that will soon not be present anymore and/or a desire to make physically present something that resides in memory. Drawing is in this respect the art of the mental trace, an art of remembrance.

In *Felix in Exile,* for instance, it is Kentridge's memory, and not his direct observation, that seems to inform the work. His animation deals with things he saw as a child, like a photograph of the massacre outside Sharpville that occurred when he was six years old:

> My father was one of the lawyers for the families of the people who had been killed. I remember coming once to his study and seeking on his desk a large, flat, yellow Kodak box, and lifting the lid off of it . . . inside were images of a woman with her back blown off, someone with only half her head visible. The impact of seeing those images for the first time . . . the shock

These aspects of *Felix in Exile*'s visual form and narrative content pose several intriguing questions. What can be said, in interpretative terms, about the microcosmic elements of a drawing (trace, mark, line) at points in time before these have fully coalesced into a finished contour or figure? And how (if at all) are these elements-in-progress related to concepts and experiences of time, history or memory? When looking at Paul Klee's notions on the drawn line, we can see a clear relation to the aspect of time. In his *Pedagogical Sketchbook* (1925), Klee explains through graphic examples the characteristics of drawing and, in particular, the line. He points out emergence as a characteristic of the drawn line and speaks in this case of the line's momentum or trajectory: 'A walk for walk's sake. The mobile agent is a point, shifting its position forward' (Klee 1953: 16). For Klee, a process is implicit in the line, which is in fact considered as a point that shifts itself forward. The line also combines past and present, because it is always in a state of becoming. At the same time, its trajectory – the trace – remains visible. In that latter respect, drawing can be considered a medium that is related to temporal movement: not only in the process of creation but also in the process of perception.

This intrinsic characteristic of drawing is emphasised by the technique of animation. The process that Klee already discerns at work in any single drawing now becomes even clearer; the gestures in lines and erasures that Kentridge made in his *Drawings for Projection*, for example, appear directly and in motion before the viewer's eyes. Moreover, with the special production technique that Kentridge used in these works (one of imperfect erasure), instead of using a clean new sheet of paper for each movement, certain stages in the drawing process that normally remain invisible are now made visible to the viewer. Indeed, Kentridge has said that he started filming his drawings not for the purpose of animation, but as a way of recording the drawing's history:

> Often I find that a drawing which is of some interest in its first impulse becomes too cautious, overworked or tame as the work progresses. A film of the drawing holds each moment. Often as a drawing proceeds, interest shifts from what was originally central to something that initially appeared incidental. Filming enables me to follow this process of vision and revision as it happens. This erasing of charcoal, an imperfect activity, always leaves a grey smudge on the paper. So filming not only records the changes in the drawing but reveals too the history of those changes, as each erasure leaves a snail-trail of what has been. (Christov-Bakargiev 1998: 61–4)

For example, when looking at the newspapers that whirl around in the sky in *Felix in Exile* (Figure 7.3), imperfect erasure allows us see traces of previous stages in Kentridge's drawn rendition of those objects and their movement in space: the history of the whole process of movement is shown. All the

Figure 7.2 William Kentridge, drawing from *Felix in Exile* (1994). Charcoal and pastel on paper, 80 × 120 cm

or photography. Similarly, his filmic characters also communicate by means of drawings and drawn lines. Different kinds of drawing elements are visible within *Felix in Exile*: drawn lines (mostly in black charcoal, but sometimes in red or blue pastel); the smudging of lines; the erasure of lines; lingering traces of the drawing process left behind due to imperfect erasure of earlier mark-making. Newspapers that move around in the frame are erased and then drawn again in the process of the ever-changing drawing, which quite literally leaves its charcoal trace behind (Figure 7.3).

Nandi draws and makes clear marks on paper, surveying the land with all kinds of specialist instruments, marking the resting place of dead bodies, and so on. Furthermore, there is a great deal of tracing visible within the film: red lines that seem to encircle dead bodies lying on the ground, wounds on human flesh and suspicious places in the landscape. These red tracings seem to mark evidence in a way reminiscent of forensic processes of criminal investigation. Another, related form of evidence-marking is performed through the appearance within the film of a seismograph that makes mechanical inscriptions of red lines on its rotating cylinder.

Figure 7.3 William Kentridge, sequence of drawings from *Felix in Exile* (1994). 35mm film transferred to video. Dimensions variable. Collection Museum of Contemporary Art Chicago, gift of Susan and Lewis Manilow, 2001.23

Figure 7.1 William Kentridge, drawing from *Felix in Exile* (1994). Charcoal and pastel on paper, 120 × 160 cm

changes that are taking, or have taken, place back home on the wastelands around Johannesburg. Viewers witness crimes that were committed and see dead and bleeding bodies scattering the local landscape. As time passes, however, the landscape itself is in constant flux, covering up everything that has happened on it. Murdered people are covered up by sand or, quite literally, by the media (in this case, newspaper pages) and slowly melt into the landscape. Crime scenes appear and disappear one after another, sometimes marked by steel rods, billboards rising from the ground, or the red markings that demarcate a suspicious area or the spot at which a corpse was found. Felix receives this information through Nandi, who surveys the African land and records everything that takes place on it with the help of all kinds of optical and measuring instruments, or even by reading information from the stars (Figure 7.2).

She then notes everything down in the form of drawings. A witness in exile, Felix looks at Nandi's drawings as they pile up or whirl round in his room. He also exchanges physically impossible gazes with her through use of a mirror and a telescope. Meanwhile, Felix's room starts to flood with water. At the narrative's end, Nandi is shot and dies, at which point Felix's abode is completely flooded with water. His connection to his homeland now gone, Felix finds himself standing in an African landscape in a pool of water (or maybe it is a pool of tears) and carrying a suitcase full of drawings.

Drawing as a physical trace

As this plot summary suggests, drawing stands at the basis of the animation in *Felix in Exile*. Kentridge chose to make drawings instead of using a more conventionally realistic production medium, such as live-action film with reference to Walter Benjamin's concepts of history and his ideas on mimesis.

FELIX IN EXILE

Made in charcoal and blue and red pastel, *Felix in Exile* is the fifth of Kentridge's *Drawings for Projection*. It was created between September 1993 and February 1994, during the period just before the first democratic elections in South Africa. Kentridge's birthplace, Johannesburg, forms the geographical setting for most of his *Drawings for Projection*. These works frequently focus on the distinctive landscape surrounding what was South Africa's first industrial centre, a physical terrain marked by exploitation of the earth, undulating hills, mines and disused wastelands. Kentridge deals with political and social issues related to apartheid-era South Africa from a personal, sometimes autobiographical, perspective. Yet he has also said that he

> never tried to make illustrations of apartheid, but the drawings and films are certainly spawned by and feed off the brutalised society left in its wake. I am interested in a political art, that is to say an art of ambiguity, contradiction, uncompleted gestures and uncertain endings. (Christov-Bakargiev 1998: 14)

This contradiction and ambiguity is personified by two important recurring characters within Kentridge's films. These two characters, Soho Eckstein and Felix Teitlebaum, are introduced in Kentridge's first film, *Johannesburg – 2nd Greatest City after Paris* (1989). Eckstein is portrayed as a prosperous, pinstripe-suited real estate developer who owns a mining town in Johannesburg's outskirts. He is a ruthless man, seemingly indifferent to his workers' wellbeing and the emotional state of his wife, another recurring character in the *Drawings for Projection* series. Teitlebaum, on the other hand, is Eckstein's opposite, portrayed naked and seen mostly from the back, contemplating the demonstrations of the exploited and the victims beaten or killed. Sympathetic and emphatic, Teitlebaum is, presumably, the alter ego of the artist himself. Yet Kentridge considers his central duo more as two sides of one character, rather than as two fundamentally different protagonists. Felix and Mr and Mrs Eckstein are all white, and thus possibly able to disregard the daily struggles for survival that the vast majority of South Africans faced under apartheid. But *Felix in Exile* also stages another and different kind of character: Nandi, a black African woman whose experiences are opposed to Felix's. In *Felix in Exile*, Soho Eckstein is absent for the first time in the *Drawings for Projection* series: instead, the experience of the observer Felix is united with that of Nandi.

Felix in Exile shows its titular protagonist confined between the walls of his hotel room or apartment (Figure 7.1). Felix receives information on the

CHAPTER 7

Drawings to Remember
Nanette Kraaikamp[1]

INTRODUCTION

This essay focuses on one animation film by the South African artist William Kentridge, *Felix in Exile* (1994). Kentridge's perhaps best-known artworks are his *Drawings for Projection*, a series of stop-motion animation films made out of charcoal drawings; *Felix in Exile* forms one entry in that series. *Felix in Exile* is a nine-minute stop-motion animation consisting of some thirty to forty charcoal drawings. Each drawing is modified little by little by redrawing and erasing lines. Because it captures each change in the drawings a few frames at a time with a 35 mm camera, watching the film is like watching drawings being created. Viewers can see the drawings literally transform before their eyes: the whole process of smudging, adding, erasing and marking is made visible (Christov-Bakargiev 1998: 61–4). The subject matter, as in many of Kentridge's works, is the traumatic history of his native South Africa. In a poetical and highly autobiographical manner, Kentridge addresses sensitive political issues regarding apartheid and tries to preserve the memory of this controversial colonial past. His *Drawings for Projection* was created from 1989 onwards, the period when apartheid was dismantled and more and more of its crimes discovered.

Felix in Exile represents a very effective artistic attempt to present both a specific local history and human memories of it. It is worth asking which elements of this animation make its inscription and/or documentation of history so effective. Are Kentridge's handmade drawings responsible for this, for instance? Can the ephemeral character of drawing more generally afford the viewer a kind of access to the past and an enhanced ability to preserve the past in memory? Drawing, after all, performs a double role within *Felix in Exile*, functioning simultaneously as both Kentridge's technical medium and primary mode of communication. Using Kentridge as a case study, this essay looks into certain notions about drawing and drawing mechanisms in order to see how these might relate to concepts and experiences of time, history and memory. *Felix in Exile*'s representation of history is explored, for example,

Part 3

Films and Filmmakers

Levi-Strauss, David (2013), 'The documentary debate', in Julian Stallabrass (ed.), *Documentary*, London/Cambridge, MA: Whitechapel Gallery/MIT Press, pp. 103–9.

One Mind, film, directed by Hyunseok Lee. UK: Loughborough University, 2011.

Macdonald, Scott (2015), *Avant Doc: Intersections of Documentary and Avant Garde Cinema*, Oxford/New York: Oxford University Press.

Peace, David (2006), *The Damned United*, London: Faber and Faber.

Rancière, Jacques (2013), 'Naked image, ostensive image, metamorphic image', in Julian Stallabrass (ed.) (2013), *Documentary*, London/Cambridge, MA: Whitechapel Gallery/MIT Press, pp. 63–8.

Rosenthal, Alan (1971), *The New Documentary in Action*, Berkeley: University of California Press.

Sira Myhre, Aslak (2010), *Masters and Servants*, Oslo: Forlaget Oktober.

Skoller, Jeffrey (ed.) (2011), 'Making it (un)real: contemporary theories and practices in documentary animation', *animation: an interdisciplinary journal*, 6: 3.

Solomon, Charles (ed.) (1987), *The Art of the Animated Image: An Anthology*, Los Angeles: AFI.

Stallabrass, Julian (ed.), *Documentary*, London/Cambridge, MA: Whitechapel Gallery/MIT Press,

Stearns, Jason (2011), 'Shocking pink', *The Guardian*, 28 May, <https://www.theguardian.com/artanddesign/2011/may/28/richard-mosse-infrared-photos-congo> (last accessed 23 October 2016).

Strøm, Gunnar (2003), 'The animated documentary', *Animation Journal*, 11, pp. 46–63.

Ward, Paul (2005), *Documentary: The Margins of Reality*, London: Wallflower Press.

Wells, Paul (1983), personal interview with Norman McLaren.

Wells, Paul (1988), *In Cold Blood* (An Adaptation for Theatre), Central Studio, Basingstoke, and touring.

Wells, Paul (1990), *In Cold Blood* (An Adaptation for Television), New Commissions Programme, Channel Four.

Wells, Paul (1997), 'The beautiful village and the true village: a consideration of animation and the documentary aesthetic', in *Art & Design*, 12: 3/4, pp. 40–5.

Wells, Paul (2007), personal interview with Marjut Rimminen.

Wells, Paul (2011), personal interview with Eric Goldberg.

Wells, Paul (2013), *The Oil Kid*, script commissioned by Stavanger Oil Museum and AGR Oil.

Wells, Paul (2014) 'Chairy tales: object and materiality in animation', *Alphaville: On-Line Journal of Film and Screen Media*, 8, Winter, <http://www.alphavillejournal.com/Issue8/PDFs/ArticleWells.pdf> (last accessed 23 October 2016).

White, Hayden (1996), 'The modernist event' in Vivian Sobchack (ed.), *The Persistence of History: Cinema, Television and the Modern Event*, New York/London: Routledge/AFI, pp. 17–38.

Notes

1. Animation has benefitted from the impact of the digital shift, in that the high degree of 'constructedness' in contemporary film production, principally through the impact of computer technologies and software, has meant that 'film' has become far closer to the condition of animation, from which it was severed in an enduringly schismatic fashion when early cinema committed dominant models of image-making to material actuality and realism rather than overt illusionism and fantasy.
2. I spoke at, and chaired a panel on animated documentary during, IDFA 2007. The panel included Marjut Rimmenen, Tim Webb, Alex Chan, Mischa Kamp and Floris Kuuyk. The debate that followed included major practitioners, many of whom refuted or denied the existence of 'animated documentary', even if allowing for 'documentary animation': nominally, animation used *within* documentary forms rather than *as* documentary forms. Interestingly, the session was couched within a broader set of talks about 'the manipulated image', or what was essentially the impact of the digital in constructing documentary films.
3. Based on the idea of 'thick description' in anthropologist Clifford Geertz's *The Interpretation of Cultures* (1973), a 'thick' text properly seeks to provide full historical contextualisation for human behaviour and social ritual so that these become transparent to external comprehension and understanding.

Bibliography

A Shift in Perception, film, directed by Dan Monceaux. Australia: Danimations, 2006.
Bernard, Sheila Curran (2007), *Documentary Storytelling*, London/New York: Focal Press/Elsevier.
Bollacker, Kurt D. (2010), 'Avoiding a digital dark age', *American Scientist*, 98: 2, March/April, p. 106.
Calvino, Italo (1987), *The Literature Machine*, London: Secker and Warburg.
Capote, Truman (1966), *In Cold Blood*, London: Penguin Books.
Cholodenko, Alan (1991), *The Illusion of Life*, Sydney: Power Publications.
Coles, Robert (1997), *Doing Documentary Work*, New York/London: Oxford University Press.
de Waal, Edmund (2010), *The Hare with the Amber Eyes*, London: Vintage Books.
DelGaudio, Sybil (1997), 'If truth be told, can 'toons tell it? Documentary and animation', *Film History*, 9: 2, pp. 189-99.
Geertz, Clifford (1973), *The Interpretation of Cultures: Selected Essays*, New York: Basic Books.
Grandpa Looked Like William Powell, film, directed by David B. Levy. USA: 2010.
Hediger, Vinzenz and Patrick Vonderau (eds) (2009), *Films That Work: Industrial Film and Productivity of Media*, Amsterdam: Amsterdam University Press.
Honess Roe, Annabelle (2013), *Animated Documentary*, Basingstoke: Palgrave Macmillan.
Kaye, Nick (2000), *Site-specific Art: Performance, Place, and Documentation*, London: Routledge.
Kriger, Judith (2012), *Animated Realism: A Behind-the-Scenes Look at the Animated Documentary Genre*, Waltham MA/Oxford: Focal Press/Elsevier.
Learned by Heart, film, directed by Marjut Rimminen and Palvi Takala. Finland: Soundsgood Productions, 2007.

landscapes work as studium, and all have what Rancière calls the 'trace of history' in their actual presence and their development as part of the consequences of oil industry wealth; all are thus inherently educational as sites of knowledge. Finally, the sequence itself (like the complete script that contains it – 'sequence *ad infinitum*') is written as a series of *transitions* and *metamorphoses* that exemplify in action Rancière's idea of a recombinant form of visual arts practice. After all, the script both encompasses and emerges from elements drawn from a diverse range of visual, material and social sources, including: Myhre's memoir; oil museum archives; primary interviews; town guides; institutional libraries, and so on. Also crucial here, though, is the script's use of associative ideas and symbolic objects: the map, the oil products, the lipstick, the graph, the doll, and so on are actively understood and utilised as *signs*. All of these things ultimately represent Stavanger as a *repository* for the production of material concerned with the oil industry and its history. They also represent the script (and, ultimately, the animated documentary-in-production) as a *site* of meaning, not to mention the dialectical move between the material culture of Stavanger itself and the aestheticisation of an animated documentary film about Stavanger as *the archive*.

Conclusion: Documentary Commons

By mobilising a polyvocal and multi-register address of the animated documentary through that form's parallels with – and echoes in – other documentary arts practices, I have sought to further validate it as a focus for new permutations in documentary per se, but also to extend the range of possibilities inherent in the idea of the 'truth claim'. The curatorial processes typically involved in making animated documentaries facilitate a dialectical move between repositories of material information and sites of meaning, thus defining an idea of 'the archive' that is relevant to the demands of the contemporary era. Animated documentary's self-reflexive character contains within it an implied recognition of the necessity to maintain qualities of democratic openness and inclusion within any and all modes (and all individual examples) of documentary practice, animated or otherwise. As such, the recent expansion of animated documentary helps to achieve a creative 'commons' of interpretive strategies that help to sustain the deep relativities of the past when set against the attempted creation of new grand historiographical narratives. To return to this essay's introductory image, it is good to see animation, its critical study and the publicly engaged model of animated documentary filmmaking finally sitting at the front of the class in my imaginary academy.

KNUT

Now, do you see?

HANNA

That's just it, Grandpa. They're things. Just endless 'things'. Do we need them all? Do they make us any happier?

Hanna pulls down a lip-stick from the circulating products to use as a 'pencil' to create a crude graph with lots of wavy lines, ascending and descending.

HANNA

Consumers, luxuries, take, take, take ... We're getting richer while other people starve.

Knut pulls down a toy doll from the circulating products.

KNUT

Consumers? Luxuries? You talk about them as if they were pure evil. I didn't hear much about it when you pestered me for new dolls as a little girl.

He places the doll in front of him. It becomes a silhouette and multiplies into a crowd of people.

KNUT

But we haven't only made things, we have made communities. We built the school you went to, the houses we live in, the roads you drive on, the bus to town and the free health care. It's built on oil, Hanna. Norway is perhaps the best country to live in the whole world today, isn't it?

Behind them and the silhouette crowd, form the vectors and rigs of city vistas building, with lights, cars, etc. We see the school, a hospital building, a bus running out of town towards a reservoir pumping fresh water in a desert area.

KNUT

We don't drill oil to destroy the world, Hanna, but to make it. You are not the only one who has fought for things, you know. We created the Unions. We tried to do the right thing. We found our voice.

HANNA

Yes, all the strikes you told me about. Norway wasn't built on oil, Grandpa. It was built by people, politicians like Bratelli and the rest, that you're so fond of. (Wells 2013)

This sequence initially refers to the Kielland disaster, in which 123 people were killed when the Kielland oil rig capsized. The memorial to that catastrophe – 'the broken link' – and many of the icons then used after it (the chain, the question mark, the 'tick', the dollar sign) work as punctum; all are, in Rancière's terminology, obtuse images. The evolving vistas and the power of singularity (*the punctum*) of the obtuse image; the educational value (*the studium*) of the document bearing the trace of history; and the combinatory capacity of the sign, open to being combined with any element from a different sequence to compose new sentence-images *ad infinitum*. (Rancière 2013: 68)

In order to evidence these conceptual premises, and simultaneously illustrate the idea of the *repository*, the *site* and *the archive*, I wish to conclude by looking at an extract from my own practice, in writing an animated documentary (Wells 2013) for the Oil Museum in Stavanger, Norway.

Based on the memoir *Masters and Servants* by politician and activist Aslak Sira Myhre (2010), and developed in collaboration with oil industry investors and historians, my script dramatises a social history of oil in Norway. It does so by playing out tensions between Knut, an oil industry veteran, and his eco-warrior granddaughter, Hanna. It is important to stress that the script was predicated on: the specificity of real places and contexts in Stavanger; real historical events (most particularly, key industry-defining tragedies); and an implied discussion of the benefits and drawbacks of the oil industry. In the following sequence, Knut and Hanna debate these latter issues:

CUT TO

Hanna and Knut standing by the Kielland tribute monument, 'Broken Link'. The large chain coupling that composes the monument transforms into a longer, wider chain, which forms a question mark.

The question mark transforms into a dollar sign, which multiplies and pours into the shape of a large 'tick' [√] and transforms again into the map of Norway. The camera homes into Stavanger on the map, which becomes defined by a metamorphosing graphic of the town's monuments from the 'Sword in Rock' (Roed) to the Straen Senteret Top Hat and Anvil to the 'Shrimp' (Hukeland) to the Myhregaarden apartments to the outline of the Oil Museum to the Kvadrat stores.

VO

[This begins as the large tick becomes the map of Norway, and continues over the following transitions]

Knut

Look round you. See the world we live in. When I was your age, Hanna, today's Stavanger would have looked improbable even in a sci-fi film. We're better off than we could ever have dreamt.

As the Stavanger statue/building graphic reaches its image of the Kvadrat store, all kinds of oil- and gas-related products pop up and spiral round Knut and Hanna (i.e., transport; packaging; technology; clothes; furnishings; household objects, etc.)

Unsurprisingly, Rancière does not recognise the animated image as the 'metamorphic image' *par excellence* (though he does mention manga in passing); he instead remains sceptical about the prospect of *any* potent model of image-making emerging or enduring within what is, arguably, an already exhausted visual culture. Ironically, though, Rancière suggests that the answer might lie in:

> the Schlegalian poetics of the witticism that invents between fragments of films, news strips, photos, reproductions of paintings and other things, all the combinations, distances or approximations capable of eliciting new forms and meanings. This assumes the existence of a boundless Store/Library/Museum where all films, texts, photographs and paintings co-exist. (Rancière 2013: 68)

Inevitably, I am attracted to the phrase 'invents between' since for any animation theorist, historian and/or practitioner, it cannot but recall Norman McLaren's seminal dictum that: 'animation is not the art of drawings-that-move, but rather the art of movements-that-are-drawn. What happens *between* each frame is more important than what happens *on* each frame' (Solomon 1987: 11). That structuring 'interval' in animation practice has come to represent two things. Firstly, the key point of intervention and creativity that mobilises each image in a spirit of its observational and applicatory 'trace' (think of Goldberg's above-quoted description of animation as a documentary process of close observation). Secondly, the animated image's historicised and aestheticised presence as an interpretive, creative and rhetorical act. The animated documentary has surely become, then, the recombinant form that Rancière alludes to – and also, as suggested earlier, *the archive* (Rancière's store/library/museum) that apprehends the texts which properly speak to a wide range of discourses relevant to contemporary historiography. Such discourses include those of appearance and disappearance; of the virtual and the material; and of the past, the present, and the possibly imminent 'no future' feared by Kurt D. Bollacker and, before him, Johnny Rotten.

The oil kid

I have long argued that theories of practice (like those advanced above by Rancière) should translate into practices of theory, in which theoretical concepts can act as tools in creative work. Seeming to draw on the work of Roland Barthes, Rancière concludes the article in which he talks about his three conceptions of the image with a consideration of the way in which the image must function if it is to properly service innovation and attain meaning. He distinguishes between 'the archive', and the methods by which the past is understood, are under threat. This in turn led me to think about the ways in which the animated documentary's model of aestheticisation was, to coin Nick Kaye's phrase once more, a 'dialectical move' that placed the virtual in circulation as a critical commentary on material culture. Put simply, much animated documentary is fundamentally concerned with the question of what can survive for posterity in the face of a lack of contemporary evidence of a given phenomenon and/or as a result of that phenomenon being rendered culturally marginal. Those questions also beg another: How might such a phenomenon be visualised and restored in later animated documentary work? Hyunseok Lee's *One Mind* (2011), for example, is an animated documentary that seeks to facilitate the experience of engaging with Buddhist art and architecture through the digital restoration of an ancient monastery. The core concept of the piece is to prompt sense memories within the virtual reconstruction of the monastery as if it were a walk-through installation.

Interestingly in this regard, Jacques Rancière has made claims for the installation as a 'theatre of memory', in which a 'double metamorphosis' takes place. The image becomes both a 'cipher of history' and a mode of 'interruption'; as a result, he argues,

> Installation art thus brings into play the metamorphic, unstable nature of images. The latter circulate between the world of art and the world of imagery. They are interrupted, fragmented, reconstituted by a poetics of witticism that seeks to establish new differences of potentiality between these unstable elements. (Rancière 2013: 65)

As is so often the case, the image, when discussed as 'art', becomes a plausibly unstable yet instructive engagement with historical evidence and a challenging interruption into what is essentially the dominant media flow of photojournalistic imagery. Yet once more, however, it remains generally unrecognised that this form of engagement-cum-interruption is the very condition of animation – and, most specifically, of animated documentary, especially in the case of a film like *One Mind*. Rancière's argument comes in the midst of his analysis of the documentary image, in which he suggests a series of closely related categorisations: 'the naked image' merely witnesses [e.g., a photograph]; 'the ostensive image' renders visual material as art by placing it within the institutional discourses of 'the gallery' [e.g., a photograph in an arts institution]; and 'the metamorphic image' plays 'with the forms and products' of visual culture and, when not concerned with 'demystification', provides a point of access to meaning seemingly not available in traditional documentary forms [e.g., a photograph that has been manipulated, re-contextualised, or re-used as part of other work]. (Rancière 2013: 65–7) interpretation of the material. Animated processes of investigation, interrogation and re-invention become both a creative practice (the making of a film) and a finished outcome (the film that is made). Further, this dialectical move ultimately shapes the 'argument' implied and articulated in (variously): the *outcome* (that is, the finished film); the *hypothesis* and its test; the 'theory' as it is tacitly synthesised in 'practice'. In these ways, animated documentary as a mode then becomes (to return to the title of Edmund de Waal's book) the revelation of the 'hidden inheritance' inherent in the phenomena that individual animated documentaries depict and deconstruct.

Never mind the Bollacker

The Sex Pistols' seminal 1977 album *Never Mind the Bollocks* did not fundamentally change my view of music, since it struck me at the time as nothing but old-school rock 'n' roll. However, its Day-Glo sleeve and 'offensive' title did challenge my view of art, presentation and packaging. To a long-time fan of double-gatefold sleeves, lyric inserts and Hipgnosis designs, Jamie Reid's cover for the Pistols seemed challengingly amateur and distinctly poor. I already knew the phrase 'Never mind the bollocks' from my London childhood: a dismissal of anything that seemed irrelevant or an unconvincing excuse for something. But Reid's typography, suggestive of an anonymous blackmail letter, and the swathes of bright colour, seriously irritated me. Where was the portrait of the band? Where was the assemblage of concert shots and tour photos? Where was the 'artistic' composition that would allow the cover to add gravitas to the music contained inside the sleeve? Yet ultimately, this cover made me realise that the precise illusionism of a given design could suggest and provoke far more than the more literal interventions of portrait photography or deliberately composed art shots were able to manage. As a sixteen-year-old, this was an important step towards my later recognition of animation as a moving image artifice analogous (but not identical) to live-action film – and thereafter, my understanding of what constituted evidence for a cultural record of something and the claims of aestheticisation within such a representational process.

The Sex Pistols' sleeve and what it taught me returned to mind when, much later on, I encountered a 2010 *American Scientist* essay written by one Kurt D. Bollacker, warning against 'the digital dark age' (Bollacker 2010). Bollacker's suggestion was that the singular failure to establish formats and contexts by which digital data might be irrevocably stored for future posterity was already resulting in wholesale loss of material – and may ultimately mean that a whole era will pass seemingly un-evidenced. At one level, this was possibly scaremongering. But on another, it constituted a clear recognition that latter's generic tropes as straightforward codes of 'objectivity'. As Kaye (ibid.: 215) notes, 'One of the first observations one might make of these documentations [of site-specific art work] is their sensitivity to their own limits, their willingness to concede the impossibility of reproducing the object'. As a form, animation fundamentally acknowledges these limits in its self-conscious re-engagement with, and re-imagining of, source materials that are thus, to use Sheila Bernard's term, made *active* (Bernard 2007: 45–7). In this way, animated documentary invites critical commentary on, public discourse around, and key investments in both the interpretation and interrogation of received and perceived personal, social and historical 'realities'.

Animation, as is clear from the nature of its language of expression in all forms, always has a distinctive relationship to the 'object'. It always takes into account the latter's mobility, shifting status and propensity for change. Kaye (2000: 215) stresses that 'Earth art, Land art, and subsequently, Body art, similarly come to treat the gallery space as a place to document or map interventions into inaccessible sites'. It is but a simple step from here to suggest that the animated documentary works in an analogous manner to the gallery (*the repository*) and the documentation situated within it (the record of *the site*). Animated documentary constantly articulates and illustrates the tensions between recording and being a creative outcome in itself. It also inherently deals with the idea of itself as *the archive*. In working with – and often, actively producing – this 'flux' of change as its very subject, animation echoes and reflects the very things it records, bringing to them what Kaye calls, in relation to site-specific art which is not present, a 'perceptual exposure' (ibid.: 215). This clearly echoes Monceaux's 'shift of perception' in his film of the same name. In essence, however, *all* animated documentary offers this very same perceptual exposure in operating as a 'non-site' to the site-specific nature of its chosen topics, preoccupations and issues. Animated documentary offers an exposure to material that has gone through a perceptual filter, and which therefore encourages a response to the discourse raised, rather than passive acceptance of an authorial aestheticisation – as arguably (and perhaps ironically) evidenced in the photographic work of Mosse. As Kaye argues:

> The site [or a work's central thematic topic, pre-occupation or issue], it follows, is not available as an 'object', for it is not static; the site is mobile, always in a process of appearance and disappearance, available only in a dialectical move which the Non-Site prompts and to which it always returns. (2000: 216)

This 'dialectical move' that Kaye describes is in essence the tension between an animated documentary's chosen material and that film's chosen

Rimmenen and Takala's *Learned by Heart* is even more sophisticated in this respect. The film falls, however, between disciplinary stools in a way that dictates only a partial recognition of its achievements. If Mosse's work is about re-dressing the dominant codes and conventions of documentary and photojournalism, Rimmenen and Takala's approach is also about redefining imagery beyond rhetorical intervention. This speaks to the oft-implied criticism that documentary photography or footage is characterised as much by what it does not show as by what it does. Their work thus illustrates the extent to which the wider mode of animated documentary addresses the idea that absence – Hayden White's above-quoted view of the 'historical event', for example, or the emptiness and lack of knowledge implied in my 'death row' photos – is complicit in the notion of repressing or forgetting material and emotional histories. Rimmenen and Takala mobilise their visual resources to recover both the physical and the emotive; to suggest the holistic picture, rather than the selective and specific. Another example of this highly characteristic aspect of much animated documentary work is Dan Monceaux's *A Shift in Perception* (2006), a film that visualises the tactile and emotional memories of three South Australian blind women, Leander, Edna and Rhonda, by re-animating a series of live-action vignettes. In this way, Monceaux does not merely suggest the 'shift of perception' that has defined the women's lived experience, but also the necessary shift of perception that is required in understanding the matters of record contained within the various objects, materials and techniques used to portray Leander, Edna and Rhonda's stories. In this instance, such things are readily present to those who can see or use them, but more absent for those who live with them, and whose lives are ultimately interpreted through them.

Interestingly, this idea of 'absence' is also crucial to the understanding of site-specific art. When an artwork is absent in the gallery, it is nevertheless recorded by its documentation. As Nick Kaye (2000: 215–16) has pointed out, apropos of Robert Smithson's art: 'Documents do not simply reflect upon the apparent contradiction of attempting to record site-specific works in another place, time, and through another medium, but act out some of the complexities of the relationship between work and site.' This is a fundamental aspect of the way in which much animated documentary is constructed, since the latter functions as a discourse between its subject, its sources and the clear artifice of its essayistic interpretation of the former. Though a seemingly obvious point, it should be emphasised that the animated documentary – and particularly an 'avant-doc' like *A Shift of Perception* – foregrounds the subjectivity, authorship and constructed-ness of the documentary form. Animated documentary ultimately challenges the documentary form's long-sustained mythologies of actuality-film-as-truth, and the closely related idea of the and socially speaking. The young girl's 'perception' translated into 'memory' is in essence used to play out the complexities inherent within a range of related binary oppositions: the personal and the political; the micro- and the macro-world; local sensation and feeling against universal forces; the meta-narrative of the construction of the form against the grand narrative of social and cultural history. Rimminen and Takala constantly recognise that their highly self-conscious employment of animation means they are using a personal tool of expression in order to speak to major historical perspectives and issues. In their view this is still a risk and a contradiction, when taking into account the kind of critical and peer reception widely accorded to animation in the documentary realm at the time when their film was made (Wells 2007). While maintaining an intense belief in animation's capacity to use the 'micro' in the service of apprehending and re-presenting the 'macro', both filmmakers still felt self-conscious about this presumption in the face of the widespread dismissal of animation per se, let alone animation's place in documentary. Only today in films like *Watcher of the Sky* (Edet Belzberg, 2014), *Montage of Heck* (Brett Morgen, 2015) and *Last Hijack* (Tommy Pallotta and Femke Wolting 2014) is animation now broadly viewed as an acceptable and almost taken-for-granted creative approach to use.

One might compare this briefly, for example, to Richard Mosse's photographs addressing the civil war in Congo. The war claimed 5.4 million lives between 1998 and 2007 and also resulted in 400,000 rapes (Stearns 2011). In a certain sense, however, visual documentation, photojournalistic and otherwise, of the conflict had become banal and taken for granted. This was perhaps because, for many years, black-and-white photography prevailed as a marker of authenticity in documentary, not to mention that fact that in war zones, images of refugees were long rendered clichéd through their repeated publication. In his work on Congo, however, Mosse used ex-military infrared stock to re-take such compositions, largely rendering any green hues in the images pink or magenta. Conceptually, this radicalises photojournalistic imagery in the service of seeing the participants afresh, and thus potentially encourages artist and audience alike to affectively re-engage with the political, economic and humanitarian consequences of large-scale civil conflict. Moreover, there is also the irony that Mosse chose to work with military photographic stock: his resulting images of conditions in Congo were thus literally facilitated by those responsible for causing those conditions, and the visual propaganda that had circulated around them, in the first place. As an artist, Mosse consciously draws attention to this fact as an integral part of his work's aestheticised reflexivity, a condition that is even more self-consciously used by documentary animators, given the already 'rhetorical' condition of using animation as a tool of representation.

To select but one random example, consider David Peace's non-fiction novel *The Damned United* (2006), a psychological study of Brian Clough's ill-fated forty-four-day-long management of Leeds United Football Club. Freely imagined from Clough's point of view, Peace's novel required primary interviews and extended authorial consultation of eight related autobiographies, four biographies, nine club histories, ten English realist novels, four soccer encyclopaedias, newspaper records and a number of match-day programmes in order to create Clough's supposedly paranoid 'inner voice'. This particular creative process – evidenced in Peace's afterword of sources and acknowledgements – operates in a similar way to that of any animated documentary when genuinely seeking to emulate 'subjectivity'.

Returning to de Waal, his text cautions against any creative approach of this sort which does not inhabit a variety of sources fully, critiquing his own descent into nostalgia about the netsuke figures and their possible exotic history, and also recognising that this attitude would represent a 'thin' text about his inheritance. What he really desired was the deep, associative, 'thick' text that would emerge from the kind of invested research process that informed Peace's work, and a pertinent representation of the netsuke figures' biography thereafter. The 'thick' text is essentially concerned with the idea that all production and exhibition contexts are *repositories*; all images and objects are *sites* of meaning; and representations of the site in relation to its repository is in effect *the archive*. I wish to argue here, then, that when de Waal (2010: 17) says that 'how objects are handed on is all about storytelling', and that the accretion of stories must be used to guard against the 'chain of forgetting', he seeks to apprehend the feeling beyond the fact of the narrative – and in consequence, seeks to attach meaning through the act of memory. It is in this – the ready apprehension of 'memory' in the service of the image and object – that the animated documentary has specific qualities and capabilities, and which activates 'the archive' as a mobile and fluid resource.

Marjut Rimminen and Palvi Takala's *Learned by Heart* (2007), for instance, is an exploration of post-Second World War Finland seen through the perception of a young girl – but also the specific form of perception *in the moment* as it is later remembered by the protagonist when she is an older woman. The film is constructed as a collage of archive footage and photographs and also animated vignettes. It is strongly influenced by the impact of the church, expressed here through hymns, and the normal everyday rites of passage in human experience as they are re-contextualised by ideological restraints. Though Finland had tentatively maintained its independence in the face of Soviet overtures, the impact of the Nazi invasion and the broader influence of larger Western economies defined Finnish experience, both individually intervention and the latter's insistence on the act of encoding. Animation as a documentary form, then, is actually an instance of re-materialising the image in the face of the idea that photography can be complicit in prevailing accounts, and thus can work to hide as much as it reveals. The 'death row' implicit in the photographic artefact becomes an explicit model of the 'come-to-life' encountered in the animated documentary. As veteran Disney animator Eric Goldberg confirms, 'Animators are born documentary makers; they have to look at everything so hard; everything must be so closely observed. Each drawing is a document recording how you know something is alive' (Wells 2011).

The hidden inheritance

Aestheticisation in animated documentary is, then, a way of arousing life-giving properties in already established material evidence. This arousal proceeds in order to understand the codes and conventions – and, crucially, the *curatorial* sensibility – necessary in any given interpretive approach that an artist uses when creating an animated documentary form. It should be noted here that this curatorial sensibility must necessarily see 'the archive' that may facilitate this practice as a fluid form; an idea I will address later in this discussion. I have written elsewhere about the meanings of objects in animation (Wells 2014), a topic that had an unlikely source in my pathological disdain for ceramics, fostered by being forced to do pottery at school. To conquer this phobic response, I read ceramicist Edmund de Waal's *The Hare with Amber Eyes: A Hidden Inheritance* (2010), a biographical account of his engagement with a collection of Japanese netsuke figures that he inherited. Again, this may at first seem a theoretically distant perspective on animated documentary, one at odds with other scholars' normative citation practice. I wish to suggest, though, that the analysis of animated documentary practice – and, indeed, of animation per se – benefits from the *polyvocal* inclusion of multidisciplinary voices and the *multi-register* inclusion of academics and non-academics whose respective tones and modes of expression may vary, but which necessarily access pertinent core knowledge and information. Though any collaborative practice, or any conglomeration of material sources may possess hierarchy in its organisational model, the central premise of this approach is to challenge any potential hierarchy by an inclusiveness that places such assumed ideas into relief. This also speaks to the documentary enterprise in democratising the hypotheses articulated through a diverse range of voices that may inform discussion of the former.

This latter position is accepted without question in other quasi-documentary arts practices and disciplines when myriad sources are required.

reflexive as it remains a self-conscious interrogation of all perceived constructions and records of material reality, or seemingly common experience agreed thereafter.

There is a set of photographs on the wall of my mother's living room that she terms 'death row'. All the people in the photographs (with the exception of her and me) are dead. 'They are the reason you're like you are', she says obtusely, leaving me intrigued and provoked at the same time. I know some of their identities – my dad, various grandparents, aunts, uncles, assorted neighbours and bystanders – but all I see is absence, silence and loss. While such photographs retain their 'truth claim', and may be traditional sources of evidence to find out about people from/in the past, they seem only to provide a lack of evidence – or, at the very most, questionable evidence.

I am immediately reminded in this regard of David Levy's film *Grandpa Looked Like William Powell* (2010), in which Levy explores how a family memento – in this case, his grandfather's autograph book from 1924 – demonstrates just how little one might know about one's relation. From this premise, his animated documentary uses the autographs, written messages and photographs of his grandfather, 'a swarthy, Jewish version of William Powell' (the 1930s film star famous for roles in *The Thin Man* [1934] and *My Man Godfrey* [1936]), as the basis for a hand-drawn animation visualising the anecdotes he had gleaned about his relative and pictorially annotating his primary research material. The literalness of a photograph of Levy's grandfather in his swimming trunks is transposed into a hand-drawn motif in the film, an 'aestheticisation' that helps the viewer to sense the 'aliveness' of the subject.

In instances such as this one, as David Levi-Strauss (2013: 107) points out:

> The idea that the more transformed or 'aestheticised' an image is, the less 'authentic' or politically valuable it becomes is one that needs to be seriously questioned. Why can't beauty be a call to action? ... To represent is to aestheticise; that is, to transform. It presents a vast field of choices but it does not include the choice not to transform, not to change or alter whatever is being represented. It cannot be pure process, in practice ... to become legible to others, these imaginings must be socially and culturally encoded. That is aestheticisation.

This idea is useful, in that it places matters of record (in whatever medium) within a broader palette of interpretative practice. The image is thus rendered as something in the service of the meaning and context that it is intended to represent. In animation, and certainly in an animated film like Levy's, the process and the outcome constitute an essential and determinedly political act of transformation, bequeathing legibility through the transparency of the

1930s embrace of Len Lye and Norman McLaren, in particular, spoke to this idea, with McLaren himself noting:

> John Grierson saw the work of the GPO Film Unit as a series of social 'publications' arguing for democracy, revealing the importance of democratic practices. Sponsoring 'art' films, and adding a commercial principle, deliberately set out to show *literally* that the 'freedom of expression' was at the heart of his social agenda. He wanted to show these films as part of political life and the economy. (Wells 1983)

Grierson's moral, social and ethical agenda essentially defined the documentary enterprise in Britain; his embrace of the avant-garde contained within it a recognition that it was important not merely to observe social practices but also to define the parameters of the 'truth claim'. This challenge posed by this history centred, in many respects, on exploring the primacy of photography in the authentication of 'documentary', and in addressing the fervent self-distancing of arts culture from animation. The latter wariness was, at one level, perverse, in that animation had been so favoured and preferred by the British Ministry of Information during the Second World War and by its successor, the Central Office of Information, in the post-war period.

To a certain extent, though, that historically specific moment of sustained institutional patronage cast documentary and public information film works – animated or otherwise – as ideologically charged and politically owned; conditions that were a seeming anathema to the artist. It becomes crucial, therefore, to identify the imperatives and outcomes of the creative process itself – the documentary work. As Robert Coles (1997: 74) insists:

> Put differently, what kind of moral or psychological accountability should we demand of ourselves, or [of those] who lay claim to social idealism, or [of] a documentary tradition that (we hope) will work towards a social good? [E xpose injustice, shed light on human suffering or contribute to a growing body of knowledge stored in libraries, in museums, in film studios[?].

It is this 'moral or psychological accountability' that, I wish to suggest, resides in the ideologically *and* artistically driven investment in making an animated documentary. The aestheticisation of any such film work is a marker of its authorial insight and its acknowledgement of 'the archive', a point I will return to later. Crucially, animation mounts a meta-critique of documentary itself while simultaneously using and re-working the documentary mode's traits and tropes in order to facilitate a rhetorical intervention within the subject at hand. This fact re-defines both the documentarian and the 'documents' and hypotheses they test, simply by virtue of using the inherent reflexivity of the animated form. It maybe useful to stress here that all animation practice is that reconciled 'high' and 'popular' culture, but that also permitted the 'visual' to take on as much validity as 'words' within any one given text. For the practitioner seeking reassurance in developing valid animated narratives and visual outcomes, this was important, in that co-opting literary credibility at a time when film, media and animation studies were non-existent or limitedly formed was critical in the advance of critically informed image-making – a practice still pertinent in the contemporary era, in which animation film-makers such as Estonian Priit Parn or Russian Igor Kovalyov want their films to be read like a novel rather than as a conventional animation/film.

Though this made me feel mildly maverick at the time, I was comforted that the same view was shared by Italo Calvino:

> The sociological-inquiry film and the historical-research film make sense only if they are not filmed explanations of the truth that sociology and historiography are saying ... For a true essay film I envisage an attitude not of pedagogy but of interrogation, with none of that inferiority complex towards the written word that has bedeviled relations between literature and cinema. (1987: 79–80)

Crucially, I had come to recognise that Capote had re-thought the novel in a way which mapped a terrain that, Hayden White (1996: 22) suggests, re-determined a historical event as: 'a hypothetical presupposition necessary to the constitution of a documentary record whose inconsistencies, gaps and distortions ... presumed to be [its] common referent itself moves to the fore as the principal object of investigation'. The 'event' itself, then, was merely an act of naming or categorisation, something that had happened that might only be recognised as 'a narrative'. Its 'facts' were explicit, but its 'truth' was necessarily embedded, unclear, and sometimes invisible. I was already persuaded that animation was predicated on the idea of being an interrogative art, its material filmic consequences *always* an interrogation of reality; *a rhetorical device* that spoke directly to the inconsistencies, gaps and distortions White highlighted, and that yet also embraced the truth of the historiographical and the sociological. This latter understanding seemed to be vindicated in the ways that I saw animation used in training and instructional films (see Hediger and Vonderau 2009), Disney's wartime propaganda, or even in later works like Svankmajer's *The Death of Stalinism in Bohemia* (1991) or Ali Samadi Ahadi's *The Green Wave* (2010).

At the same time, however, animation had also been a vehicle by which documentary and the experimental avant-garde had been fused (see Macdonald 2015), so its rhetorical aspects in this context were largely about the ways in which anti-narrative or frame rate challenged both notions of cinematic 'reality' and the external reality of the social world. John Grierson's and explored as part of that process. After Capote, I felt that the piece's emotional truth was as important as executing an accurate narrative of the murders in order to explain a seemingly motiveless crime. Equally, I wanted to reveal the presence of the authorial voice in constructing and guiding the narrative. Although my theatre version, for example, was by no means a Brechtian call-out of art's relationship to its political convictions, its 'colour script' of the piece alone signified specific rhetorical interventions. The warm yellows and ochres of John Ford's Monument Valley locations, for example, or the dark mahogany and navy blues of his cavalry communities, were used to frame Holcomb's credentials as a 'Western' town. The bright tones of L. Frank Baum's Oz were borrowed to actually represent 'Kansas', before it was drenched in the sickly greens of Hitchcock's necrophiliac nausea in *Vertigo* (1958) or the noir-ish chiaroscuro of Jacques Tourneur's *Build My Gallows High* (1947); cold, blue, riverside, spot-lit areas also reflected Smith and Hickock's desperate melancholia.

I advance this point because I had by that time become aware of 'colour scripts' through my interest in animated films, and my (then) unconscious understanding of animation as an intrinsically illusionist and rhetorical form. Working within this wider vocabulary of bright impressionist saturations and dark expressionist shadows, yet prioritising heightened naturalism in the performances, I embraced 'animation' as an art-direction tool to create theatrical 'documentary'. All of this, of course, makes notions of the 'factual', 'non-fiction' or 'objective' expression in representation a highly relative thing in itself. But this is not unrelated to the art world's initial reticence in rejecting 'documentary' as something understood to typically be in the service of institutional governance and public information, or, at the very least, of any already dominant and established 'voice' mediated to mass audiences. This schism was always illusory in many senses, but became bound up in the cultural debates that separated art from entertainment, or high from popular culture, when the popular was often the mediator of a potential avant-garde, but seemingly in the hands of explicitly named art works and not the creative insights of the journalist or documentarian (see Stallabrass 2013: 12–21).

Capote's *In Cold Blood* was art as historicism, but equally, a profoundly important statement bridging the seeming divide between my investment in the modernist literature of D. H. Lawrence, Virginia Woolf and T. S. Eliot and my discovery of Saul Bellow, Henry Miller and Norman Mailer, the latter writers proving to be – for me at least – potent visualisers of (masculine) feeling and emotion, the point of access to sex and satire. It was but a short journey to the underground comics of Robert Crumb, Marvel's Jack Kirby and Steve Ditko, *Mad* magazine and Tex Avery cartoons. This was significant in as much as I felt that I had 'flatlined' art and documentary into a continuum approach is predicated on the view that, in order to apprehend animation's versatility as a tool of documentary expression, it is necessary to see animation as an 'umbrella' for all the arts: drawing, painting, sculpture, photography, film, performance, and so on. Though this is a key preoccupation in Skoller's journal special issue, usefully expanding documentary's parameters as a genre, I wish here to explore the arts as a conduit for a *combinative* approach in using other creative disciplines that have already established their credentials within the documentary form. It is hoped that this further reinforces the emergent literature on animated documentary, while also demonstrating that already proven documentary approaches in other art forms have validated the concepts of subjectivity and aestheticisation as key documentary tools.

Death row

One of my first personal investments in the combination of 'art' and 'documentary' was Truman Capote's *In Cold Blood* (1966), a novelistic development of Norman Mailer and Tom Wolfe's pioneering 'New Journalism' based on subjective interpretations and accounts of real-life events and using 'thick' text forms of primary and secondary research.[3] This was then played out through the filter of an individualistic, quasi-naturalistic literary stylisation: an embedded emotional 'graphic' as potent as Dorothea Lange's *Dust Bowl* photographic images or the sequential photojournalism published in magazines like *Look* and *Life*. Having played the part of Detective Alvin Dewey, in an extended classroom simulation overseen by my (evidently) progressive English teacher, Frank Startup, I was immersed in 'performance art', living literature and American social history and politics. Looking back, this highly formative experience positioned me in such a way that I always subsequently saw a confluence between 'subjectivity' and 'objectivity', and a synergy between creative practice and social engagement. Richard Brooks's 1967 film version of *In Cold Blood*, which I saw only much later, sought to bring a *vérité* approach to Capote's narrative, even filming in Holcomb (the small town in which the infamous multiple murder that the writer documented took place), and in the prison facilities at Kansas State Penitentiary that housed Perry Smith and Richard Hickock, the perpetrators of the crimes in question. Brooks filmed in black and white, both to reference noir tones and conventions but also to benefit from monochrome's then-accepted veracity as the presiding visual language of documentary aesthetics and 'truth'. I later made theatre (Wells 1988) and television (Wells 1990) versions of *In Cold Blood* that sought to fuse the narrative further. John Ford's frontier communities, Capote's alleged homosexual fascination with the killers, and the key theme of the relativity of human motive, outlook and action were all referenced reflected McLaren's status within experimental animated film, in deliberately intervening in documentary modes by using the form. This lack of acknowledgement fails to recognise the progressive nature of McLaren's position *as an animator*. The implied notion of animation as cinema and film studies' 'poor relation' was first properly acknowledged and articulated in the work of Alan Cholodenko (1991). But, even as late as 2007, at the International Documentary Festival in Amsterdam (the largest festival of its kind), 'animated documentary' was viewed with a high degree of scepticism, and in most cases dismissed, even though gaining sturdy (if unexpected) defence in the persons of Werner Herzog and Nick Broomfield – both, of course, not unfamiliar with revising the predominant orthodoxies of documentary film.[2] The festival screenings of animated documentaries, curated by Gerben Schermer and Eric Van Drunen, were met with hostility by many and curiosity by others: surely forms as seemingly opposed as 'animation' (the undisputed art of the impossible, but mainly for children) and 'documentary' (the socially earnest quest for 'objectivity' and 'truth') could not be harnessed together? By instructive contrast, the DOK Festival in Leipzig has, since its emergence in 1955, long assumed a relationship between the two modes, suggesting that animation and documentary actually shared the highest degree of 'subjectivity' and that the 'document' or matter of record was a highly relative thing, far closer to art-making than the rigours of proven material evidence and academic historiography. DOK Leipzig has a comprehensive website providing information for the content of each annual festival and an accompanying film archive drawn from previous festival editions.

From early efforts in defining the animated documentary form by DelGaudio (1997), Strøm (2003), Ward (2005) and myself (1997), through to recent books by Kriger (2012) and Honess Roe (2013), and a journal special issue edited by Skoller (2011), a critical literature has developed which has provided sustained engagement with this growing area of contemporary filmmaking practice. My own interest has moved away from defining animated documentary and closer towards addressing the nature of the documentary enterprise itself – and yet further, towards considering animation as a conduit of the arts in the construction of creative tools in the service of documentary work. This has been partially pursued in my original paper at the 2011 *Animated Realities* Conference held at Edinburgh College of Art, and in my own documentary filmmaking practice since then.

Thus, while the following essay still inevitably touches upon issues of definition and deployment, it also refers back to the opening idea of animation studies sitting under-represented and under-acknowledged at the back of my imaginary class, and also to my own particular approach towards *polyvocal* and *multi-register* theories of creative practice and creative practices of theory. This

CHAPTER 6

Never Mind the Bollackers: Here's the Repositories, Sites and Archives in Nonfiction Animation
Paul Wells

INTRODUCTION: CLASS ISSUES

Imagine a classroom, say, in the old-school style of Hogwarts or Miss Jean Brodie's, and huddled up in the tightly rowed desks are academic subjects and disciplines. at the front, secure in their superiority, are the Classics and the sciences; engineering, business and architecture take their places just behind. The arts, unsurprisingly, sit by the window gazing out on other lands, nudged by the humanities and design to pay more attention, while sport comes in late, pulling its socks up. Film and media studies constantly put their hands up, eager for more attention, while, ironically, at the same time looking back and down at the sullen figure of animation studies sitting in the corner. This morning, however, animation studies is smiling. Its homework has been returned, and the red ticks in the margin have accumulated into three 'A's – 'ani-doc', 'art' and 'archives' – its place in the Academy is thus secure.[1]

When I first addressed the idea of the 'animated documentary' in the early 1990s, the acceptance of animation per se within UK university curricula boiled down to a few groundbreaking courses in production (mainly in art schools and polytechnics) and some recognition that scholars (principally American) active in the Society of Animation Studies sought to advance the idea of animation as a significant art form worthy of sustained study and analysis. The latter was hard enough: 'cartoons' were surely the flotsam of cultural practice and unworthy of attention. So, to also sully 'documentary' by association was a bridge too far. Even a seemingly open-minded earlier text such as Alan Rosenthal's *The New Documentary in Action*, which presciently included discussion of Norman McLaren's *Pas de Deux* (1967), still contained critique of 'a number of deficiencies' in McLaren's work, such as: 'the harshness of his colors', the 'too often repeated simplicity of his forms', and his 'lack of passion and fire' (Rosenthal 1971: 268). Rosenthal's critique, therefore, though possibly valid at some levels, still does not foreground what animation has specifically added to the parameters of documentary, nor

Telotte, Jay (2008), 'Animating space: Disney, science, and empowerment', *Science Fiction Studies*, 35: 1, pp. 48–59.
Titanic, film, directed by James Cameron. USA: Lightstorm Entertainment, 1997.
van Dijck, Jose (2006), 'Picturizing science: the science documentary as multimedia spectacle', *International Journal of Cultural Studies*, 9: 1, pp. 5–24.
Ward, Paul (2011), 'Animating with facts: the performative process of documentary animation in *the ten mark* (2010)', *animation: an interdisciplinary journal*, 6: 3, pp. 293–305.
Wells, Paul (2008), 'Animation and digital culture', in Martin Halliwell and Catherine Morley (eds), *American Thought and Culture in the Twenty First Century*, Edinburgh: Edinburgh University Press, pp. 291–306.
Wright, Richard (2008), 'Data visualization', in Matthew Fuller (ed.), *Software Studies: a Lexicon*, Cambridge, MA: MIT Press, p. 78.

Benjamin, Walter (1999), 'The work of art in the age of mechanical reproduction', in *Illuminations*, London: Pimlico, pp. 217–52.

Bennett, Bruce (2007), 'Towards a general economic of cinema', in Susan Bruce and Valeria Wagner (eds), *Fiction and Economy*, London: Palgrave Macmillan, pp. 167–86.

Brain, Robert and Norton Wise (1999), 'Muscles and engines: indicator diagrams and Helmholtz's graphical methods', in Mario Biagioli (ed.), *The Science Studies Reader*, London: Routledge, pp. 124–48.

Caldwell, John (2000), 'Modes of production: the televisual apparatus', Robert Stam and Toby Miller (eds), *Film and Theory: An Anthology*, Oxford: Blackwell, pp. 125–44.

Caldwell, John (2004), 'Convergence television: aggregating form and repurposing content in the culture of conglomeration', in Jan Olsson and Lynn Spigel (eds), *Television after TV: Essays on a Medium in Transition*, Durham, NC: Duke University Press, pp. 41–74.

Campbell-Kelly, Martin and William Aspray (2004), *Computer: A History of the Information Machine*, Oxford: Westview Press.

Cubitt, Sean (2005), *The Cinema Effect*, Cambridge, MA: MIT Press.

Debord, Guy (1995), *The Society of the Spectacle*, New York: Zone Books.

DelGaudio, Sybil (1997), 'If truth be told, can 'toons tell it? Documentary and animation', *Film History*, 9: 2, pp. 189–99.

Doane, Mary Ann (2006), 'Information, crisis, catastrophe', in Wendy Chun and Thomas Keenan (eds), *New Media, Old Media: A History and Theory Reader*, New York: Routledge, pp. 251–64.

Glynne, Andy (2013), 'Drawn from life: the animated documentary', in Brian Winston (ed.), *The Documentary Film Book*, London: BFI/Palgrave Macmillan, pp. 73–5.

Gunning, Tom (1990), 'The cinema of attractions: early film, its spectator and the avant-garde', in Thomas Elsaesser (ed.), *Early Cinema: Space, Frame, Narrative*, London: BFI, pp. 56–62.

Gurevitch, Leon (2015), 'The transforming face of industrial spectacle: a media archaeology of machinic mobility', *senses of cinema*, 75, June, <http://sensesofcinema.com/2015/michael-bay-dossier/industrial-spectacle-cinema/> (last accessed 19 October 2016).

Gurevitch, Leon (2016), 'Cinema designed: visual effects software and the emergence of the engineered spectacle', in Shane Denison and Julia Leyda (eds), *Post-Cinema: Theorising 21st-Century Film*, Sussex: Reframe Books, <http://reframe.sussex.ac.uk/post-cinema/> (last accessed 19 October 2016).

Honess Roe, Annabelle (2013), *Animated Documentary*, London: Palgrave Macmillan.

Ihde, Don (2009), 'From da Vinci to CAD and beyond', *Synthese*, 168: 3, pp. 453-67.

Loose Change, film, directed by Dylan Avery. USA: Journeyman Pictures, 2005.

Manovich, Lev (2001), *The Language of New Media*, Cambridge, MA: MIT Press.

Metz, Anneke (2008), 'A fantasy made real: the evolution of the subjunctive documentary on U.S. cable science channels', *Television and New Media*, 9: 4, pp. 333–47.

Metz, Christian (1982), *The Imaginary Signifier: Psychoanalysis and the Cinema*, Indianapolis: Indiana University Press.

Oxford English Dictionary (2005), Oxford: Oxford University Press.

Powers of Ten, film, directed by Charles and Ray Eames. USA: International Business Machines and Office of Charles and Ray Eames, 1977.

Scott, Karen and Anne White (2003), 'Unnatural history? Deconstructing the *Walking with Dinosaurs* phenomenon', *Media, Culture & Society*, 25: 3, pp. 315–32.

The Sinking of the Lusitania, film, directed by Winsor McCay. USA: Universal Film Manufacturing Company, 1918.

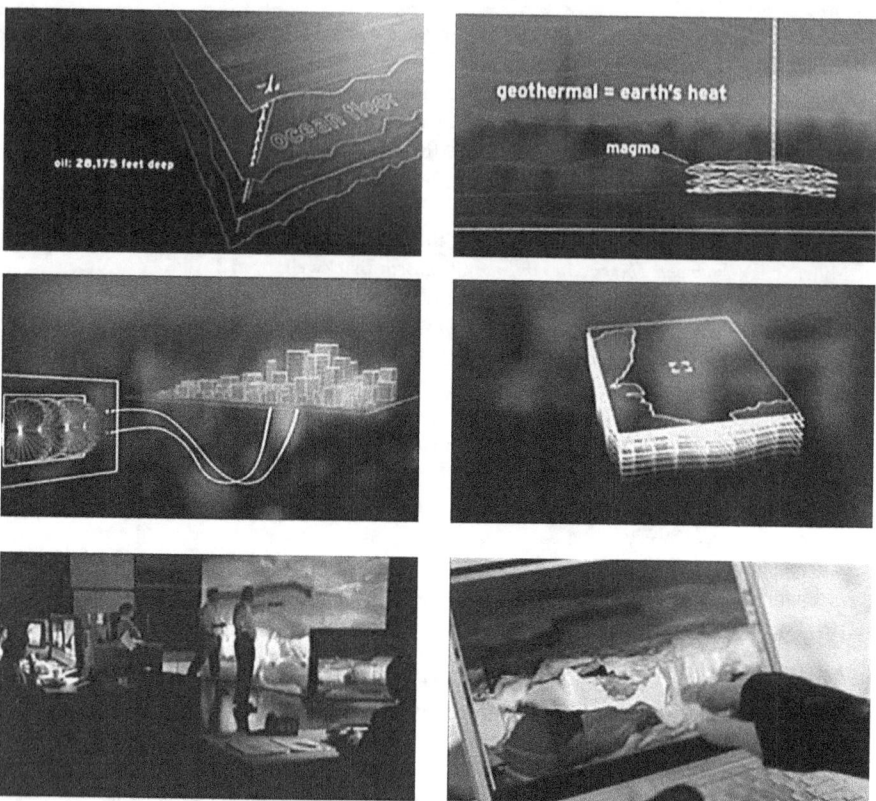

Figure 5.4a–f Stills of the simulations from Chevron's *Human Energy* commercial

NOTE

1. By 'pre-indexical' here I refer to the concept first described by Charles Peirce and later returned to by theorists from Andre Bazin to Tom Gunning and most notably by Lev Manovich that the advent of the 'single referent' image (as Manovich refers to it) bore an indexical relationship to objects captured by the chemical photographic process. For Manovich the century of photographic indexicality that characterised twentieth century visual culture was an anomaly in an otherwise largely non-indexical visual culture.

BIBLIOGRAPHY

Babbage, Charles (1851), *The Exposition of 1851; or, Views of the Industry, the Science, and the Government of England*, London: John Murray.

Beller, Jonathan (2006), *The Cinematic Mode of Production: Attention Economy and the Society of the Spectacle*, Lebanon, NH: Dartmouth College Press.

prevailing cultural discourse (in this case, the hostile narrative of ecological destruction, environmental disruption and climate change surrounding oil extraction). Instead, *Human Energy* presents a vignette of the hopefulness, positivity and the possibility of human ingenuity. Hard questions might present themselves, the commercial admits, but it argues that Chevron is using oil extraction to benefit communities and realise its consumers' potential. Rather audaciously, *Human Energy* attempts to park the company car on the lawn of traditional aid, development and even ecological charities. Perhaps most curious (though now familiar) is the way in which the commercial does this: through shots of oil engineers and scientists performing their job interspersed with Chevron's conception of what constitutes 'human energy'. Wells's 'not so special effects' (in this case, geological simulations) show the lengths Chevron is prepared to go to extract the resources its customers need to keep up the development job. Notably, and as with previous examples, viewers are treated to shots (Figure 5.4a–f) of 'experts' standing before their simulations and pointing, presumably identifying crucial aspects and technicalities unknown to the audience. This is 'human energy': the ability to devote labour and capital to the task of keeping humanity resourced.

Conclusion

To conclude, the arrival of freely available computer-generated simulation has been accompanied by the rhetorical spectacle of expertise. Individually, the many influences (scientific, engineering and/or industrial) that have fed the disciplinary and ontological construction of such a visual language may not be new. As we have seen, simulation and the spectacle of simulation have many longstanding historical precedents. However, the significance of simulation and its deployment as a form of animated documentary lies in its expansion of what animation is and can be. However, it would be a mistake to suggest that the rhetoric of animated simulation – that, through simulation, animation can now be considered a valid objective addition to the documentary form where previous forms of animation were not – should be taken at face value. Just as it is questionable to assert that animation ever really functioned in contradistinction to the supposedly indexical image, so, too, it is reductive to suggest that animated simulation based upon data models and scientific methodologies is inherently dependable in its veracity. This essay's deployment of the case study examples above suggests that the rhetoric of expertise is, amongst other things, just that: rhetoric.

The Documentary Attraction

Figure 5.3a–c Stills from *Loose Change*'s simulation sequences

aesthetic surface draw attention to that fact, that I believe the rhetoric of expertise rests. Two illustrative examples of this, drawn from very different media vehicles to Cameron's *Titanic* but which nonetheless bear remarkable similarities to it, are worth final consideration.

The first example is from Dylan Avery's 2005 documentary *Loose Change*. In this documentary, made to reveal the 'truth' of the 9/11 attacks on the Twin Towers and the Pentagon, a constant interplay between the 'credibility attached to location shooting' that Doane describes and that of the simulated visibility of the internal workings of the buildings in question are played out. The documentary opens with a plethora of archival footage (going as far back as the Second World War) before introducing handheld footage taken by civilians in New York of the attacks on the World Trade Centre. Interestingly, the film introduces footage throughout its running time via a telling motif: a flickering television in a dark room displays footage as the camera tracks toward it. This device explicitly works to introduce documentary footage as mediated and therefore of dubious veracity; a key theme for *Loose Change*, which questions the claim that documentary proof that planes struck the Twin Towers equates to proof that planes caused the buildings' collapse. *Loose Change* repeatedly refers back to simulation for authority on which to base its claim that the attacks could not have been carried out or executed in the manner popularly alleged. Indeed, what is perhaps most fascinating about this example is the way in which *Loose Change* attempts to directly challenge the credibility of location shooting with post-event simulations that, through appeals to an array of 'expertise' ('academics, engineers, physicists' as the film's opening moments put it), can utilise empirical simulation to prove that the planes could not possibly have destroyed the buildings in the manner suggested. As in the *Titanic* sequence, the aesthetic quality of simulations of the Twin Towers and subsequent adjacent buildings that collapsed is pared-down and utilitarian (Figure 5.3a–c). The authority of *Loose Change*'s simulations does not rest on an appeal to visual intricacy and production values. Rather, they reveal the buildings' inner structure, urging the viewer to approach the computer-generated simulations in accordance with the dictates of the film's voiceover and accompanying experts: as engineering diagrams that strip away artifice in the quest for 'truth'. This deployment demonstrates nothing if not the rhetoric of expertise.

This chapter's final example, a series of 2008 television commercials made by Chevron to promote their narrative of an oil company primarily concerned with the nurturing of 'human energy', derives from a very different location that, once again, bears interesting similarities to the examples discussed above. Similarly to *Loose Change*, Chevron's *Human Energy* commercial presents the animated simulation as a means of presenting an alternative narrative to revealing structural details from the inside of a computer model that draws attention to their construction.

This is not a radically new development, but the development of a continuum. Mary Ann Doane (2006) has described the way in which simulations deployed on television frequently seek to visualise events and phenomena that finished unfolding at some point in the past and/or for which no indexical record exists. At risk of complicating the present discussion's focus on animation in the cinematic context, Doane's claims regarding what she variously calls 'simulated visibility' and 'television knowledge' are well worth considering. Though Doane talks of television and 'televisibility' rather than the cinematic, her work's relevance says much about the context in which contemporary computer-generated simulations are produced. As suggested earlier, computer visualisations are produced with apparatus that utilised the cathode ray tube as the bedrock of its image output processes. As Manovich points out in his work on the genealogy of the screen, with the emergence of digital projection in the cinematic space, the exhibition contexts of cinema and television have begun to share commonalities that go beyond convergent production contexts (see Caldwell 2000, 2004).

Doane's argues that televisual simulations demonstrate the limits of empiricism:

> Television knowledge strains to make the invisible visible. While it acknowledges the limits of empiricism, the limitations of the eye in relation to knowledge, information is nevertheless conveyable only in terms of a simulated visibility – 'If it could be seen, this is what it might look like.' Television deals in potentially visible entities. The epistemological endeavor is to bring to the surface, to expose, but only at a second remove – depicting what is not available to sight. Televisibility is a construct, even when it makes use of the credibility attached to location shooting – embedding that image within a larger, over-riding discourse. (Doane 2006: 254)

But to complicate Doane's argument here, I would argue that, by acknowledging the limits of empiricism, animated simulations also rhetorically demonstrate the attempt to deploy that very same discourse as a means of providing supporting authority for documentation of an event for which indexical reference does not necessarily exist. Doane's piece describes visualisations of the brain's inner workings, but in the *Titanic* example discussed above we see viewers sat around a computer monitor and presented with a simulation of the ship's sinking reconstructed via witness accounts and (importantly) empirical data of the wreck and its structural failure patterns. Regardless of the simulation in question, however, it is in Doane's claim that animated simulations are a construct, and that the limits of the simulation's

Babbage's accompanying claim for his difference engine and analogical engines respectively was that they could perform tasks previously erroneously performed by human labour. Calculation, it seemed, was a task best undertaken by minimising the possibilities brought about by the subjectivity of human cognition.

To return to the animated simulation of today, this form of spectacle frequently functions according to a different visual register to that of the usual computer-generated visual effects spectacle found in Hollywood. In doing so, it reveals something of its rhetorical nature. Specifically, the spectacle of simulation does not require a high level of photorealism. On the contrary, it demands subpar levels of rendering, in order to signal to the viewer that what they perceive is 'simulation'. Here, photorealism would represent unnecessary attention to detail for a utilitarian computational form that must demonstrate that both processing and cognitive power have been diverted to the task of accurately performing calculations that can facilitate the quest for the 'truth'. This phenomenon has been astutely described by Paul Wells (2008: 296) as 'not so special effects', deployed, he suggests, as a means of signifying the seriousness of the business of simulation. I would argue, then, that these 'not so special effects' become rhetorical (in the sense that rhetoric is the deployment of language for persuasive and impressive effect often regarded as lacking sincerity) when they act as a visual language that does not simply function to explain the apparent facts of a situation, but also to persuade the viewer that they are party to visual information created by, and normally consumed by, the expert. The 'not so special effect' is impressive and persuasive by virtue of the fact that it offers a window for the viewer into a world stripped of the need for high aesthetic production values in service of something apparently more noble. In reality the not so special effects' primary function is to persuade the viewer and as such is rhetorical as much as it is often informative. Returning, for instance, to the simulation deployed at *Titanic*'s beginning, its aesthetic qualities and production values are markedly lower than those of the movie's conclusion, despite the fact that it would have been easy to render them in much greater detail. Aside from the obvious fact that research scientists would be unlikely to render their simulations to Hollywood-grade VFX standards, the reduced graphical complexity in this simulation (as with many others) performs the handy role of signifying utilitarianism. This returns us to notions of CG animation emerging from computer science, and in so doing highlights a broadening in animation's ontological nature. Industries involved in the emergence of computer graphics – automotive, aerospace, military, scientific, architectural, engineering and construction – deploy their graphic forms to utilitarian ends and high levels of photorealism are of little consequence. Instead, they often make a virtue of foregrounded artifice, as a guarantor of expertise should not, therefore, be regarded as wholly new and/or revolutionary. However, where pre-computational animation that immersed itself in the authority of expertise *can* be found on occasion in the twentieth century, with the twenty-first-century emergence of computer animation there is now a far greater magnitude of such material produced. Partly, this is due to the proliferating nature of the emergent animated documentary medium. It is also, however, a direct consequence of the fact that computer-animated simulation is (and has long been) so instrumental to both scientific and industrial processes. For this reason, computer animation's existence is increasingly more pervasive than that of its analogue, cel-based predecessor. This development is perhaps best described by Don Ihde (2009) in his work on what he calls 'technoscience's visualism'. This, he argues, begins to explain the contemporary means by which computer-generated imaging simultaneously contains within it traditional animated capacities and science, engineering and design practices. An illustrative example of this emergent combination can be found in the media archaeology of contemporary Hollywood movies that make a spectacle of immensely complex industrial detail in their visual effects sequences (Gurevitch 2015). Indeed, it is no coincidence that the company which now owns the visual effects industry's most-used software package (Maya) happens to be Autodesk: a company that started by selling industrial computer-automated design packages for the architectural, automotive, engineering and construction industries (Gurevitch 2016).

Intriguingly, the notion that the computational could be spectacular in its claim to precision, veracity and mathematical capacity is not new. As early as the 1850s, Charles Babbage famously wished that erroneous human 'calculations had been performed by steam' after amending a table of incorrectly computed differential equations. At that time, the word 'computer' was assigned as a noun for a form of employment (humans took jobs as computers just as they might take ones as lawyers). The apocryphal tale of Babbage's frustrated wish is often cited as the inception of his decision to design and build analogue precursors (named difference engines) of modern computers. Less often noted is the degree to which Babbage was both aware of and vocal about the spectacular potential of his computational inventions. Babbage's letters and accounts from the time reveal that he lobbied to have his computational engine placed as an 1851 Great Exhibition piece, on the grounds that it would prove a particularly popular attraction (Babbage 1851). Babbage's appeals, as related in these accounts, were that the spectacle of automated, rapid calculation, and its demonstration of the capacity to set mechanisation to the task of information processing, would constitute a spectacular attraction in its own right. In addition,

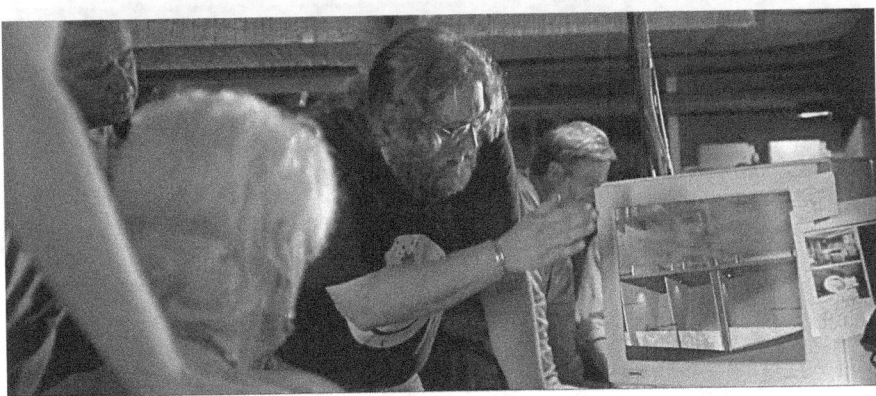

Figure 5.2d–f Stills from *Titanic*'s computer simulation scene (continued)

counter to twentieth-century theoretical notions of animation that structured indexical film documentary and fabricated animation (often associated with children's entertainment) into purportedly opposite camps. Contemporary computationally based animation that presents itself (and/or is presented)

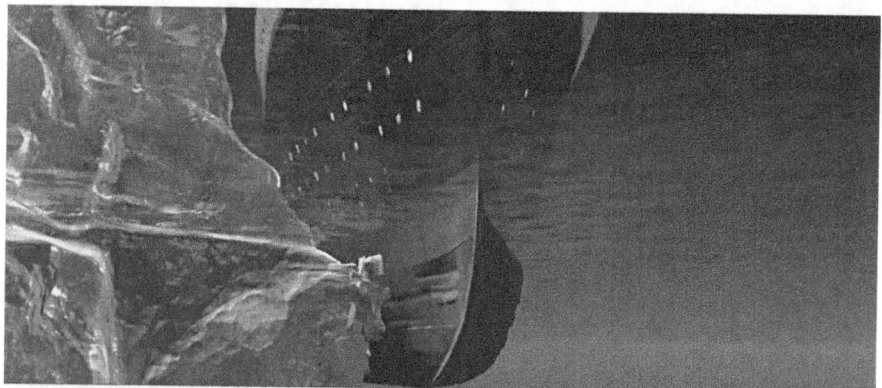

Figure 5.2a–c   Stills from *Titanic*'s computer simulation scene

Not-so-special Effects and the Animated Document

What these remarkably similar scenes point towards, then, is a history of animation deployed as the spectacle of expertise. Intriguingly, this fact runs was used both in the finished work and in many 'making of' documentaries surrounding it. *Titanic* is worth discussing, then, because it highlights the blurring of boundaries between animation, documentary and contemporary Hollywood spectacle. Most important for our overarching consideration of animation as a location of expertise in documentary contexts, however, is not the film's climactic images of the *Titanic* sinking, but a short early section in which the present-day crew of research vessel the *Keldysh* sit the now-elderly Rose (Gloria Stuart) down at a computer terminal, in order to explain to her the process by which the *Titanic* sank (Figure 5.2a–f). Repeated viewing of the scene in question reveals extraordinary similarities with McCay's *The Sinking of the Lusitania*. There is, for instance, almost a scene-by-scene correlation in the way in which the *Keldysh* crew's simulation of the *Titanic* is introduced. First, viewers are presented with a shot remarkably similar to that in which McCay and Beach pondered over an illustration. In *Titanic*, protagonists sit around a computer screen whilst marine scientist Lewis Bodine (Lewis Abernathy) explains the events that took place as the ship sank. Rather than McCay's intertitles describing associated facts and figures, viewers see Bodine present a seemingly familiar range of statistics as he narrates the sequence of events relevant to the *Titanic* being punctured below the waterline.

Like McCay's 'expert'-driven short, this sequence from *Titanic* sets up a similar contract with the audience, in which both the limitations and the possibilities of simulation are acknowledged well in advance of the anticipated on-screen event (and long after the actual historical counterpart). Like *The Sinking of the Lusitania*, what is extraordinary about this scene is the way in which it purports to provide privileged access to *Titanic*'s 'behind the scenes' workings: viewers are granted access to the simulations on which Cameron based his set-piece visual effects spectacular. The common thread between McCay and Cameron's respective works is the rhetoric of expertise. *Titanic*'s viewer is treated to the spectacle of data and knowledge as Bodine explains the facts and figures behind the eponymous ship's loss: 'the watertight bulkheads don't go any higher than E deck'; the stern is '20,000 [or] 30,000 tons' in weight, causing the ship to split in half; the stern 'finally goes under about 2:30 am'. In other words, the simulation that *Titanic*'s audience is made privy to functions to lend authority to the film's final scenes and their own particular brand of spectacle. The preparatory spectacle of data and simulation acts as a support structure for the climactic visual effects spectacle to come. Although *Titanic* was clearly not a film conceived and executed within a documentary form, it is also clear from this sequence that computer-generated simulation functions as a form of animated document that strengthens the film's claim to verisimilitude necessary for its subsequent spectacular dénouement.

Figure 5.1a–f Stills from *The Sinking of the* Lusitania (Winsor McCay, 1918)

The central fascination of the sequence described above relates to its prescient resemblance to another animated simulation of a sinking ship: that of the *Lusitania*'s sister vessel, the *Titanic*. In a striking echo of McCay's work, James Cameron's *Titanic* (1997) features multiple levels of self-reflexivity around the framing of the sinking it depicts. As Bruce Bennett (2007) points out, *Titanic*'s marketing and press materials set much store on the lengths to which Cameron and his team went to achieve historical accuracy regarding the manner of the ship's sinking. Famously, Cameron made a personal dive to the *Titanic*'s wreck to capture footage for his film; much of that footage sinking of the civilian ocean liner *Lusitania* off the Irish coast with the loss of almost 1,200 lives, is rightly regarded as a seminal historical demonstration of animation standing as a document of reality. As no contemporary filmed document of the event existed, it was decided to animate an account instead. *The Sinking of the Lusitania* is a valuable historical artefact not simply for the film's content, but because it reveals something of the way in which a self-conscious rhetoric of expertise was already emergent even in animated documentary's early history.

At the beginning of its narrative, McCay's film self-reflexively addresses, rather than obscures, the relationship between animation, filmmaker and depicted event. Rather than taking the viewer straight into an animated world of oceanic disaster, McCay opts instead to present a view of the animator's studio, the rarely seen space in which animations are created (Figure 5.1a–f). As if witnessing a cinematic equivalent of the primal scene, the viewer wondering why they have been given such privileged access to the film's production context. Intertitles swiftly explain that McCay, 'originator of Animated Cartoons, decides to draw a historical record of the crime that shocked Humanity'. After a brief live-action shot of McCay, viewers are introduced to 'Mr. Beach giving McCay the details of the sinking – necessary for the work to follow'. The following shot of McCay and Beach pointing at an illustration with a pen and stroking chins whilst deep in conversation sets up the coming animation as a considered work of collaborative expertise. A following intertitle explains that 25,000 drawings were made and photographed for this animation: another self-reflexive attempt to ground the coming animated simulation of the *Lusitania*'s sinking within a discourse of effort, research and expert labour. In effect, McCay sets up a contract with the viewer. He acknowledges immediately that his work is not indexical but instead appeals that the viewer accepts it on the basis of the research and development that has gone into its making. Next, viewers are told that the film's waves had to be animated and then presented with a representation of the sea that is surprisingly sophisticated, visually speaking: an analogue precursor to modern digital simulation. Intertitles then state that: 'From here on you are looking at the first record of the sinking of the *Lusitania*' and details of the ship's date of sailing from England and number of passengers are provided. The animated ship that follows (after an intriguingly iconographic shot of a silhouetted U-boat, framed by the edges of the paper and the desk on which the latter sits) also has an odd sense of simulation attached to its use of perspective and movement. Finally, the viewer is given a privileged underwater view (again, with an intriguingly simulated perspective) from which to witness the torpedo that sunk the *Lusitania*, before returning above water for the ship's demise.

patterns through to hair and materials simulations. Ironically, many of these scientists will admit that the simulations they initially create (with as high a degree of accuracy as possible) and the 'simulations' they ultimately deploy can be very different things. For instance, Robert Bridson, the senior principal research scientist for visual effects at Autodesk, and previously a fire and fluid flow simulation specialist at the University of British Columbia, often explains that fire-based explosions deployed in animated visual effects are not based purely upon accurate simulations: audiences simply expect explosions to look far more visually hyperbolic than they would if simulated accurately. What is most interesting about this is the way in which it reveals that the visual effects industry (whether deployed in Hollywood movies or television documentaries) utilises the idea of calculation, simulation, veracity and expertise whenever it usefully suits a claim to specialist-led verisimilitude, but conveniently drops such simulations in favour of artistically licensed animation when there is a need to satisfy audiences' expectation of visual spectacle. Here, we have a complex interplay of calculation, simulation and visualised data as spectacle in its own right on one hand, and animation, fabrication and artistic intervention to facilitate spectacular engagement on the other. It is for this reason that I am interested in the rhetoric of expertise. While simulation and its mathematically based empirical foundations may be central to much computer animation in documentary films, it is the rhetoric surrounding such animation that is really crucial. Specifically, the rhetoric of expertise supplied by animated simulation serves the wider purpose of supporting the 'authority' of a given documentary. If the simulation is a rhetorical device, however (and to some extent, how could it not be – it is difficult/impossible for most viewers to qualify the methodological basis of any simulation), then its presence should be recognised as such.

It would, of course, be incorrect to suggest that animation as documentary has not been aligned with expertise before. As both Sybil DelGaudio (1997) and Jay Telotte (2008) separately point out, a wealth of twentieth-century television material combines expert scientific and engineering knowledge and credentials with low- (and occasionally high-) budget animation. *The Johns Hopkins Science Review* animated numerous scientific developments throughout the early 1950s, while the Walt Disney Corporation spent much of the 1950s and 1960s producing various instructional animated shorts and movies for television, works characterised by a tone of authority on the subject. Earlier still, Winsor McCay's 1918 animated short *The Sinking of the Lusitania* has been referred to by so many theorists discussing animated documentary that it has become a site of ritual discursive pilgrimage for the field. McCay's film, made three years after the 1915 German U-boat has no real way of knowing how much data is being drawn upon or of what quality the data are. In this sense, while data always underlie simulation, whether or not a filmmaker or onscreen expert chooses to explicitly acknowledge and/or emphasise that data, the nature, quantity and quality of the data all remain choices to be made. In this sense we start to see differences in the way in which data and simulation are framed as spectacle in an animated documentary. Compounding this picture is the fact that an 'expert' is almost invariably introduced in situations in which the spectacle of either data or simulation (or both) are presented to a viewer. Experts often act as qualifying forces, leading the viewer through the significance of a set of data or explaining the implications of a simulation and the data that underpin it. In turn, an expert may gain their authority from this simulation and imbue a documentary with an additional claim to veracity. In all of this there is a powerful translation going on: data, simulation and expertise all become forms of spectacle. The viewer seldom has the opportunity to question or refute the data or the simulation presented in a documentary. In this sense, and while referring back to the authority of expertise, at some level such material is spectacular in nature; it must be taken on face value of what is being seen. With this in mind, we can now consider this aspect of the documentary attraction as a form of animation and simulation imbued with the rhetoric of expertise.

Documenting the Spectacle of Data

In 1966, a US military-funded group of university scientists known as MAGI (Mathematical Applications Group Incorporated) was formed in Elmsford, New York. MAGI were preoccupied with the task of simulating radiation dispersal in the event of a catastrophic incident at a nuclear facility. In 1972, with military research funding coming to an end, the group transferred their computer simulation work over from the military to the civilian domain. Consequently, the line between the use of computer-generated, high-accuracy simulation and data visualisation on the one hand and spectacular attraction on the other became fuzzy. With commercialisation, MAGI/Synthavision turned their dispersal simulation into light radiation simulation and produced a primitive version of ray tracing that modelled the way in which light (a modified variant of their original nuclear radiation) bounces off, or passes through, various materials in the process of illuminating a scene. For a contemporary example of the ray tracing process in action, look no further than Pixar Animation Studios' RenderMan software.

Spanning out beyond light radiation simulation, many of today's leading visual effects studios employ physicists, engineers, chemists and computer scientists with specialisms in fields from fluid flow dynamics, fire and smoke step further, though, and interrogate what is meant specifically by the notion of 'spectacle', the term is used frequently in relation to the cinematic (and more recently digital) image, but seldom are possible meanings defined. The *Oxford English Dictionary* definition describes spectacle as a 'visually striking performance or display', going on to note that it can refer to 'an event or scene regarded in terms of its visual impact' (OED 2005: 1699). While this is entirely accurate and appropriate, with the audiovisual image the conception of spectacle has been narrowed (via theorists as diverse as Guy Debord [1995], Christian Metz [1982], Tom Gunning [1990], Jonathan Beller [2006], and others) to refer to an economic, social and cultural impulse on the part of directors, producers and VFX animators to capture an audience's attention via visually arresting and pleasurable images. The nature of spectacle is a topic that could fill up a book in its own right. For this chapter's purposes, however, I refer to 'spectacle' not simply as an impulse geared only toward providing audiences with astonishing, arresting, and/or generally pleasurable forms of visual stimulation. Rather, in doing the former, 'spectacle' also moves toward encouraging engagement with screen content. So far as animated documentary is concerned, this argument can be refined by considering the ways in which data, simulation and expertise are explicitly deployed as specific forms of spectacle to support the rhetorical aims of documentary filmmakers.

Gunning has argued that the spectacular attraction in early cinema emerged in the absence of narrative (and was only later put to work in narrative's service) and did so under two cinematic forms: actuality and the trick film. The contemporary audiovisual landscape is quite different. Contemporary spectacle functions against a backdrop of multiplying visual forms (films, television shows, internet shorts, computer games) and also against a backdrop of multiplying production and exhibition streams (cinema, television, mobile phones, computers and more). Consequently, within these expanding forms of production and exhibition we also witness multiplying forms of spectacle: what I will refer to variously as the spectacle of data, the spectacle of simulation and the spectacle of expertise. These forms are related to, but also distinct from, each other. The spectacle of data, for instance, can take numerous forms: directly as numbers on a screen, or a quantity of data represented as a function of time and subsequently animated, or (perhaps less directly) as millions of data points of grass animated on a prairie or billions of data points of water on an animated ocean. Where the first examples above are direct references to data, in the latter ones data are an implicit but ultimately underlying factor in a simulation, demonstrating the concept of the spectacle of simulation.

Indeed, data and the spectacle of data generally underlie a simulation's claim to veracity but are often only implicit, in the sense that the viewer again within this essay's discussion of computer-generated imaging's role in documentary production.

In light of the history outlined above it is unsurprising that computers not only simulated scenarios with a direct relation to real-world outcomes but were subsequently put to use in visualising the data processed in such a way as to reflect these realities pictorially. In some ways, the story of late twentieth- and early twenty-first-century computer graphics has been one of computer scientists' and animators' quest to find ever more complex ways of simulating 'reality' in such a way as to be difficult to distinguish from the indexical, photographic alternative. The archives of SIGGRAPH (the annual global conference of the special interest group on graphics and interactive techniques) are full of research papers stuffed with mathematical calculations of the physics of light reflectance, diffusion and distortion upon every kind of surface and material one could imagine, and the solution for how to implement these calculations in a way that mimics perceived reality. Above all else, analysis of this research field quickly reveals the sheer quantity of calculation and data that has been involved in approaching an ever closer simulation of photo-real imaging over the past three decades. In this sense, photo-real simulation has gradually come to be the spectacular expression of empirical mathematical calculation made visible. Thus, we have reached an interesting moment in spectacular documentary animation. In the past, hand-rendered animation may have been regarded as running counter to the received expectations of a documentary genre premised upon indexical foundations. In the contemporary context, however, computer-generated animation is cloaked with a very different rhetoric. With calculation embedded into the computer-generated image's fabric, the rhetoric of objective empirical process can easily be infused throughout and around the latter. While I am *not* claiming that computer-generated animation really is infused with forms of empirical process, the rhetoric that surrounds the simulated image, laden as it is with the explicit exhibition of 'data', is such that it signifies 'empirical truth' to the viewer that is rhetorically drawn upon again and again.

All of this leads to a related (and very necessary) clarification of terms surrounding the multiplicity of ways in which 'spectacle' operates in relation to the animated document. This chapter's remainder considers a number of types of spectacle that, while fluid and overlapping, are not necessarily the same. In order to articulate their specific function, we need to return to a definition of spectacle in its own right. If, as suggested earlier, in early cinema the novelty of being able to animate an image made the latter an astonishing spectacle in its own right, we might reasonably go on to argue (as Sean Cubitt [2005] has) that, at a basic level, animation is inherently spectacular. To go a effects animators involved in their respective productions described their work in relation to a quest for accuracy and veracity (see Scott and White 2003; van Dijck 2006; Metz 2008).

This increasing level of access to computer-generated visual effects lies at the heart of this essay's interest in animated simulation within the documentary attraction. Past forms of animation were presented as a peculiar and anomalous potential challenge to the indexical documentary's integrity. I consider here, however, the way in which both computer graphics and simulation (not the same thing but frequently conflated in public demonstrations of the technology) are often constructed within documentary as visual forms that validate via the credence of expertise they lend. This construction has a history going back to the emergence of empirical science and the rise of scientific graphical representation employed as a visual supplement to mathematical calculation. As Robert Brain and Norton Wise (1999) have argued, diagrammatic and graphical methods were central to the past century's scientific methods not least because they were intimately interrelated to the rise of both physiological and physical research into biological function and industrial engineering. In other words, the visualisation of accurate data sets drove scientific research and engineering as well as resulting from it.

A more recent direct inheritor of this history is computer-generated imaging. This initially developed as a strand of twentieth-century computer science research and as a consequence of the need to visualise data sets. As Richard Wright (2008: 78) notes, the increasingly pressing need for data visualisation was recognised formally by the American science community in America by the late 1980s. The National Science Foundation warned of the increasing prevalence of vast quantities of data and suggested data visualisation as a means of spotting patterns in the former. In reality, data visualisation had been emerging as a field of computer science from the moment that computers were connected to cathode ray tubes and likely before. Regardless of data visualisation's history *as a field*, at a very basic level any form of image appearing on a computer screen is already inherently data visualisation, for no other reason than that it is already a computational output of data pre-structured by the machine on multiple levels. Indeed, the history of the Second World War and post-war computing is intimately bound up with the history of both simulation and data visualisation. Military interest in (and therefore funding of) computers was not only premised upon their potential as code-breaking machines but also upon their ability to perform rapid calculations of vast quantities of data in order to undertake simulations necessary for accurate weapons aiming (Campbell-Kelly and Aspray 2004). This intriguing relationship between simulated calculation and its consequent, immediate and direct applicability to reality will be considered reconfigured under the logic of the narrative. Indeed, documentary narratives subsumed the attraction perhaps even more than their fictional cousins. After all, a documentary film's claim to authority in the narrative era lay, in part, upon its refusal of sensationalism, something that the attraction, by contrast, sought to generate. Consequently, in the twentieth century the aims of documentary filmmaking were often constructed as existing in a state of tension with the appeal to spectacle. This is not to say that documentaries did not include spectacle (many frequently did), but the driving force of documentary principle dictated that spectacular material exist in service of the overall documentary narrative drive to inform. Of course, there were examples that contradicted this general rule. For instance, Charles and Ray Eames's educational film *Powers of Ten* (1977) propelled the viewer through a seemingly indexical (but in actual fact skilfully rendered) series of glass paintings of the universe at an increasing rate of acceleration. In this example, the film's educational and informational content regarding the size and nature of the universe was very much a functional derivative of the spectacle rather than a dominant driver of it. In general terms, however, a plausible argument can be made that the advent of narrative reconfigured the attraction within both documentary and fiction cinema throughout the twentieth century. By the twenty-first century's turn, though, the relationship between the documentary and the spectacular attraction was clearly shifting.

As John Caldwell (2000) has argued, the late 1990s witnessed rapid developments in digital production technologies and dropping production technology costs that allowed television producers to narrow the production value gap with cinema. Ever higher resolution, higher frame rate and improved colour gamut made high-quality digital video capture and exhibition capacities nearly ubiquitous. Documentary series such as *Planet Earth* (2007), *Life* (2010) and *Human Planet* (2011) all showcased the visually astonishing capacities of emerging contemporary production technologies. Indeed, such were the latter's capacities that short 'making of' videos (either broadcast after the documentaries themselves or added as extras in subsequent DVD releases) became a staple of documentary production. Unsurprisingly, these conditions affected post-production as well as production. In the former, documentary filmmakers increasingly found themselves within reach of digital visual effects technologies that were previously the domain of big-budget Hollywood productions. Take, for example, the BBC documentary series *Walking with Dinosaurs* (1999). At the time of its release it was frequently compared with *Jurassic Park* (Steven Spielberg, 1993). Subsequently the series has been considered by many theorists addressing the relationship between animation and documentary. What is interesting about the visual effects in both works is the frequency with which visual no matter how photo-real they may appear. This throws into question the supposedly indexical image's claim to veracity. In reality, of course, such claims were always questionable: theoretical considerations of documentary and its ontological status were as contested before digital imaging's emergence as they are now. With all of this in mind, this chapter emphasises a very different approach to the relationship between documentary and animation, and, in this case, a very specific type of animation: computer-generated simulations as both attractions and constructed visual signifiers of expertise.

While the digital attraction has received much attention as a means of framing contemporary understandings of Hollywood spectacle, less attention has been given to the place of attractions in documentary filmmaking. This is understandable given that spectacular visual effects have generally functioned within the realm of the fantastic, their existence a testament to technological and commercial virtuosity in making the simulated appear real: the opposite function of the indexical filmic document. But as a host of film theorists have pointed out, early cinema actually astonished its audience with little more than the spectacle of the moving image itself (Metz 1982; Gunning 1990). In many ways, Sean Cubitt (2005) suggests, all early cinema was a special effect: whether actuality or magic trick, contemporaneous accounts suggest cinema audiences' amazement. The importance of this tendency becomes apparent when we consider the nature and content of the early cinema of attractions. As Gunning (1990: 56) points out, early cinema was not governed by the 'narrative impulse' that was central to the medium later on. Rather, 'First there is the extremely important role that actuality film plays in early film production. Investigation of the films copyrighted in the US shows that actuality films outnumbered fictional films until 1906.'

Examples of 'actualities' are abundant in early cinema: from the Lumière brothers' seminal first works on, early films frequently contained subject matter that an unfamiliar modern viewer might deem oddly mundane. Although early filmmakers were eager to document everyday life, the novelty of the moving image was so powerful an effect that to be able to animate a document of real life was an astonishing spectacle in its own right. In early cinema, the tendency to provide actualities (in some senses precursors of the documentary form) as a staple cinematic attraction was strong on the part of filmmakers and enthusiastically consumed by audiences. Animation (and animation of the indexical photographic image particularly) was a driving force in this dynamic. It seems that just as the arrival of narrative to cinema changed the nature and function of the attraction (Gunning argues that narrative drove the attraction 'underground'), the relationship between the actuality and the attraction also changed. As with narrative cinema, so with documentary: the original one-shot documents of actuality were subsequently

CHAPTER 5

The Documentary Attraction: Animation, Simulation and the Rhetoric of Expertise
Leon Gurevitch

In her recent book *Animated Documentary* (2013), Annabelle Honess Roe points out that the two cinematic modes that her title references inevitably necessitates an examination of the ontological differences between live action on the one hand and animation on the other. Summarising a range of theory (DelGaudio 1997; Wells 2008; Ward 2011; Glynne 2013), Honess Roe explains that these ontological differences have often been presented as an opposition between the indexical, supposedly objective photographic document of the external world on the one hand, and a subjective, hand-rendered animated form that represents the intervention of the animator and their expressive artistic licence on the other. To an extent, this opposition goes back to Walter Benjamin's articulation of the 'human-hand'. In the age of mechanical reproduction and changing notions of what constituted an indexical 'document', the latter, Benjamin argued, marked a form of 'subjectivity' that was to be minimised in indexical image reproduction wherever possible (Benjamin 1999). But in a cinematic context, such discussions were never likely to be conclusive because questions of editing, camera positioning, lighting, film stock and much more meant that the human hand was rarely, if ever, absent from the construction of documentary.

In recent years theorists such as Paul Wells (2008: 295) have highlighted Lev Manovich's observation (2001:195) that in a post-celluloid new media environment, the history of the directly manipulated visual image has, after a brief century-long indexical interlude, come full circle. Manovich argues that the emergence of photographic processes meant that our image culture moved briefly away from representational forms that involved the human hand's direct intervention in their creation, gravitating instead towards a system in which the photographic machine recorded a direct index of what was in front of it. The rise of digital manipulation, however, meant that the pre-indexical[1] conditions of visual representation returned with a twist. Digital manipulation, Manovich explains, presents us a landscape in which seemingly live-action, indexical images are routinely reconfigured under a painterly logic,

Eldritch, Tristan (2011), 'Hauntology rising: folk horror and atavistic resurgence, part 1', <http://2012diaries.blogspot.co.uk/2011/06/hauntology-rising-folk-horror-and.html> (last accessed 23 October 2016).

Ellis, John (1982), *Visible Fictions*, London: Routledge.

Fore, Steve (2011), 'Reenacting *Ryan*: The Fantasmatic and the Animated Documentary', *animation: an interdisciplinary journal*, 6: 3, pp. 277–92.

Glynne, Andy (2013), 'Drawn from life: the animated documentary', in Brian Winston (ed.), *The Documentary Film Book*, London: BFI, pp. 73–5.

Grierson, John [1932] (1966), 'The first principles of documentary', in Forsyth Hardy (ed.), *Grierson on Documentary*, London: Faber and Faber, pp. 145–56.

Gunning, Tom (1995), 'An aesthetic of astonishment. Early film and the (in)credulous spectator', in Linda Williams (ed.), *Viewing Positions: Ways of Seeing Film*, New Brunswick, NJ: Rutgers University Press.

Honess Roe, Annabelle (2013), *Animated Documentary*, Basingstoke: Palgrave Macmillan.

Kahana, Jonathan (2009), 'Introduction: What now? Presenting reenactment', *Framework*, 50: 1/2, pp. 46–60.

Moore, Samantha (2015), *Out of Sight: Using Animation to Document Perceptual Brain States*, unpublished PhD dissertation, Loughborough University.

Nichols, Bill (2008), 'Documentary reenactment and the fantasmatic subject', *Critical Inquiry*, 35, pp. 72–89.

Plantinga, Carl (2013), '"I'll believe it when I trust the source": documentary images and visual evidence', in Brian Winston (ed.), *The Documentary Film Book*, London: BFI.

Rosenkrantz, Jonathan (2011), 'Colourful claims: towards a theory of animated documentary', *Film International*, 6 May, <http://filmint.nu/?p=1809> (last accessed 24 October 2016).

Seitler, Dana (2008), *Atavistic Tendencies: The Culture of Science in American Modernity*, Minneapolis: University of Minnesota Press.

Sobchack, Vivian (1999), 'Toward a phenomenology of nonfictional film experience', in Jane Gaines and Michael Renov (eds), *Collecting Visible Evidence*, Minneapolis: University of Minnesota Press, pp. 241–54.

Stiassny, Melanie (2003), 'Atavism', in Brian K. Hall and Wendy M. Olson (eds), *Keywords and Concepts in Evolutionary Developmental Biology*, Cambridge, MA: Harvard University Press.

Ward, Paul (2006), 'The future of documentary? "Conditional Tense" documentary and the historical record', in Gary D. Rhodes and John Parris Springer (eds), *Docufictions: Essays on the Intersection of Documentary and Fictional Filmmaking*, Jefferson, NC: McFarland, pp. 270–83.

Ward, Paul (2011), 'Animating with facts: the performative process of documentary animation in *The Ten Mark* (2010)', *animation: an interdisciplinary journal*, 6: 3, pp. 231–44.

Winston, Brian (1995), *Claiming the Real*, London: BFI.

– say – by animation'. In both *Andersartig* and *The Children of the Holocaust*, we are talking about *recollection* of witnessed events – with all of the subjectivity that this suggests – rather than about direct, indexical footage of those events. How we as viewers relate to the films' animated images is a key question. In both, animated imagery prevents the supposedly 'direct' viewer engagement by dint of its inherent 'reflexivity'. Yet the animation simultaneously brings a great deal of connotative power: *The Children of the Holocaust*'s graphic style, for example, echoing that of a child's story book. Clearly, this might be seen as a pragmatic design choice on the animators' part. They were, after all, aiming to communicate difficult subject matter to a young audience. But it can also be read here as a way of amplifying certain key themes and issues that are part of the 'documentariness' of the film – namely, recollection, re-visiting and re-enacting the past, and the atavistic power that the interviewees' 'thens' have over their 'nows'. If we see these animated films as being as much 'about' these difficult, emotional and psychic resonances, rather than simply being about the original historical 'events' (bombing raid kills orphans; children flee Nazis), we are more able to fully understand and appreciate how animation and documentary function together. As Honess Roe (2013: 34) puts it: 'animation, precisely because it does not require the existence of the profilmic in the same way as live action, is at greater liberty to conflate the "then" and the "now"'. It is in this 'conflation' of 'then' and 'now' that we can find the key to understanding how animation can show us otherwise irretrievable things from our collective past.

Acknowledgement

The author would like to thank Annabelle Honess Roe for her helpful critical comments during the draft stages of writing this chapter.

Bibliography

An Eyeful of Sound, film, directed by Samantha Moore. Canada/Netherlands/UK: Sapiens Productions and Wellcome Trust, 2010.

Andersartig, film, directed by Dennis Stein-Schomburg. Germany: Ocean Pictures Filmproduktion, 2011.

Carroll, Noël (2003), *Engaging the Moving Image*, New Haven and London: Yale University Press.

The Children of the Holocaust, film, directed by Zane Whittingham. UK: BBC and Fettle Animation, 2014.

Corner, John (2012), 'Temporality and documentary', in Emily Keightley (ed.), *Time, Media and Modernity*, Basingstoke: Palgrave Macmillan.

Ehrlich, Nea (2015), *Animated Realities: From Animated Documentaries to Documentary Animation*, unpublished PhD dissertation, University of Edinburgh.

documentaries that use actual historical (in other words, *live-action*) footage and the interplay is therefore between the 'then' of those images with the 'now' of the film's present. Although one can say that a *similar* strategy can be seen in some animated documentaries – especially where animated scenes are standing in (as mimetic substitution, in Honess Roe's terms) for historical scenes – it is more often the case that 'historical time' in Corner's sense is not conjured up in the same way: rather, it is done through the exaggerations, compressions and distortions that are central to animation as a form.

The viewer is, therefore, being asked to actively recognise and engage with animation as a communicative tool *and* as a way of positioning us, temporally speaking, in relation to what we are watching. I have referred elsewhere (Ward 2006) to Vivian Sobchack's discussion of Jean-Pierre Meunier's typology of filmic experience, and I think it is useful to bring a modified version of that account to the current discussion. In Meunier's typology, there are three positions or modalities on an experiential spectrum that describe our film viewing experience at any one time: 'film-souvenir', 'documentary' and 'fiction'. It is the first two modalities that concern us here. The 'film-souvenir' (or what Sobchack dubs 'home movies') are images that are 'existentially and specifically known to us already ... [they refer] to beings and things and events that exist now or once existed "elsewhere" than solely on the screen' (Sobchack 1999: 243). By 'known to us', Sobchack means directly and intimately known – in other words, the images are of events, people or places we have *directly* experienced or witnessed. Hence the term 'home movies': although the images in question may not be *actual* home movies, they fulfil the same psychological function. Meunier's 'documentary' modality addresses us via images of which we have some cultural knowledge – but also, crucially, where we *lack* some knowledge and have no direct experience of the events or people depicted. As Sobchack argues, this is 'a lack that modifies the nature of our identification with the image' (ibid.: 243). We did not witness the events or know the people depicted directly, but we are made aware that someone else did.

Although I find this model convincing as a way of understanding how we might relate to certain images, I would argue that, like Corner's discussion of documentary temporality, it is entirely predicated on *live-action* footage and the latter's indexical power to show us something directly. It is clearly problematic to think of animated images within this model – which is to say, thinking about animation as a way of connecting us to real historical events and people provides an interesting test for such a model. As Andy Glynne (2013: 73) points out, 'if documentary value is more a matter of witness than of a supposed evidential quality of the photographic image ... then witness can be illustrated by non-photographic (as well as photographic) means: even

Figure 4.2b *The Children of the Holocaust* (Fettle Animation, 2014)

with their enduring emotional resonance. This type of animation use would fall into Honess Roe's category of non-mimetic substitution. In other words, the animation acts as a 'substitute' for actual footage that either does not exist or cannot be used for some other reason, but the animators have made no real attempt to *directly mimic* what the events might have actually looked like. Indeed, compressions, graphic disjunctions, distortions of scale and so on actively draw the viewer's attention to the scene's animated-ness, and thereby emphasise the psychological power of the events depicted through animated means (Figure 4.2b).

The events depicted using animation in *The Children of the Holocaust* and *Andersartig* are framed as the memories of people remembering traumatic things that happened in their childhood. Figured in animation, this act of remembering, of looking back, gives an intriguing temporal twist to the status of the images. John Corner (2012: 69–70) draws attention to the specific temporality of documentary, noting that there are two broad registers – time as 'historical time' and time as 'durational design'. Historical time is 'the specific times at which the images and sounds were recorded, whether or not these times are made explicit to the viewer'. Time as durational design is to do with planning and pragmatic considerations such as 'how long to hold shots on the screen [and] what value to give to sequences within the overall structure'. There is a third level of temporality, phenomenological time, which is derived 'from the alignment of the "time" of what is happening on the screen with the "time" of watching'. What is at issue here is the way in which viewers relate, temporally speaking, to what is on the screen. Corner is clearly considering

In *The Children of the Holocaust* there is, then, a clear disjunction between interviewees 'telling the story' of their persecuted childhoods, accompanied by animated visuals, and the straight-to-camera live-action interviews. On one hand, we have specific, anchored case study examples clearly and strikingly visualised using animation. On the other, we have candid interviewee reflection on how 'their story' might fit into a wider historical and social fabric, using live-action, straight-to-camera interviews. In one particularly striking interview, Martin Kapel talks about the importance of studying history and understanding how the present came to be as a result of what happened in the past. He also reflects on why he does not hold those in Germany today responsible for what the Nazis did. These interviews therefore fulfil the film's wider pedagogic brief overall (we should remember that it was made for use within the BBC Learning Zone).

The animated scenes certainly work very well as visual representations in alliance with interviewees' recounted memories. When we hear Ruth Rogoff talking about her experiences of the Nazis clearing the Jews 'house by house', we see an animated scene of cross-sectioned houses with some characters cowering in one. A giant Nazi soldier enters frame right and lifts the roof off each of the houses in turn (Figure 4.2a).

Clearly, this is not meant to be an accurate depiction of 'how it happened' – it is not a 're-enactment' as we would commonly understand that term. Rather, the scene in question is a (somewhat fanciful, certainly dramatic and memorable) re-presentation of what happened. It is full of artistic license in order to connect us not only with the depicted events themselves but also

Figure 4.2a *The Children of the Holocaust* (Fettle Animation, 2014)

not be captured in the first place, or there exists some reason why any such record cannot be used.

One of Honess Roe's key examples of mimetic substitution is the BBC television series *Walking with Dinosaurs* (1999–2000), wherein CG animation is used to mimetically represent what dinosaurs may have looked like and how they might have behaved. The series is in this sense a speculative and provisional 'documenting', but one that the programme-makers are at pains to point out is based on detailed empirical evidence derived from fossils. Much of the way in which this type of programme addresses us as viewers – with the animated sequences constituting a fundamental part of this address – involves emphasising the forensic nature of the re-enacted scenes. This is a form of animation-as-reconstruction – with all of the connotations that the term 'reconstruction' implies. The temporal relationship that Nichols identifies in relation to re-enacted scenes – that we must, in the process of viewing, *recognise* that a version of the 'then' is impinging into the 'now' – is even more pronounced in these animated scenes, simply because their reconstructed nature is part of the mode of address. The scenes are clearly 'indexed', to use Noël Carroll's term (2003: 169), as a form of 'looking back', using animation as a way to give us privileged access to something that would otherwise be inaccessible.

A different approach to 'looking back' can be seen in the animated documentary *The Children of the Holocaust* (2014), made by Fettle Animation for BBC Learning Zone. The film uses interview testimony with six now-elderly Holocaust survivors, recollecting their experiences of fleeing the Nazis when they were children. There are self-contained sequences that start with a title card bearing a survivor's name and year and place of birth (for example, 'Ruth Rogoff. Born 1933. Zwickau, Germany'), followed by the elderly interviewee's voice reflecting back on the time when they encountered the Nazis, how they escaped, and where they ultimately settled down. In this sense, the soundtrack's function is very much the same as in *Andersartig*, though in the case of *The Children of the Holocaust* it is the real/actual people we hear, not a voice actor. This fact is anchored for the viewer by each animated sequence being followed by a live-action interview with the person who has just been heard on the soundtrack. Instead of 'telling their story' as they have just done on the soundtrack to an animated sequence, the interviewees reflect more generally on why they think the Holocaust took place, and why it is important to never let it happen again. In the case of Ruth Rogoff, for example, she considers how her memories of her experiences – the fact that she escaped and many others did not – have shaped her as an adult. At one point she states that she always has water and something to eat in the car, and that this is 'definitely a throwback to the fear of hunger'.

Although the use of animation might present problems for some, in terms of its status as re-enactment, animation's freedom from the photographic indexicality we would be bound to within a live-action re-enactment is what gives it its power. Indeed, this is clearly emphasised by *Andersartig*'s appropriation and 'spectralisation' of the class photograph. In this respect, it is perhaps more accurate to talk about this (or any?) animated documentary using the term 're-imagining' rather than 're-enactment', simply because the latter term has too many connotations of closely observed, detailed, often forensic reconstruction of a scene or event. But using a term like 're-imagining' instead emphasises the purely imaginative force of the images and sounds and how the animator uses them. Clearly, there is 'imagination' at work – in the broad sense of imagination as a synonym for 'creativity' – but what we cannot – indeed, *should* not – evacuate from our viewing experience of *Andersartig* is that it is based on actual events that happened to actual people. It is in this fantasmatic and atavistic re-imagining that the power of the animation resides.

Animated Documentary as a Form of 'Re-enactment'

Before proceeding further, we need to grapple a little more with the idea of animation and how it might be used to 're-enact' certain events. I have written elsewhere (Ward 2011) about how the process of animation can constitute a form of performative re-enactment in relation to animated films that purport to show real events or people. Alongside the welcome contribution of Steve Fore (2011) to the discussion, Annabelle Honess Roe (2013: 22–6) discusses the functions of re-enacted scenes in animated documentaries, linking them to an overall typology of this kind of animation – either as mimetic substitution, non-mimetic substitution or evocation.

The last of these categories, evocation, refers to work such as Samantha Moore's *An Eyeful of Sound* (2010) which very effectively evokes what it is like to have synaesthesia, a condition where senses appear to 'overlap' or become 'confused' – a common example being where people hear a sound and their brain visualises it as a colour or pattern of some kind. Some of Moore's other work deals with how animation can represent brain states such as phantom limb syndrome or prosopagnosia (face blindness). The point with such animation-as-evocation is that it is 'capturing' something which literally cannot be seen and has never 'existed' in a witness-able way. One might say that it is an attempt to use animation to visualise or 'enact' something that is not readily visible, and never has been visible. In the case of mimetic substitution and non-mimetic substitution, the animation is used as a 'stand-in' for something else, either because a record of the events could

Figure 4.1a–c The 'fading' school photo from *Andersartig* (Dennis Stein-Schomburg, 2011)

famous journeys, and obsolete cultural rituals) or flip through our own scrapbooks and photo albums. (Seitler 2008: 13)

It is this relationship between the present and the past that interests me here, and how we connect the past to the present through animated documentary. Clearly, this is not through 're-enactment' in the commonly accepted sense of the term, but there *is* a highly charged temporal relationship – the atavism of a past returning to haunt us in the present – that is intensified through the heightened juxtapositions and transformations that we see in animation.

Let us consider an example: the animated documentary *Andersartig* (2011), directed by Dennis Stein-Schomburg. *Andersartig* translates from German as 'different' or 'the different one'. This animated short is based on the memories of Hildegard Wolgemuth, recollecting an incident during the Second World War when the orphanage she was living in was bombed by the Allies. We hear her words (in this case delivered by the voice of an actor, Anna Magdalena Becker) remembering how she was 'different' from the other children, how she kept to herself. On the day of the bombing, all of the children run to take shelter in a basement. Hildegard hesitates at the top of the steps and then runs away and takes refuge elsewhere. A bomb makes a direct hit on the orphanage, killing everyone in the basement. She survives, the only one out of a group of twenty-five children.

The style of *Andersartig*'s animation is deliberately 'ghostly', with figures that are transparent or 'unfinished' and indeterminate. The voice-over's detached air therefore emphasises what appears to be spectral apparitions caught in a repeating time warp (Nichols refers at one point in his article to how re-enactments play out an 'uncanny sense of a repetition of what remains historically unique' [2008: 74]) and this captures perfectly the languid feel of routine ruptured by a life-changing event. The bombing of the orphanage occurred only once as an historical event, but this stylised animated re-enactment draws out the ways in which single events can resonate and repeat through a lifetime of memories. As Wolgemuth's recollection reaches its conclusion, we see a still image of a class of students, clearly rotoscoped from a class photo. As she reveals she was the only survivor that day, her fellow students fade to white and disappear, leaving her as the sole figure in the frame (Figure 4.1a–c).

Andersartig, and other animated documentaries like it, explicitly draw upon memory and recollection. There is often a spectral quality that the animation provides – but I think it is more precisely a fantasmatic or atavistic 'throwback' that we are talking about here, one where the viewer is magically propelled into one time-space whilst simultaneously being held in another.

refer to a physical trait that re-appears in the modern day, such as humans with tails or whales with legs: these traits did once exist in humans and whales, but have long since disappeared. Melanie Stiassny (2003: 10) notes that:

> Atavism commonly refers to the reappearance of a character state typical of a remote ancestor in an individual that really shouldn't have it. That is to say, the state has been lost, or more commonly transformed, long ago within the history of its lineage ... Central to the concept of atavism is the notion of an underlying continuity spanning considerable phylogenetic distances.

The concept of atavism has also been developed in relation to cultural phenomena – for example, in discussions of violence and degeneracy in society (where people are said to be behaving 'primitively'), or in the ways that horror films connect us with the past. A similar trajectory can therefore be seen to that outlined by Stiassny's evolutionary biological sense of the term: the return of something that *should not be there* (or that should have 'moved on'), but that links back to, and forms continuities with, the distant past.

One could likewise argue that *all* magic is 'atavistic', in that it appears to link back to a more 'primitive' sensibility in a similar way to horror stories: ghosts, the unknown, the magic of blow books, possessions and other superstitions. Blogger Tristan Eldritch (2011) states:

> The logic of horror is far closer to animism than linear causality; its environment is always defined more in terms of heightened, subjective atmosphere than objectified physical geography. The most quintessential assertion horror can make is: all the rational assumptions that give you a sense of security in this world are actually apt to crumble in the blinking of an eyelid; every iota of confidence and conviction you have acquired as an adult is null and void in the face of the unknown. Horror, then, reactivates instincts, beliefs, and ways of viewing the world that our mainstream societal norms have consigned into the past.

The important thing to emphasise here is that atavism refers to a *temporal* relationship – a sense of the 'then' impinging or re-emerging into the 'now'. Writing about the cultural shifts of modernity in the USA in the nineteenth and early twentieth centuries, Dana Seitler argues that modernity itself is atavistic, noting that the shifts seen in that period led to 'a paradox: modernity sought a break with the past, but that break necessitated the past's return'; furthermore, 'atavism is a "reproduction" and a "recurrence" of the past in the present' (Seitler 2008: 1–2). She also adds:

> The desire for a connection to the past is a strong one. To verify this, all we need to do is look at the popularity of reenactment culture (restaging wars,

coincident with the actual time (and often space) of the events portrayed'. Fore makes an argument for animated documentaries in fact inherently relying on re-enactment, simply because of the nature of animation production. In this sense, the very idea of reflexivity that is deeply embedded into Nichols's article – the idea that the viewer needs to recognise the status of re-enacted scenes in a specific way, and that this is a form of fantasmatic projection – is amplified and sharpened by that process's mediation through animation.

The temporal shifting that is inherent to any re-enactment is of central interest here – and how this is engaged with by the viewer. Of specific importance is the sense that what is being viewed is, as Nichols intimates, *recognised* as a representation of some previously occurring or enacted event and is not contemporaneous with other elements of the documentary (or, indeed, with the here-and-now of the viewing context). The 'fantasmatic' that Nichols draws attention to is triggered by a temporal uncertainty in how we relate to what we are seeing. As noted earlier, this is associated with a psychic pleasure (hence 'fantasmatic' – linked to 'fantasy' and the 'fantastic') and a sense of the past encroaching on – and commingling with – the present. Viewer uncertainty about the temporal provenance of the scene can also be connected conceptually to what Tom Gunning (1995: 115) identifies in a different context as the credulous spectator's reaction to the 'magic' of early cinema, when confronted with some 'attraction' that appears to transcend known reality: 'I know very well ... but all the same'. It is also similar to Gregory Bateson's observation, cited by Nichols (2008: 73), about the recognised difference between play fighting and real fighting – it is akin to saying, in a strange sense, 'The thing that I am watching is *not* the thing that I am watching'. This apparent paradox has deep roots in the history of representation: think, for example, of René Magritte's famous painting *The Treachery of Images* (1929) with its image of a pipe and the accompanying legend '*Ceci n'est pas une pipe*'. The apparent paradox also encompasses film and animation, and is part of what John Ellis has referred to as the 'present absence' (1982: 59) inherent in audiovisual media. Cinema, for Ellis, conjures up the impossible tense 'This is was' (ibid.: 97). Honess Roe cites Ellis in her discussion, and notes that one of the reasons for indexicality's power in debates around authenticity in documentary could be its 'quasi-magical quality of bringing something past into the present' (2013: 36).

Such a 'quasi-magical' sense of 'This is was' clearly links to Nichols's discussion of re-enactment and the fantasmatic. It also brings me to another key concept that I wish to draw into my discussion of animated re-enactments: atavism. The literal meaning of the term is derived from the Latin *atavus* (for 'remote ancestor' or 'forefather'). In evolutionary science, an 'atavism' can sense – or sophistry, depending on one's perspective: there seems to be no contradiction or paradox at play in opposing staged/prior on one hand and unstaged/contemporaneous on the other – is considerably more complex than it first appears. This is because the point's central importance lies not in the ontological status of the imagery per se, but in the viewer's *recognition* of the imagery's ontological status. In other words, it is all to do with how the viewer relates to the images, and recognises that they have a specific *temporal* relationship to what those images depict.

Jonathan Kahana (2009: 50) engages with Nichols's argument, although he discusses the concept of re-enactment from a slightly different perspective via its basis in 'enactment'. He notes that there are a range of definitions of enactment, including those that refer to simple speech acts (to declare or ordain something, for example). These forms of enactment are 'their own audience and have immediate significance. To enact in these senses of the term is to render a judgment, make a decision, or establish a fundamental principle' (ibid.: 52). There are other senses of enactment, however, where a material and human transformation of some sort must take place before it can be said that enactment has occurred. These forms of enactment – which would include playing a part or role for an audience – put more emphasis on staging, presentation and the effect on the audience. Kahana continues:

> Enactment in these senses is both a temporal and spatial process, one that can not only figuratively but also literally take place, and one that covers a social distance ... suggest[ing] an impermanent and intersubjective process, a rhetorical or mimetic effect dependent upon another's belief in or reaction to the act-ing in question. (2009: 53)

In other words, as Kahana points out, the staging, presentation and effect on the audience are what is important about these instances of enactment: enactment is performative. Re-enactment, as the term suggests, involves a repetition or reproduction of something that has previously been enacted (and this may or may not be captured on/mediated by film or TV). This will further complicate what is already, as Kahana notes, a 'temporal and spatial process'. Kahana is also explicit in drawing attention to the *rhetorical* dimension of enactment and re-enactment and how this is predicated on belief on the part of the viewer: a sense that the meaningfulness of enactment (and its repetition in re-enactment) resides in the context in which it is viewed.

Animation scholar Steve Fore has most recently applied Nichols's notion of the fantasmatic subject and re-enactment in relation to his reading of Chris Landreth's celebrated animated film *Ryan* (2004). As Fore (2011: 277) notes, re-enactment is the 'staging of events for the camera that are important to the broader argument of the documentary filmmaker, but which are not 'judicious' or 'sincere and justifiable' use of re-enacted scenes. These were often of the quotidian variety (people going about their daily business) and there appeared to be no problem with re-enactments precisely because they gave the filmmaker and viewer access to a previously witnessed, everyday scenario or set of actions that were not filmed at the time. The widespread use of re-enactment in Griersonian documentaries therefore links their re-enacted scenes to a serious and often didactic ('expository', to use one of Nichols's famous documentary categories) discourse. Such a documentary discourse is, on the face of it, seemingly very far removed from animation as a form.

What Carl Plantinga (2013: 40) correctly calls 'the default position' when considering certain images is 'for most of us to believe that under certain conditions, both moving and still photographs provide evidence that something looked or occurred in a certain way'. In other words, there is an assumption – with that caveat 'under certain conditions' – that such images provide evidence of one kind or another. As Plantinga goes on to point out, there are complex philosophical reasons why this is the case; likewise, it is important to stress that 'evidence' of something and 'proof' of something are not one and the same thing. Plantinga's stance in relation to documentary is an important basis for the following discussion, especially when he talks about how documentary images should be understood as 'rhetorical evidence' and how 'staged, re-enacted or recreated scenes' *might* function as evidence (ibid.: 44). What I would like to examine in more detail is, precisely, how animation and certain forms of re-enactment function together, and how their interaction impacts on the viewer.

In his discussion of re-enactment's role and function in documentary, Bill Nichols talks through some of the ways in which this mode raises problematic questions. Seemingly straightforward, the re-enactment, or 'the more or less authentic re-creation of prior events' (2008: 72) turns out to be considerably more complex. As Nichols puts it:

> Re-enactments occupy a strange status in which it is crucial that they be recognised as a representation of a prior event while also signalling that they are not a representation of a contemporaneous event . . . The re-enacted event introduces a fantasmatic element that an initial representation of the same event lacks. Put simply, history does not repeat itself, except in mediated transformations such as memory, representation, re-enactment, fantasy – categories that coil around each other in complex patterns. (Nichols 2008: 73)

The key to Nichols's argument regarding re-enactments is that re-enacted images 'forfeit' the indexical link to the *original* event and this triggers a recognition in the viewer of the status of what they are viewing – it is at one and the same time recognised as *a staged representation* of a *prior* event and *not an un-staged representation* of a *contemporaneous* event. What sounds like common outlined by Bill Nichols (2008), is linked to a psychoanalytic understanding of 'fantasy' and how a pleasurable experience can be derived from the 'retrieval' of something past; crucially, though, this does not mean a literal retrieval of an actual object, but is bound up with the complex psychic pleasures and contradictions that temporal distance can engender. This links to 'atavism', which, simply put, refers to an instance of something from the past impinging on the present. I shall return to these two concepts presently. First of all, we need to spend some time outlining what is meant by the term 're-enactment'.

PROBLEMS WITH DEFINING RE-ENACTMENT

For some, the very idea of re-enacting events is controversial and might, theoretically at least, disqualify something from being considered a 'documentary'. I say theoretically because in practical terms, one would have to disqualify a great many films and television programmes if a strict 'no re-enactment' rule was put in place and followed to the letter. As Honess Roe (2013: 3) points out, citing the received wisdom view (actually a summary of views she has heard from undergraduate students) of what a documentary should be: 'the presumption goes that documentaries should be observational, unobtrusive, truthful, bear witness to actual events, contain interviews and, even, be objective'. As she goes on to make clear, however, if we take John Grierson's famous definition (1966: 147) of documentary as 'the creative treatment of actuality' (an argument that is at odds with the received wisdom view that she mentions encountering frequently) then there is nothing to disqualify either re-enactment or animation as perfectly viable forms of expression for telling stories 'about the events, experiences and people that exist in the actual world' (Honess Roe 2013: 3). The 'received wisdom' view of documentary is, of course, a version of what was proposed by those filmmakers that Bill Nichols (2008: 72) refers to as the 'vérité boys' when he notes that re-enactments used to be a 'staple element' of documentaries until they were 'slain' by the introduction and widespread adoption of observational tropes.

Even among people who acknowledge that re-enactment *is* acceptable in documentary, we might find some resistance to *animation*-as-re-enactment. The very notion of re-enactment would tend to make us think of a *live-action capturing* – albeit an attenuated one, precisely because it *is* re-enacted and not captured directly – of some past event that is historically, politically and/or socially important (otherwise, why bother re-enacting it?). In other words, the re-enactment appears to be strongly associated with the 'sober' discourse of documentary (live-action) indexicality. As is made clear in Brian Winston's (1995: 120–3) discussion of the Griersonian documentary tradition, the British documentary movement thought nothing of what Winston calls the

CHAPTER 4

Animated Documentary, Recollection, 'Re-enactment' and Temporality
Paul Ward

It now seems uncontroversial to talk about the hybrid category 'animated documentary' – though there is still considerable debate over what might belong in such a category, and about the accuracy of the term. Honess Roe (2013) offers the most comprehensive overview of this complex and contentious field. As one would expect with a still-emerging area of scholarship, there are discussions about animated documentary's limits: should we include animated games, nanotechnological visualisations and/or explorations of fantasy or memory? New work is emerging all the time (see, for example, Ehrlich 2015; Moore 2015), and Rosenkrantz (2011) provides an interesting recent discussion of some of the theoretical differences of opinion within the field. Despite the growing critical literature, more work is needed in delineating how people understand or relate to – in a word, how they *experience* – what might be commonly defined as animated documentary. This chapter's approach is to examine some animated documentaries and focus on how they position the viewer in relation to the events they depict. More specifically, I am interested in how animation (or animated scenes in an otherwise live-action documentary) may or may not be perceived as a form of 're-enactment', and also in the complex web of temporal relations brought into play by thinking of animated documentary scenes in this way. As we shall see, the term 're-enactment' is more complex than it first appears – it cannot simply be reduced to the simplistic sense of an 'action replay' of events, but raises all sorts of questions about performance, agency, point of view and, in particular, temporality.

Central to my discussion, therefore, are the ways in which some animated documentaries, in their re-presentation of past events, foreground and heighten the temporal relations at play. This will entail opening out how we think about animated representations of real historical events to include their 'fantasmatic' and 'atavistic' dimensions. The point of discussing these two concepts is to emphasise the fact that we are not talking about a simple 're-presentation' of something that happened, but rather, a complex interrelating of past events and present viewing experience. The 'fantasmatic', as

Part 2

Defining Terms and Contexts

Ritchin, Fred (2009), *After Photography*, New York: W.W. Norton & Company.
Scott, A. O. (2008), 'Inside a veteran's nightmare – *Waltz with Bashir*', *International New York Times*, 25 December, <http://www.nytimes.com/2008/12/26/movies/26bash.html> (last accessed 22 October 2016).
Shale, Richard (1982), *Donald Duck Joins Up: The Walt Disney Studio during World War II*, Ann Arbor, MI: UMI Research Press.
Shay, Christopher (2010), 'The Taiwan company that's turning news into cartoons', *Time*, 23 August, <www.time.com/time/world/article/0,8599,2012166,00.html> (last accessed 22 October 2016).
Skoller, Jeffrey (2011), 'Introduction to the Special Issue "Making it (un)real: contemporary theories and practices in documentary animation"', *animation: an interdisciplinary journal*, 6: 3, pp. 207–14.
Smith, Terry (2009), *What is Contemporary Art?*, Chicago: University of Chicago Press.
Sobchack, Vivian (2004), *Carnal Thoughts*, Berkeley: University of California Press.
Sofian, Sheila (2005), 'The truth in pictures', *FPS Magazine*, March, pp. 7–11.
Strøm, Gunnar (2003), 'The animated documentary', *Animation Journal*, 11, pp. 46–63.
Virilio, Paul (1994), *The Vision Machine*, Bloomington: Indiana University Press.
Waltz with Bashir, film, directed by Ari Folman. Israel/France/Germany/USA/Finland/Switzerland/Belgium/Australia: Bridgit Folman Film Gang, Les Films d'Ici and Razor Film Produktion GmbH, 2008.

Boykoff, Pamela (2010), 'The blurry lines of animated "news"', *CNN*, 2 February, <www.edition.cnn.com/2010/WORLD/asiapcf/01/30/taiwan.animated.news/index.html?iref=allsearch> (last accessed 22 October 2016).

Burnett, D. Graham (2013), 'In lies begin responsibilities', in Elizabeth Armstrong (ed.), *More Real? Art in the Age of Truthiness*, Minneapolis: Minneapolis Institute of Arts, pp. 190–209.

Capino, Jose B. (2004), 'Filthy funnies: notes on the body in animated pornography', *Animation Journal*, 12, pp. 53–71.

Cheng, Benjamin Ka Lun and Wai Han Lo (2012), 'Can news be imaginative? An experiment testing the perceived credibility of melodramatic animated news, news organizations, media use, and media dependency', *Electronic News*, 6: 3, pp. 131–50.

Crary, Jonathan (1990), *Techniques of the Observer: On Vision and Modernity in the Nineteenth Century*, Cambridge, MA: MIT Press.

Davidson Russell (2009), 'A waltz and an interview: speaking with *Waltz with Bashir* creator Ari Folman', *CC2K*, 20 January, <http://www.cc2konline.com/component/k2/item/1654-a-waltz-and-an-interview-speaking-with-waltz-with-bashir-creator-ari-folman> (last accessed 22 October 2016).

Ehrlich, Nea (2015), *Animated Realities: From Animated Documentaries to Documentary Animation*, unpublished PhD dissertation, University of Edinburgh.

Garrett, Stewart (2010), 'Screen memory in *Waltz with Bashir*', *Film Quarterly*, 63: 3, pp. 58–62.

Globalised Slavery: How Big Supermarkets are Selling Prawns in Supply Chain Fed by Slave Labour, film, directed by Chris Kelly. UK: *The Guardian*, 2014.

Grierson, John (1966), *Grierson on Documentary*, Los Angeles: University of California Press.

Groys, Boris (2008), 'The topology of contemporary art', in Terry Smith, Okwui Enwezor and Nancy Condee (eds), *Antinomies of Art and Culture: Modernity, Postmodernity, Contemporaneity*, Durham, NC: Duke University Press, pp. 71–80.

Guantánamo Bay: The Hunger Strikes, film, directed by Various. UK: Sherbet, Fonic and *The Guardian*, 2013.

Guerin, Frances and Roger Hallas (eds) (2007), *The Image and the Witness: Trauma, Memory and Visual Culture*, London: Wallflower Press.

Harsin, Jayson (2009), 'The responsible dream: on Ari Folman's *Waltz with Bashir*', *Bright Lights Film Journal*, 31 January, <http://brightlightsfilm.com/the-responsible-dream-on-ari-folmans-waltz-with-bashir/#.V72x8JN940p> (last accessed 22 October 2016).

Honess Roe, Annabelle (2009), *Animating Documentary*, unpublished PhD dissertation, University of Southern California.

Honess Roe, Annabelle (2013), *Animated Documentary*, Basingstoke: Palgrave Macmillan.

Lind, Maria and Hito Steyerl (eds) (2008), *The Greenroom: Reconsidering the Documentary and Contemporary Art*, Los Angeles: Sternberg Press.

Manovich, Lev (2008), 'Introduction to info-aesthetics', in Terry Smith, Okwui Enwezor and Nancy Condee (eds), *Antinomies of Art and Culture: Modernity, Postmodernity, Contemporaneity*, Durham, NC: Duke University Press, pp. 333–44.

One Iranian Lawyer's Fight to Save Juveniles from Execution, film, directed by Various. UK: Sherbet and *The Guardian*, 2012.

Osborne, Peter (2013), *Anywhere or Not at All*, London: Verso.

Peaslee, Robert Moses (2011), 'It's fine as long as you draw, but don't film: *Waltz with Bashir* and the postmodern function of animated documentary', *Visual Communication Quarterly*, 18: 4, pp. 223–35.

Raiti, Gerard (2007), 'The disappearance of Disney animated propaganda: a globalization perspective', *animation: an interdisciplinary journal*, 2: 2, pp. 153–69.

and documentary. Only by understanding how and why reality is represented in a certain way and the many questions these representations raise, can we hope to reach insights about what constitutes our 'contemporary'.

Acknowledgement

The author thankfully acknowledges the anonymous peer review feedback from *animation: an interdisciplinary journal* received on several of the ideas included in this chapter.

Notes

1. Available at <https://en.wikipedia.org/wiki/Category:Animated_documentary_films> (last accessed 3 November 2015).
2. Available at <www.vimeo.com/channels/docoanim/videos> (last accessed 2 November 2017).
3. Information taken from 'Animated documentary', available at <www.animateddocs.wordpress.com/about/> (last accessed 25 April 2014) and 'Facebook animated documentary discussion group', available at <www.facebook.com/AnimatedDocumentary> (last accessed 2 November 2017).
4. Available at <www.animateddocs.wordpress.com/about/> (last accessed 2 November 2017).
5. Available at <www.youtube.com/results?search_query=animated+documentary> (last accessed 2 November 2017).
6. It is worth noting that this too is part of the discussed paradigm shift where animation is increasingly accepted in nonfiction visual culture. If and when animation's acceptance as credible representation is complete, rather than an in-between status straddling fiction and nonfiction, viewers may cease to question animation and its constructedness. As a result, animated imagery may eventually be seen as similar to photography in the sense that it is expected and accepted as showing events when in fact it does not really show anything, only acting as an illustration of what is being said.

Bibliography

ABC News (2015), 'TomoNews uses animation to depict news stories satirically', *ABC News*, 14 October, <http://www.abc.net.au/news/2015-10-15/tomonews-uses-animation-to-depict-news-stories/6855546> (last accessed 3 November 2015).

Adewunmi, Bim (2014), 'UK's child refugees tell their unique stories', *The Guardian*, 18 June, <www.theguardian.com/society/the-womens-blog-with-jane-martinson/2012/jun/18/uk-child-refugees-stories> (last accessed 22 October 2016).

Alberro, Alex (2009), 'Questionnaire on "The Contemporary"', *October*, 130, pp. 55–60.

Blocker, Jane M. (2009), *Seeing Witness: Visuality and Ethics of Testimony*, Minneapolis: University of Minnesota Press.

simultaneously emerged and extended within multiple fields of life that deal with factual information, such as documentary, journalism, data visualisation, science and cartography (as seen in our daily use of GPS technologies, whether we stop to think of this as animation or not). Put simply, animation infiltrates many aspects of daily life, illustrating, or even creating, information upon which we have come to depend.

Animation's contemporarily indeterminate and intermediate stage of development and cultural status is precisely what demonstrates the fact that increasing recent use of animated images, aesthetic modes and production technologies in nonfiction moving image works marks an important point of transition in present-day visual culture. As a medium and visual language positioned between the assumptions of the past and the possibilities of the future, animation can enjoy the advantages of its continued popular association with fiction (which means that animation's use in nonfiction may generate shock and/or marketing value). Meanwhile, animation can also contribute to the contemporary aesthetics of nonfiction by expanding visuality. Animation can show that which may otherwise not be visually representable, be this because it was not filmed at the time of occurrence; is subjective in nature; is physically internal and infinitesimal (cellular structures, for example); or is infinitely large and extra- or supra-terrestrial or virtual in nature. Animation may also act as a tool to think with, such as in its contemporary uses within scientific visualisations of patterns or theoretical ideas.

The proliferation of animated nonfiction is part of a more general rise of innovative and non-mimetic aesthetics within nonfiction creative practices. Examining those characteristics of contemporary visual culture that may explain these changes can lead to a deeper understanding of the relationship between current conceptualisations of what constitutes 'the real' and what may act as credible (although constantly shifting) mediations and representations of 'reality'. As nonfiction aesthetics change and expand, new criteria for legitimisation and believability come into play. As a result, the principles on which to base the truth value of any given signifier become multiple and, potentially, increasingly murky. In an ultra-visual world characterised by the omnipresence of screens, media disinformation and evolving aesthetics of representation, a world within which visual imagery represents but also shapes realities, enhanced skills of visual analysis are crucial for contemporary consumers of information. By the continual development of new tools and theories with which to analyse emergent portrayals of information, an improvement of collective visual literacy and criticality is made possible. Presenting animation's use in nonfiction as a complex and interdisciplinary field of inquiry illuminates the break with past assumptions and indicates directions for future thinking surrounding our concepts of visuality, reality no longer sufficient for documentary or factual representation, since it is limited to capturing material referents. The credibility of images based on the notion of mimesis has today been exposed as complexly qualified. If reality is no longer physical in any simple and pure sense, then the aesthetic modes and production technologies best used to depict it are no longer necessarily photographic. Photography is no longer automatically sufficient and/or dominant as an aesthetic of documentation once humankind lives in mixed realities where the virtual and the physical intertwine. Since virtual reality requires pictorial representations that can employ many visual styles, and which must move in order to depict processes and user input, animation becomes central. New aesthetics are thus required to depict contemporary mixed realities, while the virtual culture redefines the credibility of animation and its relation to reality, nonfiction, evidence and realism. Due to the many contemporary cultural characteristics that help to explain the present-day proliferation of non-mimetic aesthetics such as animation, its longstanding association with fiction weakens because contemporary viewers have become accustomed to seeing animation in diverse contexts – and also to seeing varied visualisations that break with traditional photographic aesthetics. As a result, animation has become a ubiquitous contemporary medium and aesthetic, one so familiar that it becomes increasingly easy to read (and, therefore, to accept) as legitimate when employed in nonfiction contexts and projections.

Conclusion: The Indeterminate and Intermediate Nature of Contemporary Animation

This essay has sought to map out and explore some of the contemporary characteristics that may explain the recent rise in the production of, and theoretical interest in, animated nonfiction. Whilst defining the contemporary is, of course, a huge endeavour, I have chosen to focus on certain key technological developments that have shaped today's information age and current visual culture. Those developments shed light on the shifting cultural and epistemological role and status of animation today, illustrating the fascinating in-between status that animation currently holds: a break between past and future, somewhere (and something) between fact and fiction, or a convergence of the two. Animation in nonfiction today has a contradictory, and thus captivating, nature. While the use of animation in nonfiction is a growing trend, elements of photography's historical status as the prized aesthetic of nonfiction still endure. As such, animation is both an increasingly used *and* insistently questioned visual language. While animation is still used as entertainment and can still warrant a sense of spectacle and fantasy, it has placed in direct contact with them. Viewing the world through non-human visual perceptions questions how things are 'really' seen (and thus 'should' be depicted). If the perceiver is no longer necessarily human, and thus the central criterion for 'realistic' representation is no longer solely the human eye, this helps validate the idea that a significantly more varied range of visual stylisations today is (and, in the future, may even more be) considered believable in multiple instances and contexts.

Fifthly, what we might term the virtualisation of culture requires the omnipresence of screens through which all virtual actions and spaces in the digital realm are mediated. Screens thus act as a kind of portal into 'other' and extended aspects of today's real: increasingly, the latter might best be understood as a mixed phenomenon that combines diverse virtual and physical elements. Once virtual screen worlds become interactive and the screen consequently functions as interface, the worlds depicted on the latter no longer remain *on* its surface in any simple and literal sense. The screen instead invites embodied viewers dynamically to act within these worlds to which it facilitates access. In this sense, the *on*-screen world becomes an *in*-screen world, within which the figure of the user-viewer plays an active role. Whereas in the past (and even as recently as the 1990s), it would have been easier to define 'reality' as intrinsically and predominantly physical (and thus, photographable), this is no longer the case in the early twenty-first century. Daily actions are increasingly screen-mediated; new visual representations are thus needed in order to construct and transmit information throughout digital, in-screen, virtual worlds. In current virtualised computer culture, images are used as a symbolic language that renders visible abstract data or processes with which humans engage and act upon. This remains the case even if many of the images we consume do not signify anything that exists in physical form. In other words, many aspects of contemporary digital-virtual culture appear only on-screen; as such, they require forms and strategies of representation that exceed the terms of the photographic-mimetic representational mode reliant on the assumption of materiality. The growing virtualisation of culture thus serves to explain animation's analogously expanding role as a signature twenty-first-century visual language (Ehrlich 2015).

The ramifications of the contemporary cultural characteristics listed above are vast. This is not to claim that reality was ever limited to physical matter in a strict sense, since the former has always included (and been shaped by) non-physical elements such as language. But, by concentrating on the virtualisation of culture – by which I mean the pervasive nature of screens and online platforms of activity – I wish to demonstrate that realities today are mixed to include both the physical and the virtual. Once reality exceeds the physical, photography (and visual realism more generally) is viewers have become accustomed to receiving data in modern-day screen-based information cultures.

Thirdly, the ongoing contemporary rise in the visual representation of information is closely linked to contemporary information culture. Within the latter, animation not only enhances visuality but is also central to the way in which information is packaged and presented to viewers. Lev Manovich (2008: 340) introduces the concept of 'info-aesthetics' in this regard, explaining that the current culture of mass information requires and creates new aesthetic preferences, forms and iconologies. The exponential growth in available information means that new ways of presenting and receiving that information must evolve. Like data visualisation, animation can condense and simplify vast amounts of data and, due to its dynamic nature, is ideal for the representation of processes. Through its infinite array of formal styles combined with movement, animation is visually arresting, an immensely important attention-grabbing feature in an era of 'too much data'. Put simply, in a period when viewers are surrounded by information that is mediated by screens and visualised in many different ways, there is a marked shift away from mimetic and naturalistic representational modes. A wealth of innovatively stylised aesthetics has entered the realm of information culture, a fact which may serve to partially explain the enhanced visibility of animation today.

Fourthly, there is the existence of a phenomenon that Paul Virilio (1994) has labelled 'machine vision'. Machine vision occurs when machines that are independent of human operators 'see' and record material that is then shared with other machines, until a world image is constructed that functions further and further outside human experience or cognisance. Virilio describes this phenomenon as the proliferation of images created by machine viewpoints. Synthetic images, products of info-graphic software and data visualisation all lead to a process of computer-aided design. Contrary to how photography was in the past prized as a literal 'eyewitness to events', the way in which information is visually presented today becomes progressively more distant from the manner in which viewers would have seen events directly themselves if physically present in the specific place and time of that event's unfolding. Instead, the images of machine vision are heavily and characteristically mediated and visualised by technological means, such as satellites and military imaging from battlegrounds. This strengthens the idea that contemporary viewers are becoming increasingly accustomed to visual information presented in non-mimetic ways, through a range of emergent aesthetics that break with human vision (as much animation has long done). Machine vision questions the presumed superiority and desirability of mimesis as an imitation of referents based on how human vision perceives the latter when produce an easily manipulated image, thus further weakening photography's traditionally privileged truth value. Furthermore, as image-making technologies continue to develop and animation becomes ever more capable of producing photorealistic imagery, as in films such as James Cameron's *Avatar* (2009), what may appear photorealistic may actually be animated. This fact destabilises the assumed veracity of photography and the mimetic all the more. Thus, whether trickery is openly announced or not, the fact that audiences are aware that images *can* potentially and easily prove deceptive means that popular doubt in visual artefacts, even those that appear photorealistic and mimetic, is growing. 'Is it real?', that well-known reaction to photography (whether spectacular or mundane), embodies this contemporary cultural characteristic perfectly. Animation's main historical point of structuring comparison, next to which it may once have appeared essentially artificial or fictional in nature, is today significantly debased. As a result, a space has been created for other and new documentary aesthetics that, historically speaking, have been seen as less legitimate than certain photographic counterparts.

BELIEVABLE STYLISATIONS: THE RISE OF INNOVATIVE AND NON-MIMETIC AESTHETICS IN NONFICTION

Several aspects of contemporary visual culture potentially situate animation as less associated with fiction, positioning it instead as a more familiar (and, therefore, less 'foreign' and/or artificial) form of representation in nonfiction contexts. Firstly, the growing practical ease and accessibility of animation production technologies means that more animated works can now be made by non-professionals able to bypass the extensive artistic and technological know-how once necessary for animation production. Secondly, the escalating pervasion of surveillance culture, the ever-present cameras that people continuously use for the purposes of personal documentation, entails that present-day viewers have become accustomed to the idea of always having ready access to visual footage of reported events. The ubiquity of recording and surveillance devices that characterises contemporary culture evokes a consequent expectancy of image availability on the part of audiences. The question then arises: What is to be done if/when such imagery does not exist? Animation is an ideal creative device in such cases. The medium enables the unlimited visual representation of events free from photography's required visual capturing of a specific occurrence at the time of its unfolding, no matter how the results of that initial capture may be manipulated subsequently. This reinforces the increasingly significant role to be played by animation in expanding and enhancing the existing visual field and in better facilitating the delivery of information visually, which is how value as a documentary aesthetic makes way for new aesthetics of documentary and nonfiction, such as animation. Scholars such as Fred Ritchin in his aptly named book *After Photography* (2009), for example, have made it startlingly clear that photography requires interpretation. Thus, photographs can easily take on a range of unexpected manipulations and meanings.

For instance, photographic imagery may surprise viewers by being used to convey information that is not necessarily visible. Consider, for example, Colin Powell's testimony to the UN in 2003, which utilised satellite imagery that did not actually *show* weapons of mass destruction, but which was still used to provide justification for the invasion of Iraq (Blocker 2009: xvi). Alternatively, photography may also be used to convey meanings that seem to contradict initial readings of a particular photographic image. How else to explain the fact that home video images of the attack on Rodney King by Los Angeles policemen in 1991 were eventually deemed insufficiently authentic evidence when drawn upon in court (Guerin and Hallas 2007: 3)? Whereas photography is often perceived as evidence, showing viewers something that was visually captured, in these examples what exactly was shown was evasive, emphasising the extent of interpretation necessary even when engaging with photographs. Animation, on the other hand, does not hide the fact that it is constructed and can thus visualise information without pertaining to show or capture in the same way.[6] Although 'credible' visual depictions of nonfiction phenomena are perhaps still most often associated with photography, current cultural, epistemological and technological circumstances paint a more complex picture. When considering animation as an alternative mode of nonfiction representation, it is vital to understand that, once animation's main structuring point of comparison starts to become increasingly destabilised, animation's long-assumed artificiality is opened up for significant reconsideration as well.

Indeed, it could be argued that photography has today become ever more similar to animation: neither medium can be argued to inherently contain indisputable evidence of something; both mediums rely instead on interpretation in order to create meaning. The difference, of course, is that animation more obviously flaunts its incorporation of interpretative elements and practices, which is part of its inherent stylization as a medium. Photography is increasingly distanced from any automatic sense of transparency because, once it is acknowledged that the medium and individual examples of it may have multiple meanings, any uncomplicatedly direct link between realities and their recording by photographic means becomes open to doubt. This becomes all the more true with the development of digital photography, whereby analogue photography's physical link to its represented referents is replaced with units of information recorded and restructured in order to corporality depicted onscreen, despite its different visual appearance. Viewers project onto animated bodies as if they were filmed physical bodies similar to their own. Animation's sufficient closeness to the viewer's corporeal sense of self reinforces its advantageous (and still increasing) use in a wide range of contemporary nonfiction contexts and projects.

In order to understand some of the reasons why animation has now become substantively (albeit not comprehensively) mainstream in a range of contemporary nonfiction contexts, several key cultural characteristics of the contemporary moment must be considered. As Jonathan Crary (1990: 2) notes of epochal shifts in visual culture, traditional forms may change yet also linger while new strategies of visualisation emerge and expand. This is precisely the framework within which to best explain the recent rise of animated nonfiction. Two broad contemporary cultural characteristics and considerations are salient here: the first concerns the demise of the photographic and the mimetic, while the second relates to the consequent rise in non-mimetic forms of visualisation, such as animation.

'IS IT REAL?' THE DEMISE OF THE PHOTOGRAPHIC AND THE MIMETIC

The growing, yet still surprisingly hesitant, use and reception of animation within nonfiction is, as already noted, in part predicated on animation's traditionally presumed artificiality and consequent association with fiction. However, it is crucial to keep in mind that something can only be deemed fictional and/or artificial in comparison to that which is *not* deemed so. Therefore, identifying and examining photography as animation's structuring point of comparison is crucial. Photography's traditionally perceived strength lies, alongside other things, in mimesis (the accurate capture of the physical appearance of referents) and indexicality (the physical connection between a sign and its referent most often associated with analogue photographic technologies). These characteristics most obviously link nonfiction photographic depictions such as documentaries to the world beyond them. Consequently, they have also often been used to validate such depictions' claims to truth. Nonetheless, despite photography's pervasive presence in everyday life and its long-privileged position with regard to claims of evidentiary status, the medium's authenticity has been questioned and theorised in many different ways. Photography's status as a privileged mode of conveying documentary information has been in decline since at least the 1970s. This process was only accelerated with the development of digital photography. In fact, new digital production methods and a growing awareness of potential image manipulation conceptualise digital photography as a new medium, i.e., post-photography. The undermining of photography's assumed privileged truth important to bear this in mind when considering the case of *The Guardian*'s animated videos, because the latter are journalistic works that also include photographic imagery of the protagonists whose experiences and situations were being reported on. This fact perhaps suggests that, despite animation becoming increasingly accepted as a useful and legitimate representational choice within certain nonfictional contexts, it is not yet considered a *wholly* reliable journalistic mode: hence the inclusion of photographs within the reports in question. Tellingly, those latter images actually illustrate nothing of the content the reports describe and do not really act as any substantive form of evidentiary proof: they merely show the faces of people whom the reports identify as active and/or affected protagonists. The truth-value of these photographs is, therefore, completely assumed and convention-based, linked as it is to the habitual identification of photography with reliable visual evidence. The photographs are no more a confirmation or documents of events reported than the animation preceding them. They are, nonetheless, still perhaps accepted as more believable corroborating evidence. What an illustrative example such as this highlights is the transitional status of animation today: increasingly used as a credible form of news reportage while simultaneously remaining subject to longstanding assumptions about the existence of other, more worthy, credible and established modes of documentary investigation and representation.

It is also interesting in this regard to note that *The Guardian* website includes a warning at the onset of the Guantánamo Bay and Thai fishing videos: 'contains scenes some viewers might find disturbing'. Such echoes of the concerns that NMA's animated news items might potentially offend and/or mislead some viewers suggests that animated news images may in fact be perceived and experienced as 'true enough' to provoke difficult sensations in a significant number of viewers. This in turn raises questions as to the link between ethics, documentary viewing and bodily identification with onscreen protagonists, as theorised by Vivian Sobchack. Sobchack claims (2004: 173) that an ethical view of events onscreen develops through the spectator's bodily identification with the protagonist witnessed. That identification is based on the spectator's understanding of their potentially shared physical pain and mortality, thus differentiating documentary spectatorship from the experience of watching a fictional representation. If the horrific violence of juvenile executions, force-feeding, and the torture and murder of enslaved individuals may seem 'disturbing' to viewers, the human fact and impact of such cruelty has clearly not been disregarded, despite the reporting of such actions and events taking animated form. As Jose B. Capino (2004: 55–6) has suggested in relation to animated pornography, animated bodies are able to provoke physical responses in viewers, who recognise and relate to the animated news sequences are indeed so obviously fictitious and comical on one hand, how can they simultaneously be seen as possessing enough truth value to be able to influence (let alone 'wrongly') public opinion about the so-called 'real' on the other?

Although much 2010 established media coverage of NMA emphasised the allegedly 'comical overtones' or 'cartoon-like' qualities frequently ascribed to animation, a 2012 study analysing the effects of using animation in news reports found that animated formats neither enhance nor dampen news credibility (Cheng and Lo 2012). This implies that the ways (actual or possible) in which animation is used and received depend on changing cultural conventions. 'We're still being laughed at', said NMA officials in 2010, while also predicting that by 2012 their clips would not simply be known abroad as amusing novelty animations; rather, they would increasingly become the norm for TV news (Shay 2010). Such predictions have to some extent come true: the use of animation in factual reporting is now clearly an increasing journalistic norm, not a marketing scam or quirky choice (again, think of the animated visualisation of events preceding a plane crash as reported on the news, for example). Most viewers today are quite familiar and comfortable with such uses of animation: NMA has, for instance, worked with the BBC and Reuters on joint animation projects, mostly on the topic of refugees (ibid.). In sharp contrast to CNN's original disdain, many subsequent reviewers of animated journalism now acknowledge animation's advantages as a practically and ethically efficacious means 'to maintain anonymity of the individual but to give a strong sense of visual metaphor about the experiences they've had, but can't film' (Adewunmi 2014).

Currently more mainstream and authoritative than NMA, for example, *The Guardian* website has since 2012 included an animated report on lawyer Mohammad Mostafaei's battle against executions of juveniles in Iran in *One Iranian Lawyer's Fight to Save Juveniles from Execution* (2012) and the animated video *Guantánamo Bay: The Hunger Strikes* (2013), based on detainees' personal testimony. In 2014, as part of its coverage of human trafficking in the Thai fishing industry, *The Guardian* also produced *Globalised Slavery: How Big Supermarkets are Selling Prawns in Supply Chain Fed by Slave Labour*, a horrifying exposé consisting of long animated sequences based on testimonies from people affected. Significantly, *The Guardian* was actively involved in the *production* (as opposed to simply the online hosting) of these videos. This fact demonstrates the existence of increasingly widespread professional and popular acceptance of animation as simply another form of legitimate news reportage and investigation.

Nonetheless, animation's continued connection in the minds of many to diverse ideas and practices of fictional narrative also remains apparent. It is

This lukewarm, ambivalent reception illustrates the nature of many contemporaneous debates and assertions regarding the 'in-between' nature of animated nonfiction, compared with more clear-cut traditional distinctions made between animation/fiction and photography/fact. As recently as 2010, for example, Howard Kurz, *Washington Post* media critic and host of CNN's *Reliable Sources*, remarked: 'Let's not confuse a bunch of cartoons with what people in the news business do' (Boykoff 2010). NMA's Jimmy Lai argued in response, however, that, despite certain details perhaps appearing visually inaccurate, the images in much of *TomoNews*'s output were in fact based on other media reports. The images in question thus maintained the integrity of the news content depicted by the channel's output (ibid.). Of course, the question as to how far details of real-world phenomena may be changed and their representations altered whilst still maintaining an overarching sense of integrity of content resonates with John Grierson's famous definition of documentary as the 'creative treatment of actuality' (1966: 13). In this sense, animated news is not necessarily so different from varied other forms of nonfiction, journalism and documentary. This point is ever more relevant today, when hybrid documentary forms such as docudrama, mockumentary and reality TV have become mainstream and shows such as *The Colbert Report* (2005–15) or *The Daily Show* (1999–present) emphasise the growing inclination towards the convergence of information and entertainment in infotainment. In fact, many online audience comments in response to CNN's sceptical, self-regarding reportage on NMA reflected unfavourably upon the sensationalism of many other (non-animated) news channels today. 'News is a joke', 'journalism is dead anyway' and 'facts are a thing of the past' were all article reader comments posted in response to Howard Kurz's public pronouncements (Boykoff 2010); such utterances might be seen as suggestive precursors of the 'fake news/alternative facts' discourse systematically developed and exploited by politicians such as Donald Trump later in the decade. Is it such a surprise, then, that animated news is one phenomenon to have emerged from widespread contemporary audience disenchantment with established news outlets and providers?

NMA's news agency is suggestive not only because it demonstrates how extensive the contemporary use of animation for nonfiction purposes is becoming. It also exposes some of the central theoretical themes that are related to popular reception of this kind of animated work. On one hand, this form of news reportage is described by some as 'lacking in accuracy', possessing 'comical overtones', and as 'a bunch of cartoons' (Boykoff 2010). On the other hand (and ironically), however, NMA was also fined for its news coverage being overly graphic, exposing themes, stories and issues that might, it was claimed, offend and wrongly influence viewers (ibid.). But if *TomoNews*'s that breaks with past conventions (and/or that makes us notice and reflect upon the latter), signalling a shift or change from past to future. Reconsidered in this context, the often-supposed 'strangeness', or contradictory nature, of animated nonfiction indicates such a shift. This is because it breaks with past conventions of documentary aesthetics based on photography and introduces new possible forms of representation to the field.

Cartoons or News?

Turning now to specific case study examples, *TomoNews* by Next Media Animation (NMA), a Taiwan-based broadcasting channel launched in 2009, produces more than thirty computer-animated dramatisations, positioned on a continuum between the humorous and the informational, of news events every day. Initially targeting the Hong Kong and Taiwanese markets, these videos now average more than 4.1 million hits a day, making NMA the second most watched news channel in Hong Kong (Shay 2010). In October 2015, Guy Podmore, *TomoNews*'s International Content Editor, explained that many of NMA's animated news stories are now intended for the US market and wider English-speaking world, displaying a massive expansion in the channel's audience since 2010 (ABC 2015). Most (though not all) of the videos incorporate animation, giving *TomoNews*'s online broadcasts a distinctive visual edge. The channel's intensive use of animation not only enables the visual inclusion within its broadcasts of that which is not photographed, but also plays an important marketing role, arguably serving to increase both the visibility of, and potential new audience interest in, the channel's output. 'Subscribe now and never watch boring news again', the *TomoNews* website's introductory video states. It is worth noting that this description actually manifests the unique historical and cultural moment where animation is situated in-between fact and fiction. As long as animation is associated with fiction, its use in nonfiction is perceived as novel or 'quirky enough' to prevent the animation itself from being boring whereas if/once animation is fully accepted as imagery of nonfiction, it too may be considered as 'boring news', potentially marking the moment for an additional and necessary change in representation. From conception through production to publication, each news story on *TomoNews* uses motion capture technology and takes less than four hours to create in animated form. This fact sheds light on the ongoing development of animation production techniques, which may have been significantly time-consuming in the past but today can allow quick and unlimited visualisation of content on a rolling basis (ibid.).

Despite their clear local success, *TomoNews*'s signature tactics have frequently been criticised and still raise doubt in many commentators' minds.

anxiety about the loss of the real through the loss of indexicality (Osborne 2013: 128). This is because the latter was previously depended upon as a marker of the real in analogue photographic imagery (Burnett 2013: 194). That same sense of unease may also be used to explain the rise of various forms of documentary practice in recent decades. As Maria Lind and Hito Steyerl (2008: 12) explain, documentary is a genre that typically emerges or re-emerges in a time of crisis. It is, therefore, no surprise that in the post-1989 and post-9/11 ages, documentary proved a prevalent (and cross-disciplinary) cultural form, covering such varied topics as: globalisation, migration, surveillance, the 'War on Terror', political, epistemic and economic instabilities and popular uprisings. The continuing interest in documentary works suggests that, despite the haziness of their claims to 'truth', there still exists a belief that they can serve as a field through which to search for meaning in present predicaments. As technologies and forms of visual representation change, visual mediations of realities change as well. An ongoing 'documentary quest for ever more authentic representations of the real' (ibid.: 15) may therefore help explain the increasingly creative and experimental nature of many documentaries today, including animated documentary film works.

However, since animation has already been used in much earlier nonfiction filmmaking, the question remains: What makes recent animated documentaries seem 'new' or 'contemporary' as an aesthetic of information? First and foremost, the staggering growth in the quantity of animated nonfiction moving image works in very recent years demonstrates that the scale of present-day creative recourse to animated modes and imagery easily exceeds that witnessed during any earlier period of moving image history. Secondly, past uses of animation in nonfiction contexts often relied on animation's traditional association with fiction and fantasy (think, for example, of Disney's *Seven Wise Dwarfs* [1941], where the dwarfs from the same production company's feature-length *Snow White* [1937] march to the Post Office in order to purchase War Savings Certificates). Today, however, the power of this association has lessened considerably, as seen in recurring uses of animation to re-enact unfilmed events in the news, such as a plane crash, where no allusion is made to animation's historical use in fictional or humorous contexts. A relevant consideration in this regard is the fact that the technological evolution of animation production essentially changes animation's nature. This means that much contemporary animation can be seen as qualitatively different from that of earlier periods, thus making its overarching affect one that feels very much 'of the moment'. Finally, the meaning of newness is, as explained by Boris Groys (2008: 78), context-based: newness as something that is recognisably different from what has gone before. In other words, the new and contemporary is something novel, original and/or unusual. It is something a pervasive visual cultural mode today. Given that animation does have a longer (albeit often infrequent and/or marginalised) history of being used in nonfiction fields such as education and propaganda (see Honess Roe 2009: 42–58; Honess Roe 2013; Raiti 2007; Shale 1982), what is it about contemporary culture that might explain the above-noted shifts and changes in animation's creative, critical and cultural status, reception and believability? And, with more specific regard to the increasing proliferation and prominence of animated nonfiction and documentary, why *now*?

Defining Contemporaneity

An explanation of 'Why now?' requires further understanding of what this 'now' actually is. We need, therefore, to ask a series of interrelated and overlapping questions: What is 'the contemporary'? What is the relationship between the conditions of contemporaneity and emerging visual cultural tendencies, given that the latter form the backdrop to increasing interest in and use of animation in nonfiction moving image practices? And, what is it that makes animated documentaries seem, to many artists and audiences alike, such a supposedly 'new' and 'contemporary' visual cultural mode? In what follows, I attempt to map an understanding of contemporaneity that illuminates the rise of animated documentaries by borrowing from theorists who propose the digital revolution in visual culture as one central characteristic of the contemporary.

We tend to believe that anything produced in the present is *always* contemporary. However, the issue is not quite so simple. As Terry Smith (2009: 2) claims, the topic of 'the contemporary' is actually 'an interrogation into the ontology of the present, one that asks: What it is to exist in the conditions of contemporaneity?' The ways in which the contemporary is symbolised and historicised is what shapes its identity: different theorists define and demarcate the latter (and thus, also the former) in different ways (Alberro 2009: 60). Focusing on visual culture, for example, Peter Osborne's discussion of contemporary art maps out several possible periodisations of 'the contemporary': since the end of the Second World War in 1945; since the 1960s; and/or since the end of the Cold War in 1989. Each periodisation brings with it its own distinctive geopolitical and aesthetic defining characteristics (2013: 18–20).

When asked to define contemporaneity, Alex Alberro (2009: 56–7) describes the years after 1989 as characterised most obviously by globalisation, the fall of the Berlin Wall and with it the end of the Cold War, the new information and communication technologies of the internet, and the ensuing shift from the analogue to the digital. The rise of digital culture is central to an understanding of the present moment since it generated an ontological visual culture is at an interesting turning point, poised between fiction and fact – or perhaps combining the two. On one hand, animation's traditional popular association with fiction is less dominant, since it is now increasingly used in nonfiction contexts. But on the other, animation is still widely practised and consumed as a form of escapist and spectacular entertainment and, as I will demonstrate, it has yet to be fully accepted as a credible visual depiction of factual information. This latter fact emphasises two things: the problematic (not least because persistent) supremacy of photography as the assumed default aesthetic of nonfiction filmmaking, and also the transitional status of animation today.

In this chapter I try to understand the emergence, popularity and reception of animated nonfiction in recent years. In order to do so, it uses the expanding trend of animated news footage and reportage as an illustrative case study. Such moving image material is a close cousin of the animated documentary, but due to its generally mainstream (and thus, purportedly authoritative) journalistic sources, it may also be more familiar (and thus, potentially acceptable) to viewers. This growing visibility of animation in nonfiction reflects a contemporary paradigm shift – the rising acceptance of animation over photography in nonfiction, even though animation breaks with visual realism and was historically associated with fiction – a profound change in perception of the way events can be represented and still be accepted as viable and believable. This has massive implications since it exposes the decline in photography's assumed truth value, makes way for new aesthetics of documentary, and consequently *raises questions about the tools that viewers have to interpret the meaning and credibility of visual signifiers more generally*. The paradigm shifts my following case study uncovers will be positioned and analysed within what I see as the major contemporary changes in nonfiction representation, changes that are characteristic of today's wider visual culture. Specifically, such transformations include: technological shifts that have reshaped both contemporary visual culture and visuality (such as virtuality, screen culture, machine vision, the information era and ubiquitous surveillance); the tension between past visual cultural conventions and new trends (for example, ongoing changes in the theorisation of photography's traditionally assumed evidentiary status and the slowly but steadily increasing acceptance of non-photorealistic imagery as legitimate and credible documentation and testimony in many nonfiction fields of practice).

Animation as a medium is currently perceived in a paradoxical manner. Its advantages as a mode of informational representation are increasingly recognised, while traditional understandings of it as an essentially (and intensively) fictional mode of representation simultaneously persist. It is, therefore, important to understand what it is about animation that has made it such between animation and reality. By contrast, this essay starts from and works with the proposition that animated nonfiction in fact questions and challenges the conventionally perceived difference between animation and photography. The essay also works with the idea that animated nonfiction frequently reflects upon different modes of representation that are deemed 'more real' and believable as legitimate documentation.

While the use of animation in documentary works may still have seemed oxymoronic to many as recently as 2008 (see, for example, Scott 2008), the amalgamation of factual content with animated imagery is becoming increasingly widespread (be it within journalism, science, informatics or documentary film). By October 2014, for example, Wikipedia, under the category 'Animated documentary films', listed forty-two separate works.[1] Vimeo's online Doco-anim channel was created in 2012 and, at the time of writing, listed 155 videos.[2] The 'Animated documentary' Facebook discussion group was created in 2011; by 2017, it had over 2,000 members.[3] An associated website created in 2013 regularly shares updates about new animated documentary films, events and publications, listing hundreds of animated documentary films.[4] A search for the keywords 'animated documentary' on YouTube in November 2017 led to no fewer than 6,740,000 results.[5] The latter encompassed the documentary *Life, Animated* (Roger Ross Williams, 2016), about how Disney animations helped an autistic boy learn to communicate with the outside world; an *Animated Introduction to Cancer Biology* (Cancerquest, 2013), labelled as a 'full documentary', that teaches how cancer forms and spreads; and *Nowhere Line: Voices from Manus Island* (Lukas Schrank, 2015), an award-winning documentary about asylum seekers detained in Australia that is based on interviews with them. The category of 'animated documentary' thus includes works that engage differently with animation: as the topic of the film and as a way to depict subjective perspectives in *Life, Animated* about Disney animations and autism, as an informative/educational visualization of scientific content about cancer, and as a way to provide visual imagery for audio interviews in *Nowhere Line*. This elucidates the varied engagement with animation in nonfiction as well as the blurred boundaries between documentary and different fields of nonfiction today.

The categorisation of individual films as animated nonfiction and/or animated documentary obviously depends on different (and often competing) critical definitions and classificatory criteria. It is evident, however, that a significant rise in the creative practice, academic study, public display and dissemination of animated nonfiction has occurred in recent years (see, for example, Strøm 2003; Sofian 2005; Honess Roe 2009, 2013; Skoller 2011). However, what makes animated nonfiction such an enticing and timely topic to consider is the fact that animation's role in today's highly technologised

CHAPTER 3

Indeterminate and Intermediate or Animated Nonfiction: Why Now?

Nea Ehrlich

INTRODUCTION: THE SEARCH FOR ANIMATED DOCUMENTARIES

The reception of animated nonfiction is complex. 'It's interesting . . . but it's not *real*!' is a frequent comment I have heard since embarking on research into animated documentaries. An extensive discussion of possible definitions of 'animated documentary' clearly exceeds the scope of this chapter. But, in order to clarify, I refer here to animation as 'moving imagery only visible on-screen' and my research focuses particularly on non-naturalistic aesthetics within this overarching definition. This definition may draw criticism since it seems to sidestep the specificities of animation techniques and styles. Specific styles matter and can signify, misrepresent or emphasize different aspects of the information portrayed. However, it is not my intention here to analyse animation styles which are as varied as the techniques and levels of creativity of the animators. This classification encompasses the wide variety of animation techniques and styles whilst most clearly differentiating animation from photography: as imagery that is generated rather than recorded. As we shall see, this is a central and recurring issue in animation's use within nonfiction works.

On one hand, those familiar with one or two animated documentaries (usually, Ari Folman's *Waltz with Bashir* [2008] and Marjane Satrapi and Vincent Paronnaud's *Persepolis* [2007]) generally agree that they are thought-provoking. But on the other hand, when people try to explain *why* this is so, their chosen terminology often becomes muddled with that frequently used to describe photographic imagery. Judging by popular press coverage (film reviews, filmmaker interviews, awards ceremony reportage) of the Oscar-nominated *Waltz with Bashir*, it very often seems that the film's photographic imagery alone is considered 'real', whereas the rest is 'animated': as if only a photographically indexical relationship to a material context could constitute documentary footage of 'real' phenomena (see Harsin 2009; Davidson 2009; Garrett 2010; Peaslee 2011). This reinforces the conventional distinctions frequently made between animation and photography, as well as those drawn

Halas, John and Joy Batchelor (1949), 'European cartoon: a survey of the animated film,' *The Penguin Film Review*, 8, pp. 9–14.

Honess Roe, Annabelle (2011), 'Absence, excess and epistemological expansion: towards a framework for the study of animated documentary', *animation: an interdisciplinary journal*, 6: 3, pp. 215–30.

Honess Roe, Annabelle (2013), *Animated Documentary*, New York: Palgrave Macmillan.

How we Breathe, film, directed by Anon. USA: Bray Studios Inc., 1920.

The Inner Life of the Cell, film, directed by John Liebler and XVIVO. USA: XVIVO and Harvard University, 2006.

Ivanov-Vano, Ivan (1989), *Kadr za Kadrom*, Moscow: Iskusstvo.

Marchant, Beth (2006), 'Cellular visions: *The Inner Life of a Cell*,' *Studio Daily*, 20 July, <http://www.studiodaily.com/2006/07/cellular-visions-the-inner-life-of-a-cell/> (last accessed 21 October 2016).

The Mechanics of the Brain, film, directed by Vsevolod Pudovkin. USSR: Mezhrabpom-Rus' 1926.

Mihailova, Mihaela and John MacKay (2014), 'Frame shot: Vertov's ideologies of animation', in Karen Beckman (ed.), *Animating Film Theory*, Durham, NC: Duke University Press, pp. 145–66.

Norling, John A (1927), 'Animated technical drawings', *Transactions of the Society of Motion Picture Engineers*, 9: 31, pp. 601–7.

Norling, John A. and Jacob F. Leventhal (1926), 'Some developments in the production of animated drawings', *Transactions of the Society of Motion Picture Engineers*, 3, pp. 58–66.

Orgeron, Devin, Marsha Orgeron and Dan Streible (2012) (eds), *Learning with the Lights Off: Educational Film in the United States*, New York: Oxford University Press.

Ostherr, Kirsten (2012a), 'Cinema as universal language of health education: translating science in *Unhooking the Hookworm* (1920)', in Nancy Anderson and Michael R. Dietrich (eds), *The Educated Eye: Visual Culture and Pedagogy in the Life Sciences*, Lebanon, NH: University Press of New England, pp. 121–40.

Ostherr, Kirsten (2012b), 'Operative bodies: live action and animation in medical films of the 1920s', *Journal of Visual Culture*, 11: 3, pp. 352–77.

Ostherr, Kirsten (2013), *Medical Visions: Producing the Patient through Film, Television and Imaging Technologies*, Oxford: Oxford University Press.

Posner, Miriam (2011), *Depth Perception: Narrative and the Body in American Medical Filmmaking*, unpublished PhD dissertation, Yale University, Ann Arbor: ProQuest/UMI, Publication No 3497006.

Reichert, Ramón (2009), 'Behaviorsm, animation, and effective cinema: the McGraw-Hill industrial management film series and the visual culture of management', in Vinzenz Hediger and Patrick Vonderau (eds), *Films that Work: Industrial Film and the Productivity of Media*, Amsterdam: Amsterdam University Press, pp. 283–302.

Renov, Michael (2004), *The Subject of Documentary*, Minneapolis: University of Minnesota Press.

Saettler, L. Paul (1990), *The Evolution of American Education Technology*, Englewood Cliffs, NJ: Libraries Unlimited.

Van Riper, A. Bowdoin (2011), 'Introduction', in A. Bowdoin Van Riper (ed.), *Learning from Mickey, Donald and Walt: Essays on Disney's Edutainment Films*, Jefferson, NC: McFarland, pp. 1–13.

Ward, Paul (2005), *Documentary: The Margins of Reality*, London: Wallflower Press.

Wells, Paul (1997), 'The beautiful village and the true village: a consideration of animation and the documentary aesthetic', *Art & Design*, 12: 3/4, pp. 40–45.

NOTES

1. This study focuses exclusively on drawn animation. However, stop motion was also used in early educational and instructional cinema, albeit more rarely. See, for example, the films of F. Percy Smith, particularly *How Spiders Fly* (1909).
2. In the early stages of the First World War, John Randolph Bray produced army training films which relied on the then cutting-edge technology of rotoscoping in order to clarify the operation of different types of weaponry (Crafton 1993: 158). Walt Disney, early in his career, directed two commissioned films dedicated to dental hygiene: *Tommy Tucker's Tooth* (1922) and *Clara Cleans Her Teeth* (1926) (Honness Roe 2013: 9). In Britain, F. Percy Smith's Kineto War Map series (1914–16) used animated map sequences to trace the war's progress (Ward 2005: 83).
3. While Pudovkin directed the film, the animated segments were created by Ivan Ivanov-Vano and Yuri Merkulov.

BIBLIOGRAPHY

Bissonnette, Sylvie (2014), 'Scalar travel documentaries: animating the limits of the body and life', *animation: an interdisciplinary journal*, 9: 2, pp. 138–58.

Bordwell, David (2008), 'Directors: Kuleshov', *Observations on Film Art*, 8 July, <http://www.davidbordwell.net/blog/category/directors-kuleshov/> (last accessed 21 October 2016).

Cabarga, Leslie (1976), *The Fleischer Story*, New York: Nostalgia Press.

Communication: A Film Lesson in 'General Science', film, directed by Anon. USA: Herman DeVry, 1927.

Cosmos: A Spacetime Odyssey, television series, directed by Brannon Braga, Bill Pope, Ann Druyan and Kevin Dart. USA: Cosmos Studios, Fuzzy Door Productions, National Geographic Channel and Six Point Harness, 2014.

Crafton, Donald (1993), *Before Mickey: The Animated Film, 1898–1928*, Chicago: University of Chicago Press.

Curtis, Scott (2004), 'Still/moving: digital imaging and medical hermeneutics', in Lauren Rabinowitz and Abraham Geil (eds), *Memory Bytes: History, Technology, and Digital Culture*, Durham, NC: Duke University Press, pp. 218–54.

DelGaudio, Sybil (1997), 'If truth be told, can 'toons tell it? Documentary and animation', *Film History*, 9: 2, pp. 189–99.

Deriabin, Aleksander (2001), 'Vertov i Animatsiia: Roman, kotorogo ne bylo', in *Kinovedcheskie zapiski*, 52, pp. 132–44.

Doane, Mary Ann (2009), 'The voice in the cinema: the articulation of body and space', in Leo Braudy and Marshall Cohen (eds), *Film Theory and Criticism*, Oxford: Oxford University Press, pp. 318–30.

The Einstein Theory of Relativity, film, directed by Dave Fleischer. USA: Out of the Inkwell Films, 1923.

Fleischer, Richard (2005), *Out of the Inkwell: Max Fleischer and the Animation Revolution*, Lexington: University Press of Kentucky.

Gaycken, Oliver (2012), 'The cinema of the future: visions of the medium as modern educator, 1895–1910', in Devin Orgeron, Marsha Orgeron and Dan Streible (eds), *Learning with the Lights Off: Educational Film in the United States*, New York: Oxford University Press, pp. 67–89.

chapter has touched upon the limitations of live-action cinema, but what about those of animation? *How we Breathe*, for example, demonstrates how a cell absorbs oxygen from the air by having the oxygen (represented by tiny white dots) move and cluster towards the cell. This animated drawing is labelled as a 'highly magnified view of cellular structure from the human body.' Here, as in most similar films from the silent period, the viewer is expected to freely accept this drawing as *the* view, that is, as a completely adequate substitute for what one would see under a microscope. Indeed, as Kirsten Ostherr (2012b: 356) has observed, early scientific shorts 'erase the distinctions between different types of footage, editing animated and direct photography sequences together without drawing attention to the referential shift'. The effectiveness of this film's educational strategy hinges on the audience's unconditional acceptance of a drawn approximation of a given phenomenon as a representation of the same order as a photograph of the same. Herein lies the fundamental intentional fallacy of animated scientific representation: the conscious and constant de-emphasis of the fact that the drawn image, for all its pedagogical advantages, cannot actually capture scientific phenomena, but only convey their essence. Even here, the Holy Grail of complete access to the known world remains within sight, but not within reach.

In that sense, the myth of the total representational freedom offered by animation in educational and instructional nonfiction films is just that – an ideal. Scientific animation can be as constrained as live-action filmmaking, albeit in distinct ways. For instance, the extreme simplification of the drawn image in instructional films is a double-edged sword; while it guarantees accessibility, it significantly undermines scientific credibility. It is precisely such constraints that contribute to the disconnect between representational claims and representational capabilities discussed above. My goal here has been to emphasise the inherent complexity of, and reveal the fascinating ifs and buts that accompany, any attempt to discuss animation's response to the epistemological and representational challenges posed by observable (and non-observable) phenomena. In revealing – or, sometimes, failing to reveal – the world in its visual intricacy, animation also necessarily exposes the elaborate, problematic and sometimes contradictory inner workings of its own signifying mechanisms.

Acknowledgement

The author would like to thank Charles Musser for his feedback on an early draft of this essay, which was originally written for his course Historical Methods of Film Study.

roundings and external stimuli. In an interview, Dr Alain Viel, who consulted on the scientific information included in the short, praises the ability of the film's animation team 'to transform all the structural information and the very detailed sequence of molecular events ... assembled in a storyboard into a visually pleasing work of art' (Marchant 2006). This dual emphasis on faithful scientific illustration and artistic mastery betrays a tendency to look at such films *as* films, and not simply as supplemental visual aids.

Showmanship is not the only characteristic of early nonfiction film animation that has endured to the present day. Despite the infinitely more sophisticated animation tools at its disposal, *The Inner Life of the Cell* also echoes silent instructional animation's preference for simplification, even at the expense of scientific accuracy. Lead animator John Liebler admits to prioritising visual clarity over absolute faithfulness:

> What we did in some cases ... was subtly change the way things work ... the reality is that all that stuff that's going on in each cell is so tightly packed together that if we were to put every detail into every shot, you wouldn't be able to see the forest for the trees or know what you were even looking at. (Marchant 2006)

As the fundamental pedagogical requirements (such as legibility) that early twentieth-century animation fulfilled remain the same today, contemporary computer-generated instructional shorts continue to respond to them in similar ways, preserving the legacy of clarity.

Finally, as Sylvie Bissonnette (2014: 144) has demonstrated in her study of animation in scalar travel documentaries, contemporary educational media continue to take advantage of the drawn image's capacity to 'provide viewers with a sense of scopic mastery over the invisible'. Today, as almost a century ago, 'films that explore the body's interior can turn the miniature into gigantic landscapes by magnifying cells and molecules up to the size of the screen' (ibid.: 144). What is more, like the other contemporary examples discussed above, such penetrative films offer animated models whose precision becomes secondary to the dual goal of clarity and entertainment (ibid.: 140).

Conclusion

In view of the enduring legacy of key approaches and functions of animation in silent instructional and educational films, it is worth briefly revisiting some of the claims animation made for itself during that period. This is done in order to tease out a more complete picture of the drawn image's place in the context of education and cinematic representation more broadly. This

The Enduring Legacy of Silent-Era Instructional Animation

The combination of pure entertainment and science seen in *The Eisenstein Theory of Relativity* has remained a leading model for educational programmes today. In fact, one may argue that spectacular educational television shows such as *Cosmos: A Spacetime Odyssey* (Brannon Braga, Bill Pope and Ann Druyan, 2014), a successor of the popular, Carl Sagan-presented 1980 series *Cosmos: A Personal Voyage*, are direct descendants of the Fleischers' early efforts to popularise issues in physics and astronomy. As suggested by its title, which evokes science fiction more than actual science, the most recent *Cosmos* (like its predecessor) mixes in a considerable dose of theatricality, narrative whimsy and awe-inspiring visual display with hard scientific fact, glamorising science in order to make it more palatable through entertainment. Crucially, the show owes much of this to its mesmerising computer-generated visual effects, which not only allow the audience to peek into deep space and sub-molecular worlds, but also create purely entertainment-oriented displays and spaces. These include the sleek digital interior of the 'The Ship of the Imagination' (whose name itself is an example of a Fleischerian artistic flourish), a science fiction-inspired pilot's cabin of sorts that allows the show's host, astrophysicist Neil deGrasse Tyson, to 'travel' through space and time, taking viewers along for the ride. deGrasse Tyson is the voice (and face) of scientific authority missing from early nonfiction cinema. His narration, along with his status as a celebrity scientist, adds gravitas and legitimacy to the information delivered. At the same time, however, his role in the programme recalls the performative aspects of early animation. Like American cartoonist and animator Winsor McCay, who impressed early cinema audiences in *Gertie the Dinosaur* (1914) by imbuing the eponymous animated prehistoric beast with personality (Crafton 1993: 112–16), deGrasse Tyson adds anima to science. His performative approach to scientific delivery in *Cosmos* speaks to the enduring legacy of the figure of the expert who can convincingly traverse the divide between scientific authority and skilful showmanship. Like his silent-era predecessors, deGrasse Tyson does not simply communicate knowledge; he performs it and engages with it, framing science within a narrative of fascination, discovery, and adventure.

Cosmos: A Spacetime Odyssey is produced for television and, as such, needs to offer entertainment value in order to continue attracting viewers. Still, the idea that educational works should hold aesthetic appeal has taken root beyond this particular medium. Take, for instance, studio XVIVO's *The Inner Life of the Cell* (2006), a visually elaborate, beautifully rendered, eight-minute digitally animated instructional short produced for Harvard students of biology and meant to illustrate how white blood cells respond to their sur-

The following incident illustrates the creative treatment of scientific fact in such early educational films. Max Fleischer, who produced his brother's film *The Einstein Theory of Relativity*, worked closely on it with Garrett P. Serviss, then a popular science writer for the *New York American*. The two men got into an argument over Fleischer's decision to include the intertitle 'When you see the stars twinkle'. Serviss was outraged because, as he pointed out, 'the stars do not "twinkle"; it is merely an illusion'. In his defence, Fleischer offered the following argument: 'Poets make pictures. They paint with words, but give you a mental picture nevertheless, and since the world has poets and people like poetry, in my opinion, it is correct to say that "the stars twinkle"' (Cabarga 1976: 13). For Fleischer, 'correct' does not mean 'scientifically correct'. In fact, whether or not the stars actually do twinkle is irrelevant, since the image holds the expressive power that the filmmaker (significantly, described here as a 'poet') is striving to achieve. In a film produced by a poet, scientific accuracy becomes secondary to art.

Perhaps more than most of its contemporaries, *The Einstein Theory of Relativity* vividly demonstrates that science can and does function as an attraction on screen. The film features sensationalist rhetoric in its intertitles. The latter offer the following unverifiable anecdotal titbit to court interest: '[Einstein] makes the astounding assertion that "Space is bent"! [*sic*] This is an idea which Einstein said only twelve men in the world could understand.' This statement is at once an exaggeration, a sales pitch and an implied challenge. Explaining this complicated concept is set up as a thrilling achievement. Will this film prove Einstein himself wrong? This is bona fide scientific suspense. Additionally, the film announces that 'the miracles of yesterday are the commonplaces of today', but its rhetorical treatment of technological inventions actually does present these as miracles instead of demystifying them. The plane is likened to a 'magic carpet'; the X-ray is described as 'eyes that pierce solids'; the telegraph is compared to 'listening in on a thousand-mile whisper'. Thus, scientific discovery is coded as a spectacle, an on-screen curiosity worthy of a Méliès trick film. In fact, the sequence which shows 'our pilot' being launched into space by a cannon evokes *A Trip to the Moon* (1902) with its theatrical, non-realistic depiction of a space mission. The entire section dedicated to the illustration of planetary movement simultaneously draws on and fuels people's fascination with space as the mysterious final frontier full of secrets and untold wonders, inserting fiction next to science and emphasising the occasionally blurry epistemological border between the two concepts. At the film's end, science is abandoned altogether, as the viewer is left with the uncertain, yet undeniably romantic promise of time travel ('a man is shot from Earth to overtake the speeding years').

in colour. In the beginning of the sequence, a drawn circle shown against a black background appears white. Gradually, a horizontal animated wipe from left to right changes the background to white, causing the circle to look grey. While the transition could have been instantaneous, the wipe is more persuasive in demystifying the effect because it allows the audience to see the circle change before their eyes. Here, the duration of animated movement becomes a key pedagogical tool.

Finally, another significant aspect of movement that these films take advantage of is its spectacular quality. The pedagogical significance of movement's ability to attract and focus viewer attention was noted by contemporary directors. In 1927, J. A. Norling (1927: 601) wrote that 'the use of animation makes prosaic charts, maps, and graphs into living pictures, increasing their interest value a hundred fold'. The idea that movement adds *anima,* or soul, to instructional material is also evoked in Ivanov-Vano's memoir. Ivanov-Vano cites the work of puppet master Vladislav Starevich – particularly his attention to movement and detail and his ability to infuse imagery with a soul – as the inspiration behind his own approach to scientific animation in *The Mechanics of the Brain* (Ivanov-Vano 1989: 25).

TWINKLING STARS: THE ROOTS OF EDUTAINMENT

The concept of edutainment, as discussed by A. Bowdoin Van Riper (2011: 2), refers to films 'designed to educate as well as entertain: to actively convey factual information about the real world, while using it as a backdrop for comedy or drama, that, in turn, [leaven] the educational elements of the production'. While, as Van Riper notes, this term was first popularised by the Disney studio in the late 1940s in relation to their own corpus of nonfiction films, the edutainment phenomenon's roots can be traced back to the silent era. Early cinematic educators appreciated the importance of making scientific presentation appealing to viewers and exhibitors alike. In the twentieth century's early decades, popular science was still treated as something of a curiosity, making the boundaries between documentary and entertainment even more fluid than they are today. After John Randolph Bray formed the Bray Pictures Corporation in 1919, he announced that his company had developed 'a means of presenting *spectacular effects in popular science*' (emphasis mine) (Crafton 1993: 160). As this rhetoric suggests, despite the genre's overall propensity for straightforward, clear instruction, some educational and instructional shorts succumbed to a lingering air of showmanship, allowing for the occasional directorial gesture of artistic flourish.

illustration, they also add a key additional component to this type of diagram-based instruction: movement. Early cinema often engages animation's ability to elucidate non-recordable processes through the addition of movement to drawings and diagrams. Much of the animation in these scenes is very basic, in keeping with the general spirit of simplicity. For instance, simple animation is often used effectively to illustrate flow in these films – be it the flow of an electrical current, blood or any other substance – by means of moving lines, arrows or dots. It is precisely the genuine motion, so conspicuously missing from print illustration, which helps convey a sense of the dynamism and duration of any process instead of simply offering a snapshot series of the latter's separate stages frozen in time. The viewer does not have to imagine motion anymore – they can simply observe it.

For instance, in *How we Breathe*, the reduction of oxygen quantity in blood travelling back to the heart is visualised by gradually thinning white stripes (Figure 2.2). The drawing's design is basic and straightforward; what is aimed at here is not so much representational scientific accuracy, but rather the accessible presentation of a known fact. By manipulating the white stripes' movement and size (their colour undoubtedly chosen for its immediate legibility, as it stands out against the background), the film offers a visual shorthand for its main idea, using animation to successfully capture the smooth, gradual nature of the illustrated process.

In some cases, movement is tasked with more complex expository goals. In *The Einstein Theory of Relativity*, animation is used to illustrate relativism

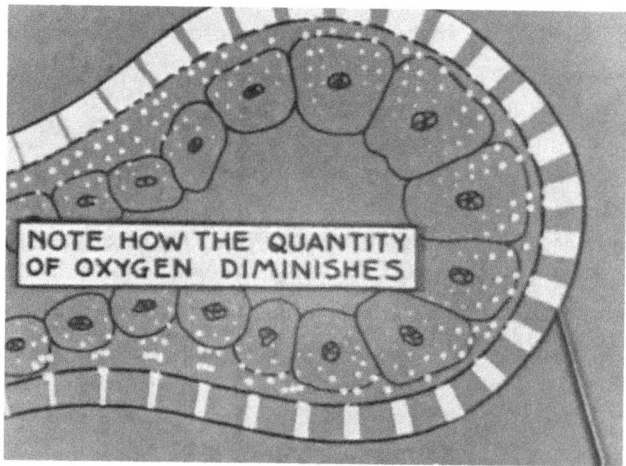

Figure 2.2 Minimalist representation of diminishing oxygen quantity as moving white stripes ensures clarity in *How we Breathe* (1920) (Source: YouTube, Jeff Quitney channel, <https://www.youtube.com/watch?v=pnaiUDsSCY8>)

point, which the use of conventional photographic images does not allow as easily' (Reichert 2009: 292).

Take, for instance, the way in which the Bray Studios' educational film *How we Breathe* illustrates the fact that the heart pumps oxygen to the body's cells. The viewer is presented with a schematic outline of a heart and an anatomically simplified rendition of an aorta against an empty white background. Two simple oval shapes at the aorta's far end are clearly labelled 'cells'. Simultaneously enlarged for visibility and reduced to only two in number in order to convey the idea with minimal visual clutter and complexity, these cells exemplify the ways in which the drawn image plays with parameters such as relative size and detail in order to achieve optimal clarity. Here, anatomical authenticity (in terms of shape, detail, visibility to the naked eye, relative placement inside the body, and so on) is sacrificed in favour of legibility and easy comprehension. In films like these, oversimplification, while not scientifically precise, nevertheless makes for effective, easily memorable illustrations, thanks to its purposeful minimalism.

Overall, animation's expository function in educational films calls for a specific drawing style characterised by schematic, understated and straightforward imagery. While one might expect explanatory drawings to tend towards photorealism, images in these films are predominantly iconic. This enables them to function as visual shorthand, evoking the necessary concept, and also makes them more readily accessible and recognisable. These drawings often have thick, clearly defined outlines and predominantly solid colouring. There are no extraneous details or embellishments; in the visual language of animation, instructional films favour telegraphic delivery. Basic geometric shapes are often used, as for example in *The Einstein Theory of Relativity*, which features a sequence depicting planets as simple white circles. There is no room for individuality: artists' personal style is suppressed in favour of bland, pragmatic illustration. Visual appeal and artistic flourish become secondary to clarity. Thus, this mode of expression marks a triumph of functionality over aesthetics; while commercial animation often hopes to inspire wonder, this type of imagery aspires to engender comprehension.

THE FLOW OF KNOWLEDGE: ADDING *ANIMA* TO SCIENTIFIC ILLUSTRATION

In addition to its minimalism and tendency towards simplification, another notable feature of silent-era instructional animation is its kinship with print media. Indeed, the majority of these films use visual tools that today remain staples of manual and textbook illustration, such as text boxes, labels and arrows. However, while instructional cartoons borrow the visual language of

Down with Detail: Achieving Clarity through Visual Simplification

While animation is often called upon to go beyond visible surfaces in this type of filmmaking, it is another of the advantages that it offers – namely, the opportunity to simplify representation and eliminate visual clutter – that proved central to the visual strategies of silent instructional films. Scott Curtis (2004: 220) has argued that legibility is a key concern shared by the respective disciplines of medicine and film studies, as the need to create an image that contains the most relevant details and is easily accessible to an audience is imperative to both. The importance of legibility to scientific visualisation in silent cinema cannot be overstated; in the absence of sound, questions of comprehension and accessibility become even more central, as the image itself now exclusively carries the burden of emphasising and highlighting essential points through a combination of graphics and text. In the 1920s, observers on both sides of the Atlantic praised animation for being particularly well-suited to achieving a level of clarity conducive to the successful transmission of specialised information to laypersons. Sukharebsky argued that animated imagery further enhanced the 'visibility' (*naglyadnost*) specific to cinema; Tyagai suggested that educational cartoons could offer a more easily comprehensible and readily accessible alternative to foreign-language technical literature, thanks to their emphasis on the visual over the verbal (Mihailova and MacKay 2014: 154). In the United States, J. A. Norling and J. F. Leventhal (1926: 61) described animation as 'probably the most valuable of any form of motion pictures' in the educational field, thanks to its ability to capture and amplify the intricacies of different processes.

But what is it that makes animation so suitable for explanatory discourse? A closer look at silent educational and scientific films reveals several ways in which the drawn image facilitates comprehension. Compared to live-action footage, which captures objects placed in front of the lens as they are (that is, in their entirety), animated drawings provide the opportunity to selectively simplify the image by eliminating any distracting or irrelevant background elements and emphasising details essential for the explanation of a given phenomenon. Even in the case of rotoscoping, the animator can choose to leave out or exaggerate certain aspects of the physical referent more freely than a live-action director. This flexibility and ease of visual manipulation facilitates drawn imagery's explanatory power by focusing audience attention on essential points. In other words, the increased degree of control over representation that animators enjoy translates into a pedagogical advantage, since 'in educational films in particular, a thought can be brought to an exact audience a glimpse into the scientist's method. Similarly to its American counterparts, this movie uses live-action footage of a dog to set up the visual lesson; eventually, these shots are replaced with a stylised drawing which visually resembles an X-ray image. The dog is outlined in black silhouette and the audience is shown a drawing (in sharply contrasting white) of the brain areas responsible for vision and movement (labelled and marked by animated arrows). A thick line drawn from the brain to the paw represents the connection between stimulus and the resulting action. Later, animation reveals how the brain's centres, if stimulated simultaneously, send a signal and make the paw move. While this account of Pavlovian conditioning is rather crude and excessively simplified, it is nevertheless valuable as an example of animation's use in early nonfiction. Here, animation makes highly abstract scientific concepts comprehensible and introduces mass audiences to contemporary cutting-edge research in an accessible manner.

This is not to say that animation's penetrative gaze in early nonfiction filmmaking is directed exclusively towards the body's interior. In Bray Pictures' *The Story of Coal* (1920), animation digs beneath Earth's core in order to reveal – through a series of schematic, labelled drawings – the process behind coal's formation. Nor were interiors – be they corporeal or geological – the only frontier inaccessible to silent-era live-action cinema but open to animation. With the drawn image's help, educational films of the period also bring viewers closer to outer space. *The Einstein Theory of Relativity* (1923) depicts imagery that would remain inaccessible to a camera for several more decades, such as Earth's appearance from the viewpoint of a person in space. The film provides basic illustrations of astronomical concepts that cannot be recorded, such as the movement of planets in their orbits. In an era when space exploration still belonged to the realm of science fiction, a film like this enabled contemporary audiences to visualise – albeit in rudimentary and imprecise terms – a set of cosmological objects and phenomena that otherwise remained firmly out of reach and, crucially, to engage with them in the context of learning.

Animation's penetrative gaze does not simply reveal other worlds, however; it also brings to light crucial questions about the boundaries of cinematic representation by highlighting the fundamental limitations of live-action footage as an instructional tool. In other words, by circumventing the camera's failure to capture certain phenomena and objects due to a variety of factors (such as miniature size and excessive distance and speed) these films also implicitly foreground that failure. To quote Sybil DelGaudio (1997: 194), '"documenting the undocumentable" becomes both a practical and a philosophical concern, directly challenging myths, not only about the "knowability" of the world, but also about cinema's capacity to represent it'.

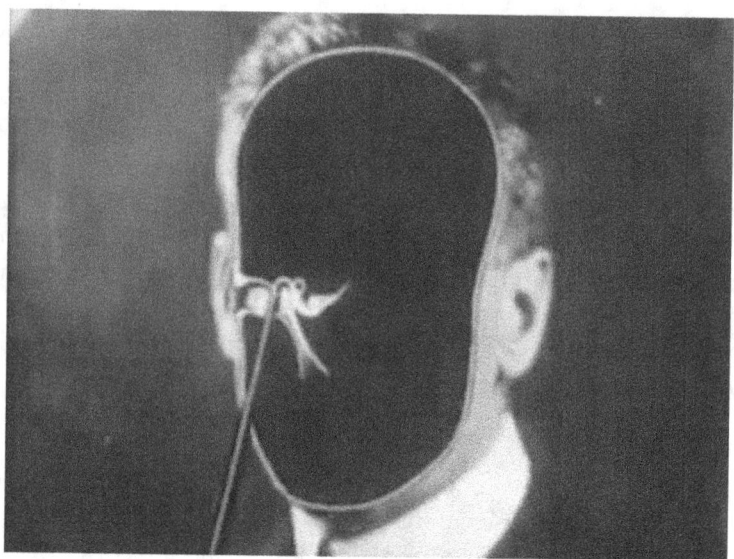

Figure 2.1 Animation's penetrative gaze in *Communication: A Film Lesson in 'General Science'* (1927) (Source: YouTube, 'Public Domain Movie serials, Film serials and Chapter plays' channel, <https://archive.org/details/Communic1927>)

for the image of the inner parts of the man's auditory system, this particular scene's focus. This representation's pedagogical advantage is at least twofold. Firstly, it allows the audience's gaze to reach beyond the visible part of the ear and explore its otherwise inaccessible innards (it is not without reason that John Halas and Joy Batchelor (1949: 10) describe this mode of expression as 'penetrative'). It also obscures all irrelevant visual data in order to avoid clutter and focus attention on the ear's structure. Furthermore, this shot serves as an orienting setup for the next drawing, which offers a 'zoomed-in' (that is, enlarged) detailed diagram of the same cross-section of the ear's insides first shown. In that sense, while animation does not actually enable the viewer to *see* inside the ear, it does offer a stylised and simplified approximation instead. By doing so, animation removes the aura of mystery from the body's insides and achieves a stark clinical sterility in its minimalistic representation that was inaccessible to live-action cinema of the time.

Animation's penetrative gaze is not only useful in illustrating internal structures; it was also often employed in order to elucidate the working mechanism behind invisible processes taking place inside the body. For instance, Soviet director Vsevolod Pudovkin's *The Mechanics of the Brain* (1926)[3] – a self-described 'popular science picture in six parts' that deals with the subject of Russian physiologist Ivan Pavlov's famous conditioning experiments – takes advantage of the drawn image in order to offer the from beyond the frame. This is similar to the self-figuration identified by Donald Crafton (1993: 134) in early fictional animation: while no human hand or figure enters the frame, the presence of an authority figure is implied. As Paul Wells (1997: 41) has observed, this 'deployment of an "expert"' is now a well-established convention of instructional films, within which it is 'either played out in voiceover or through a particular character'.

Visualising the Invisible: Animation's Penetrative Gaze

Despite this quasi-spectral presence of the voice of knowledge, it is the drawn image that serves as the crux of silent educational and instructional films' pedagogical approach. These films employ animation in a variety of ways, such as illustrating scientific processes, providing a closer look at the human body, and clarifying the structure, properties and functions of contemporary technological inventions. However, regardless of the specific context, animation's main function in early nonfiction cinema is to compensate for and go beyond the representational limitations of photographic media, by depicting what is challenging (or, in most cases, impossible) for film to record. This phenomenon has been most thoroughly examined in the context of medical films, as this type of instructional productions readily highlights both the necessity to depict actions and objects that are challenging to capture on camera and the means by which animation helps address this issue.

As Miriam Posner (2011:100) has noted, getting a shot of the human body's insides was not strictly impossible in the 1920s. But in practice, it proved extremely challenging due to bulky and unsophisticated shooting equipment. Moreover, the results often remained unsatisfactory due to technical problems such as lack of clarity and definition, minimal legibility and visual clutter. Furthermore, Kirsten Ostherr (2012b: 370) argues that, in physicians' circles, photography was not sought after for its authenticity, but rather, was 'implicitly faulted for simultaneously showing too much detail to be pedagogically useful and too little detail to transcend the limits of the bodily surfaces that the surgeon was expected to see through'. For these reasons, silent-era instructional medical films, such as those produced by the late-1920s collaboration between the American College of Surgeons (ACS) and Eastman Kodak, relied on animated imagery in order to peek inside the human body (ibid.: 356).

General interest science shorts dealing with similar subjects also relied on animation for similar purposes. Take, for example, a representative sequence from *Communication: A Film Lesson in 'General Science'* (1927). First, the viewer is shown a close-up photograph of a man's face. In the next shot, a drawing providing an inside view of the head is overlaid on top of the man's face (Figure 2.1). The drawing depicts the head as an empty black space, save kinetic properties to ensure comprehension and legibility. For this reason, they provide productive case studies for analysing the ways in which moving drawings, diagrams and dissections enhance, influence and fit within educational discourse. Thus, this essay also aims to keep the silent nature of these films in focus, moving beyond an understanding of the absence of sound as simply an early technological stage in the history of cinema as it offers a discussion of silent instructional cartoons' long-lasting impact over the relationship between animation and nonfiction.

I do not mean to suggest that the type of filmmaking at this chapter's heart completely rejects the spoken word or precludes its use in cinematically enhanced instruction. While educational shorts such as Dave Fleischer's *The Einstein Theory of Relativity* (1923) were screened theatrically to general acclaim, others, like *The Story of Coal* (Unknown, 1920), subtitled 'Studies in Chemistry', were more overtly oriented towards a school context (Fleischer 2005: 34). If shown in a classroom setting, the latter type of silent educational film did in fact benefit from a teacher's supplemental instruction. Still, and perhaps surprisingly, a close reading of several examples suggests that the circumstances of delivery did not ultimately produce great variation in these films' approach to animation as an educational medium. Despite the difference in exhibition contexts, silent instructional films share a stable common set of characteristics and functions. As the following discussion shows, they are designed to be fully legible without the help of the spoken word, so that verbal explanation becomes an additional tool, not a necessity.

There are several ways in which these films rely on the drawn image in order to offer alternatives to verbal instructions. Text boxes containing clarifying notes or labels are often included next to images, providing an additional semiotic layer to the illustration and functioning as a silent-era substitute for voiceover. *Communication: A Film Lesson in 'General Science'* (Unknown, 1927), part of the *School Films* series produced by the Herman DeVry company (one of the earliest companies to produce educational films), incorporates written notes that would have been delivered by an instructor, such as 'the arrows indicate an electric current' (Saettler 1990: 99). Similarly, in the Bray Studios educational film *How we Breathe* (1920), the role of commentator is often taken over by a label; in a sequence dedicated to the heart, the label invites the viewer to 'note how the quantity of oxygen diminishes' within blood on its way back to the heart. Unlike fiction films of the period, wherein verbal information is delivered almost exclusively in intertitles, such examples blur the silent-era boundary between the purely textual frame and the drawn one.

Finally, the pointer stick that appears in many of these films, while seemingly disembodied, nevertheless functions as a widely recognisable stand-in for an invisible instructor, clarifying concepts and guiding viewer attention saw the production of a number of pioneering educational shorts that took advantage of the representational possibilities offered by the drawn image (DelGaudio 1997).[2]

In Russia, for example, the beginnings of animation are tied to nonfiction filmmaking. Soviet film writer Lazar Sukharebsky devoted a section of his book on educational cinema to praising the advantages of animation as an illustrative medium, especially in the context of teaching children (Mihailova and MacKay 2014: 154). Elsewhere, Dziga Vertov in 1918 included an animated map in the twentieth *Kino-Nedelya*, and later used animated maps in other films (Deriabin 2001: 132). In his memoirs, animation director Ivan Ivanov-Vano recalls that, in the 1920s, the first films produced at the animation department at the Mezhrabpom-Rus' studio (the first formal animation department in Russia) were instructional ones meant to provide clear and simple accounts of important industrial and agrarian processes (Ivanov-Vano 1989: 23). Lev Kuleshov also experimented with animation in his nonfiction films, such as *Forty Hearts* (*Sorok Serdets*, 1930), which featured drawn segments created under Ivanov-Vana's supervision and argued in favour of electrification of the Soviet countryside via what David Bordwell (2008) has described as 'faux-naïve animation'.

VOICELESS INSTRUCTION, OR THE IMPORTANCE OF BEING SILENT

While most of these nonfiction films have been discussed in scholarly literature, they have rarely been examined specifically in light of their lack of sound. In contrast, much has been written about the importance of sound – and the voice-over in particular – in more recent documentary filmmaking. Paul Ward (2005: 98) suggests that 'there is "realism" or indexicality to the sound that does not reside in the image'. Similarly, Mary Ann Doane (2009: 324) calls the voice a 'guarantee of knowledge', arguing that its 'irreducibility to the spatiotemporal limitations of the body [makes it] capable of interpreting the image, producing its truth'. While this emphasis on the persuasive power of speech is the norm today, Michael Renov (2004: 97) has observed that, during the 1920s, artists relied most heavily on the power of the visual to convey their meaning, since by then, 'the codes of visual expression had become exquisitely refined [ensuring that] even abstract notions [could be made] concretely visible in the image'. It was only with the arrival of sound that emphasis in nonfiction filmmaking shifted to the realm of the verbal.

With that in mind, this chapter focuses exclusively on silent films because they necessarily favour vision over all other senses, according a privileged position to the moving drawn image as an educational tool. In the absence of voiceover narration, these movies rely on early animation's aesthetic and

CHAPTER 2

Before Sound, there was Soul: The Role of Animation in Silent Nonfiction Cinema
Mihaela Mihailova

INTRODUCTION

In today's world, animated imagery is constantly used to convey information in a variety of contexts, from weather reports to flight training simulators and classroom biology videos. As Annabelle Honess Roe (2011: 220) has observed, animation's elucidatory role has been so widely embraced that it is now largely taken for granted. Indeed, the pervasiveness of the drawn image in contemporary nonfictional contexts and academic programmes has caused viewers – and many scholars – to become desensitised to this particular function of animation. As a result, many fascinating questions about the relationship between cinema and teaching and the limits and challenges of visual representation of scientific phenomena remain insufficiently explored. Following excellent recent efforts (Orgeron et al. 2012; Ostherr 2013), this chapter aims to defamiliarise the role and functions of the drawn image in scientific and educational media by going back to the silent period and studying a selection of educational shorts in order to identify and examine the roots of certain foundational trends, methods and approaches that have shaped contemporary nonfiction animation.[1]

Oliver Gaycken (2012) notes that, at the dawn of cinema, before its status as entertainment had been solidified, filmmakers, businessmen and the press thought of it as an educational medium. In the early 1910s, Thomas Edison was occasionally known to proclaim that films would soon replace textbooks (ibid.: 68). At the turn of the teens, American reformers 'envisioned the cinema as a place where the medium's "impressionable" audiences – usually understood as children, immigrants, and women – could learn about useful things like science, history, and civics'(ibid.: 83). By the 1920s, animation in particular was already accepted as the 'default medium for communicating with the "average person"', according to contemporary pedagogical theories (Ostherr 2012a: 126). This was by no means a strictly American phenomenon: on both sides of the Atlantic, the silent period

NFB (n.d.), '*Walking*', *nfb.ca*, <http://www.nfb.ca/film/walking/> (last accessed 24 October 2016).
Nichols, Bill (1991), *Representing Reality: Issues and Concepts in Documentary*, Bloomington: Indiana University Press.
Nichols, Bill (1994), *Blurred Boundaries: Questions of Meaning in Contemporary Culture*, Bloomington: Indiana University Press.
Nichols, Bill (2001), *Introduction to Documentary*, Bloomington: Indiana University Press.
The Order Electrus, film, directed by Floris Kaayk. Netherlands: Microbia Productions, 2005.
Our Friend the Atom, film, directed by Hamilton Luske. USA, Walt Disney Productions, 1957.
Paget, Derek (1998), *No Other Way to Tell It: Dramadoc/Docudrama on Television*, Manchester: Manchester University Press.
Pinzon, Monica (2009), *Beyond Human and Science Documentaries: Molotov Alva and Waltz with Bashir as New Study Cases in the Representation of Reality*, unpublished Master's thesis, Montana State University.
Plantinga, Carl (2005), 'What a documentary is, after all', *Journal of Aesthetics and Art Criticism*, 63: 2, pp. 105–17.
Pouliot, Louise and Paul S. Cowen, (2007), 'Does perceived realism really matter in media effects?', *Media Psychology*, 9: 2, pp. 241–59.
Rawson, Philippe (1987), *Drawing*, Philadelphia: University of Pennsylvania Press.
Renov, Michael (ed.) (1993), *Theorizing Documentary*, New York: Routledge.
Rhodes, Gary D. and John Parris Springer (eds) (2005), *Docufictions: Essays on the Intersection of Documentary and Fictional Filmmaking*, Jefferson, NC: McFarland.
Roscoe, Jane and Craig Hight (2001), *Faking it: Mock-documentary and the Subversion of Factuality*, Manchester: Manchester University Press.
Ryan, film, directed by Chris Landreth. Canada: Copperheart Entertainment and National Film Board of Canada, 2004.
Ryan, Marie-Laure (2006), *Avatars of Story*, Minneapolis: University of Minnesota Press.
The Sinking of the Lusitania, film, directed by Winsor McCay. USA: Universal Film Manufacturing Company, 1918.
The Trouble with Love and Sex, film, directed by Zac Beattie and Jonathan Hodgson. UK: Sherbet and BBC, 2011.
Tsuruya, Mayu (2006), *Sensô Sakusen Kirokuga (War Campaign Documentary Painting): Japan's National Imagery of the 'Holy War', 1937–1945*, unpublished PhD dissertation, University of Pittsburgh.
Verschaffel, Tom (1987), *Beeld en geschiedenis, Het Belgische en Vlaamse verleden in de romantische boekillustraties*, Turnhout: Brepols.
Walking, film, directed by Ryan Larkin. Canada: Columbia Pictures Corporation and National Film Board of Canada, 1968.
Waltz with Bashir, film, directed by Ari Folman. Israel/France/Germany/USA/Finland/Switzerland/Belgium/Australia: Bridgit Folman Film Gang, Les Films d'Ici and Razor Film Produktion GmbH, 2008.
Wind, Edgar (1938), 'The revolution of history painting', *Journal of the Warburg Institute*, 2: 2, pp. 116–27.
Wolfe, Tom (1973), *The New Journalism*, New York: Harper and Row.

Cheng, Benjamin Ka Lung and Wai Han Lo (2012), 'Can news be imaginative? An experiment testing the perceived credibility of melodramatic animated news, news organizations, media use, and media dependency', *Electronic News*, 6: 3, pp. 131–50.

Chiu, Vivian (2014), 'Media researchers say animated news reports are detrimental to youngsters', *South China Morning Post*, 6 January, <http://www.scmp.com/lifestyle/family-education/article/1396777/media-researchers-say-animated-news-reports-are> (last accessed 24 October 2016).

Coleman, A. D. (1991), 'Joan Fontcuberta' (interview)', *Journal of Contemporary Art*, 4: 1, <http://www.jca-online.com/fontcuberta.html> (last accessed 24 October 2016).

Decker, Christoph (1994), 'Grenzgebiete filmischer Referentialität. Zur Konzeption des Dokumentarfilms bei Bill Nichols', *Montage/AV*, 3: 1, pp. 61–82.

Do-it-yourself, film, directed by Eric Ledune. Belgium, 2007.

Eason, David L. (1982), 'New Journalism, metaphor and culture', *Journal of Popular Culture*, 15: 4, pp. 142–9.

Hall, Alice (2003), 'Reading realism: audiences' evaluations of the reality of media texts', *Journal of Communication*, 53: 4, pp. 624–41.

Honess Roe, Annabelle (2013), *Animated Documentary*, Basingstoke: Palgrave Macmillan.

Horwatt, Elijah (2008), 'New media resistance: Machinima and the avant-garde', *CineAction*, 73/4, Summer, pp. 8–14.

Keeble, Richard and Sharon Wheeler (2007), *The Journalistic Imagination: Literary Journalists from Defoe to Capote and Carter*, London: Routledge.

King, David (1997), *The Commissar Vanishes: The Falsification of Art and Photographs in Stalin's Russia*, New York: Metropolitan Books.

L'image manquante/The Missing Picture, film, directed by Rithy Panh. Cambodia/ France: Catherine Dussart Productions, Arte France, Bophana Production, 2013.

LaMarre, Heather L. and Kristen D. Landreville (2009), 'When is fiction as good as fact? Comparing the influence of documentary and historical reenactment films on engagement, affect, issue interest, and learning', *Mass Communication and Society*, 12: 4, pp. 537–55.

Landesman, Ohad (2013), *Reality Bytes: Reclaiming the Real in Digital Documentary*, unpubished PhD dissertation, New York University.

Lefèvre, Pascal (2013), 'The modes of documentary comics', in Dietrich Grünewald (ed.), *Der dokumentarische Comic – Reportage und Biographie*, Berlin: Ch. A. Bachmann Verlag, pp. 50–60.

Lefèvre, Pascal (2016), 'No content without form: graphic style as the primary entrance to a story', in Neil Cohn (ed.), *The Visual Narrative Reader*, London: Bloomsbury Academic, pp. 67–88.

Lo, Wai Han and Benjamin Ka Lung Cheng (2013), 'Fuelling the debate: predictive relationships among personality characteristics, motives and effects of melodramatic animated news viewing', *Journal of Applied Journalism and Media Studies*, 2: 1, pp. 135–60.

Massironi, Manfredo (2002), *The Psychology of Graphic Images: Seeing, Drawing, Communicating*, Mahwah, NJ: Lawrence Erlbaum Associates.

Meakins, Felicity (1998), 'Err, new boundaries for fiction?! *ER*'s 'live' episode', *M/C: A Journal of Media and Culture*, 1: 1, <http://journal.media-culture.org.au/9807/er.php> (last accessed 24 October 2016).

Mendick, Robert and Edward Malnick (2011), 'BBC accused of routine 'fakery' in wildlife documentaries', *The Telegraph*, 18 December, <http://www.telegraph.co.uk/culture/tvandradio/bbc/8963053/BBC-accused-of-routine-fakery-in-wildlife-documentaries.html> (last accessed 24 October 2016).

My Trip to Liberty City, film, directed by Jim Munroe. Canada, 2003.

that those creators and their creations construct for the viewing audience. Especially in the case of hybrid film forms such as animated documentary, this interplay is both complex and diverse.

NOTE

1. Another important consideration to stress is that a particular film need not belong entirely to one of Nichols's modes but can instead include elements of several. As a general rule, however, Nichols (2001: 100) argues that 'the characteristics of a given mode function as a dominant in a given film: they give structure to the overall film, but they do not dictate or determine every aspect of its organisation'. That said, other scholars, such as Matthew Bernstein, argue that some combinations of Nichols's modes are logically incompatible on epistemological grounds: 'A documentary cannot be said to present a consistently logical argument if it employs practices that embody both scepticism (as in the reflexive mode) and confidence (expository or observational mode) about its capacity to understand and represent the "real world". Alternately, the same textual features, such as interviews, can have different valences in different films' (Bernstein 1994: 5).

BIBLIOGRAPHY

A is for Autism, film, directed by Tim Webb. UK: Fine Take Productions and Channel 4, 1992.
Abeel, Erica (2008), 'On the verge between reality, fantasy and dreams: "Waltz With Bashir" director Ari Folman', *IndieWire*, 18 December, <http://www.indiewire.com/article/on_the_verge_between_reality_fantasy_and_dreams_waltz_with_bashir_director_> (last accessed 24 October 2016).
Au, Wagner James (2008), 'Making "Molotov": how the man behind the HBO/Cinemax special created his avatar-based documentary, and why', *New World Notes*, 15 May, <http://nwn.blogs.com/nwn/2008/05/making-molotov.html> (last accessed 24 October 2016).
Augustin, M. Dorothee, Birgit Defranceschi, Helene K. Fuchs and Florian Hutzler (2011), 'The neural time course of art perception: an ERP study on the processing of style versus content in art', *Neuropsychologia*, 49: 7, pp. 2071–81.
Aumont, Jacques (1990), *L'image*, Paris: Nathan.
Barnouw, Erik (1993), *Documentary: A History of Non-fiction Film*, New York: Oxford University Press.
Bernstein, Matthew (1994), '*Roger and Me*: Documentaphobia and mixed modes', *Journal of Film and Video*, 46: 1, Spring, pp. 3–20.
Brown, Matthew Cullerne (1998), *Socialist Realist Painting*, New Haven, CT: Yale University Press.
Burton, John W. and Caitlin W. Thompson (2002), 'Nanook and the Kirwinians: deception, authenticity, and the birth of modern ethnographic representation', *Film History*, 14: 1, pp. 74–86.
Busselle, Rick and Helena Bilandzic (2008), 'Fictionality and perceived realism in experiencing stories: a model of narrative comprehension and engagement', *Communication Theory*, 18: 2, pp. 255–80.

not abandoned. For instance, while the tanks and the uniforms of the soldiers in *Waltz with Bashir* may look quite realistic, not all of the interviewee voices viewers hear are the original ones of Folman's interviewees. Moreover, while the film locates these interview dialogues within a range of seemingly documentary settings (a moving car, a house, a bar, and so on) all these conversations were in reality taped in a sound studio. According to Folman (Abeel 2008), previous experiences with animated documentaries showed that many spectators were not tolerant of location sound in animation. Moreover, two out of his nine main interview voices were performed by actors, because some interviewees got cold feet, preferring not to have the sound of their own voices discussing their war experiences present within the finished film. While *Waltz with Bashir*'s script was written on the basis of more than 100 testimonials, the completed work claims to represent only the personal memories of Folman and a small group of his friends. Thus, though the film's central themes incorporate and support a degree of reflexivity, the latter does not necessarily extend to Folman's filmmaking practices and many of the key creative and/or logistical choices that he made within these.

Conclusion

As this brief illustrative discussion of Nichols's documentary categories and modes has shown, it is important to look at how documentary forms are used in relation to filmmakers' particular documentary strategies. It is evident, for example, that Nichols's expository mode has a different effect in an animated documentary work like *Do-it-yourself*, compared to a very different expository animated documentary such as *Our Friend the Atom*. There are also animated documentaries that mix several of Nichols's documentary modes. A famous example of this is Chris Landreth's *Ryan*, a work that that employs characteristics of at least three of Nichols's modes: expository, participatory and performative. Landreth's documentary short about another animator (Ryan Larkin) is not presented as some kind of objective biography. Instead, it explicitly shows the human interaction between both animators, within which aspects of Landreth's personal history (his mother was an alcoholic) pushes him to question aspects (including alcohol use) of Larkin's. Ultimately, we can conclude that four out of Nichols's six documentary modes offer useful critical tools to further analyse, discuss and typify the field of animated documentary. More generally, it remains essential, as Roscoe and Hight (2001) argue, to always analyse the dynamic interplay between the animated documentary filmmaker's intentions, the resultant formal aspects of the animated documentaries those figures make, and the specific terms of the role general processes at work in society'. Performative documentaries' subjective accounts of reality primarily address the viewer in emotional and expressive terms. Tim Webb's *A is for Autism* (1992), wherein autistic people tell their own story in drawings, music and testimonials, can be considered as an animated documentary example of the performative mode. Every visual design in the film originated from a drawing made by one of the autistic participants; their oral testimonials enable them to recount their thoughts and feelings. Moreover, the soundtrack's piano and flute music was recorded and part-composed by two autistic performers.

Another animated documentary example of the performative mode is the 2008 theatrical feature *Waltz with Bashir*. Director Ari Folman explained in interview (Abeel 2008) why he chose animation for his account of the early-1980s Lebanon War:

> I had the basic idea for the film for several years, but I was not happy to do it in real-life video. How would that have looked like? A middle-aged man being interviewed about events that happened 25 years ago – and without any archival footage? SO BORING! But if it could be done in animation with fantastic drawings, it would capture the surreal aspect of war. If you look at all the elements in the film – memory, lost memory, dreams, the subconscious, hallucinations, drugs, youth, lost youth – the only way to combine all those things in one storyline was drawings and animation. You know, the question most frequently asked since Cannes is 'why animation?' And it's a question that's absurd to me. I mean, how else could it have been done?

A crucial theme of *Waltz with Bashir* involves the subjective aspect present within human accounts of the reality of war. The viewer is at first invited to experience what it is to be a battlefront soldier, but towards the film's end the focus shifts to the experience of refugees held in camps. The film's dominant presentation of the Lebanon War constructs the conflict as something quite surreal: only at the work's end is live-action archive material included. An interesting example of the film's deliberate changes of perspective (subjective to objective, or vice versa) is found in its Beirut airport scene. Initially, everything appears normal (planes ready to take off), but this situation turns out to have been the subjective, distorted view of the film's main character (the young Folman himself). From the moment he realises what is really going on, *Waltz with Bashir*'s visuals suddenly also show the wholesale destruction in and around the airport.

As Nichols (2001) explains, performative documentaries embody a paradox: they stress their own tone and expressive qualities, while also retaining a referential claim to depict the historical real. In the performative mode, the documentary image's indexical bond is subordinated, but which the filmmaker themselves can participate. A *pseudo*-participatory mode is, however, conceivable in animated contexts, such as the virtual worlds of games. The Machinima technique, for example, uses real-time 3D graphics engines to create film works. Pinzon (2009: 15) compares Machinima with documentary filming in our reality: '[Machinima makers] are still aiming their cameras at worlds that already exist and to some extent function independently of the filmmaking process. Unlike traditional animation, more exists outside the frame than what the audience sees.' Through use of avatars, a documentary maker can explore a game's imaginary world through discourses appropriated from the participatory documentary (Horwatt 2008). An example of this is *Molotov Alva and his Search for the Creator* (Douglas Gayeton, 2007), a film which tells the story of a man's passage from his 'real' analogue life in California into a new digital existence inside Linden Lab's virtual world *Second Life*. The film pretends to be a video diary kept in the online world, but in fact, viewers do not know to what extent the virtual encounters the film depicts are spontaneous or scripted and thus set in stone (Au 2008).

Another example of the pseudo-participatory mode is Jim Munroe's *My Trip to Liberty City* (2003), where an avatar from the well-known game *Grand Theft Auto 3* is used to explore the fictional world of Liberty City. Contrary to the avatar's expected criminal role, the film's player chooses that his avatar does not take a car and thus participate in a criminal mission. Instead, the avatar explores Liberty City on foot: an unusual activity within the scripted goals of *Grand Theft Auto*. In interview, Munroe explained his unusual choices in this regard:

> I never feel like getting into a car is the best way to see a city. The best way is to walk around and get to know it. For instance here I found this little nook in an alley and sure enough there's a stairwell there that leads up to this beautiful rooftop; something I never would have found in a car . . . This film does not use the lingua franca of gamer-made machinima films, nor does it have the insider humour of shows like *Red Vs Blue*. Instead, *My Trip to Liberty City* has some elements in common with the work of video artist Mike Hoolboom, who refers to his work in the 1990s as 'documentaries of the imaginary'. (Horwatt 2008: 13)

By exploring this virtual space by means of his touristic avatar, Munroe uses *Grand Theft Auto* in a way not explicitly intended by the game's designers. We could categorise Munroe's film as a pseudo-participatory mode because he participates in a programmed universe, not the real analogue world.

For Nichols (2001: 130–1), the performative mode of documentary raises questions about what knowledge is and 'sets out to demonstrate how embodied knowledge provides entry into an understanding of the more typically works to maintain the continuity of the dominant spoken argument or perspective. In contrast to Nichols, however, it might be preferable to speak of the '*linguistic* argument', because in silent-era documentaries no spoken word could be heard (except if someone was performing in the film theatre). Early cinema audiences could, however, read text contained within intertitles.

The expository mode stresses the impression of objectivity and well-supported argument; it facilitates generalisations and large-scale argumentation with regard to a particular expository film's documentary subject matter. Animated material may be part of the varied supporting sources (for example, interviews, still images, archive footage) that are assembled to support the central argument and persuade the audience of that particular point of view. Animation is most often used when it proves impossible for a camera to register certain aspect(s) of a documentary subject. For instance, animations can show the inner structure of an atom, as in *The Einstein Theory of Relativity* (Dave Fleischer, 1923), or show what supposedly took place during an event at which cameras were not present, as McCay's *The Sinking of the* Lusitania. Another reason to use animation within the expository mode is to guarantee some privacy for interviewees testifying about intimate topics: as, for example, in *Aldrig som första gången!*, or *The Trouble with Love and Sex*. Viewers who posted a comment for the director after seeing *The Trouble with Love and Sex* seemed to accept this drawn animated documentary not only as plausible, typical and/or factual but also as emotionally moving. From reception research, it is known that viewers do not always need a visually realistic image in order to ascribe realism to a particular documentary film or film scene (Hall 2003; Pouliot and Cowen 2007; Busselle and Bilandzic 2008; LaMarre and Landreville 2009). A satirical use of the expository mode is found in Eric Ledune's *Do-it-yourself*, where the voiceover light-heartedly presents, in the style of a pedagogical training video, quotes from an old CIA torture manual. A visual motif of fish helps place the cruel documentary subject matter in a totally different context: it becomes clear that the film's real aim is not the initially ostensible pedagogical one, but rather, a sardonic critique of torture. The expository mode can take many different shapes and tones and aim at a very broad range of goals, including the ironic use of documentary words, images and sounds.

Turning to Nichols's participatory mode, it is one in which the documentary maker (and film crew) interact openly with a given film's subject. The participatory mode, Nichols (2001: 115) argues, shows viewers how a filmmaker reacts when placed in a given documentary situation and also how that situation alters as a result. On one hand, the participatory mode tends towards impossibility in documentary animation, because in the latter typically foregrounds a fabricated, fictive diegetic world, not the real world within pattern and set of conventions of its own. Furthermore, Nichols does not always clearly define his categories (he tends to focus on the analysis of concrete illustrative examples instead) and they have also evolved over time. In the early 1990s, for example, it seems that Nichols saw only four documentary categories, or was using a different terminology to that employed within his later work (for a period, he used to speak of an 'interactive' documentary mode) (see Nichols 1991, 1994).[1] I will now consider to what extent Nichols's remaining four categories are applicable to animated documentaries, incorporating brief analysis of an illustrative example for each.

For Nichols (2001: 103), 'poetic' documentaries 'draw on the historical world for their raw material but transform this material in distinctive ways'. The poetic mode sacrifices the conventions of continuity editing and the sense of a very specific location in time and place to the overriding goal of exploring associative and pattern-based forms of meaning-making, as in the early twentieth-century city symphony subgenre of documentary film). Illustrative examples of the city symphony model in animation form might include *Brussel Winter* (Jonas Wellens, 2009) and *Passer Passer* (Louis Morton, 2013). Another film that could be categorised as 'poetic' animated documentary is Ryan Larkin's *Walking*, which tries to catch and reproduce the motion of people perambulating. As the National Film Board of Canada (NFB, n.d.) describes the film: 'The springing gait of youth, the mincing step of the high-heeled female, the doddering amble of the elderly – all are registered with humour and individuality, to the accompaniment of special sound.' Of course, it remains difficult for the viewer to know the extent to which each of Larkin's animated walking figures refers to a real person's activity, or if they instead originate primarily from his imagination as a filmmaker. Viewers *can* evaluate, however, the extent to which an animated way of walking seems plausible and/or realistic. *Walking* explores associations and patterns that involve temporal rhythms and spatial juxtapositions. By its formal characteristics, *Walking* stresses mood, tone and affect much more than displays of formalised knowledge or rhetorical acts of persuasion.

The second of Nichols's remaining documentary categories is the expository mode, arguably the most dominant mode in documentary history, 'assembl[ing]' as it does 'fragments of the historical world into a more rhetorical or argumentative frame than an aesthetic or poetic one' (Nichols 2001: 105). Expository films adopt either a voice of God (the speaker is heard but never seen) or a voice of authority commentary (the speaker, usually an expert in a relevant field, is both heard and also seen, as, for example, with the German scientist Heinz Haber in Disney's *Our Friend the Atom*). The expository mode relies heavily on an informing logic predominantly carried by the spoken word with visual imagery playing a supporting role. Editing style different documentary goals: 'to record/reveal/preserve', 'to persuade/promote', 'to analyse/interrogate' and 'to express'. Due to constraints of space, I discuss in detail here only one such attempt at overarching categorisation of the documentary field: that developed by Bill Nichols (2001). Nichols identifies six subgenres or 'modes' of documentary film and video representation: 'the poetic', 'the expository', 'the observational', 'the participatory', 'the reflexive', and 'the performative'. In what follows, I assess the extent to which these categories can usefully apply within discussion of animated documentaries.

Two of Nichols's categories pose a problem from outset. These are the observational and the reflexive modes. Nichols defines (2001: 109) the former as a documentary approach that simply observes what happens in front of the camera without overt authorial intervention. Think, for example, of live-action documentary movements such as direct cinema or *cinema-vérité*. In a narrow sense, this observational mode is, *ipso facto*, impossible in the field of animation: the latter always implies some sort of visible intervention on the filmmaker's part. Nichols's other problematic category in relation to animated documentary is his reflexive mode, within which, he argues (ibid.: 125), 'The processes of negotiation between filmmaker and viewer become the locus of attention'. Through emphasis on film's expressive nature and the use of anti-realist cinematic techniques, the reflexive mode asks the viewer to attain a heightened form of spectatorial consciousness, seeing a given documentary for what it is: a construct or representation. Jonas Odell's animated documentary *Aldrig som första gången!/Never like the First Time!* (2006), where each central interviewee's testimonial is depicted in a specific visual style tailored to that testimonial's tone, is a good example of the reflexive mode in action. Indeed, one could simply argue that the reflexive mode is integral to almost *all* animated documentary, since animation's inherent stylisation entails that the viewer of any given animated documentary is most likely aware of the work's fabricated nature from the very start.

In fact, empirical research (Cheng and Lo 2012; Lo and Cheng 2013) suggests that some viewers of contemporary animated news seem quite unaware of that material's potentially reflexive qualities, especially with photorealistic uses (including lens blur) of CGI. One such researcher explains: 'We're worried that animation news may affect . . . youngsters' judgment of reality. Those who lack independent, analytical thinking are easily influenced' (Chiu 2014). Nevertheless, it does not seem useful to treat Nichols's reflexive mode as a separate category in the animated documentary field. Christoph Decker (1994: 79) similarly questions whether the reflexive mode can be treated as an independent entity, because it concerns all other documentary modes and functions as a textual strategy, rather than constituting a distinctive formal

Bond, 2012]) or for viral online distribution (for example, *The Bold and the Beautiful in 6 Minutes* [The Beautiful Lab, 2010]) have comparatively short running times: something like a maximum of sixteen minutes, and frequently well under. A handful of other works, especially those produced for television broadcast (*The Trouble with Love and Sex* [Zac Beattie and Jonathan Hodgson, 2011]), run for anything up to one hour. Only a few examples, such as *Persepolis* (Vincent Paronnaud and Marjane Satrapi, 2007), *Waltz with Bashir* and *L'image manquante*, are feature-length films gaining theatrical distribution.

- *Various presentation formats (single screen versus multiple screens)*: while animated documentaries are usually produced and consumed as one-screen products at film festivals, on television or on the internet, some works produced for gallery or site-specific exhibition instead use multiple screens or projections (Rose Bond's *Illumination #1*, for instance, made use of the windows of the historic Portland Seamen's Bethel Building when exhibited there).
- *Varying degrees of interactivity*: animated documentary films' relationship with their viewer can range from no interactivity (as in much mainstream cinema), through pre-scripted, partial interactivity (as in games with a designated objective and play mechanics or rules), to more extensive, participant-controlled interactivity (as in multi-user virtual worlds such as *Second Life*).

The animated documentary is, therefore, an enormously diverse field with blurred and mutable boundaries. It may thus prove difficult to move with full confidence significantly far beyond this essay's brief introductory catch-all definition: animation production techniques used in combination with some prototypical codes, conventions and claims associated with live-action documentary. Instead of trying to formulate a working definition that is exhaustive and all-encompassing, therefore, it is arguably more productive to instead attempt to establish the most prominent formal categories or modes of animated documentary.

POSSIBLE CATEGORISATION OF ANIMATED DOCUMENTARIES

In pursuing that aim further, it is worth noting that several eminent documentary scholars have proposed some kind of overarching category model for documentary film more generally. Erik Barnouw (1993) presents vaguely descriptive categories such as 'Prophet', 'Explorer', 'Reporter' and 'Painter'. Carl Plantinga (2005) distinguishes between three forms of documentary voices ('formal', 'open' and 'poetic'). Michael Renov (1993) proposes four

or have combined heterogeneous styles within a single work (as in Ryan Larkin's *Walking* [1968]).
- *Combinations of different types of source material*: many films are partly animated but also include other types of images, such as archive material (as in the final sequence of *Waltz with Bashir* [Ari Folman, 2008]), specially shot live-action footage (as in *Our Friend the Atom* [Hamilton Luske, 1957]), or a wider combination of various image types (as in *Couleur de Peau: Miel* [Jung Henin and Laurent Boileau, 2011]).
- *Various tonalities*: some animated documentaries (such as *L'image manquante*) deploy an explicitly serious-minded tone; others (such as *Do-it-yourself* [Eric Ledune, 2007]) are ironic or bluntly satiric; some are self-reflexive in gesturing toward their artificial materiality (as in the work of William Kentridge), while others are not.
- *Diverse truth claims*: some animated documentaries fake their diegetic 'reality' for humorous purposes, even to the extent of becoming mockumentaries (as in *The Order Electrus*). Other films are non-committal regarding the extent of their historical truth value (as in *The Man with the Beautiful Eyes* [Jonathan Hodgson, 2000)]. Most animated documentaries, however, explicitly claim some form of documentary veracity. *L'image manquante*, for instance, states that it wants to show, through hand-carved wooden figures in dioramas, the 'missing picture' of the Khmer Rouge's cruel dictatorship in Cambodia. Sometimes, the viewer can check a given animated documentary's claims to veracity to a certain degree, but often, the viewer can only rely on the film's truth claims themselves. That said, many animated documentaries may still find it harder to advance truth claims (and have these accepted), compared to live-action counterparts. That this state of affairs is an evolving one can be gauged from the fact that, in recent years, animated sequences have become increasingly used in journalistic contexts: the Hong Kong and Taiwan-based production company Next Media Animation specialises in that field.
- *Varied degrees and quantities of fictional elements combined with factual counterparts*: many animated documentaries combine a rather traditional documentary soundtrack (for example, a testimonial or interview by a real person about events they have experienced) with animated imagery. Others (for example, *Chainsaw* [Dennis Tupicoff, 1998]) use a fictional storyline to link to factual material.
- *Absence versus presence of the artist*: the animated filmmaker can try to hide their presence within the work (as in *Walking with Dinosaurs*), or to make it manifestly clear (for instance, in *Ryan* [Chris Landreth, 2004]).
- *Different durations*: the majority of animated documentaries, being either works designed as art installations (for example, *Illumination #1* [Rose

child during the Holocaust: subjective human experience is presented as an integral part of the 'objective' historical past.

To an arguably greater extent than classical live-action documentary filming conventions, more obviously artificial animation techniques do more than just illustrate a given documentary narrative – they also deliver some form of comment or perspective on it. Of course, a live-action documentary can (and often, does) make formal choices (such as framing) that work towards the same effect. However, the photographic quality and look of live-action documentary scenes almost always seem more naturalistic to viewers than fabricated, animated equivalents created by means of any number of visibly constructed production techniques. Such handmade animated visuals have by necessity a dual nature – both an attempted analogue for documentary phenomena and a creatively expressive remediation of the same (see, for example, Rawson 1987; Aumont 1990; Massironi 2002; Augustin et al. 2011; Lefèvre 2016). Moreover, this dual nature is of relevance for the creator's perspective and also that of the viewer. The creator of an animated documentary does not simply re-present in visual terms: they also interpret, implying a visual ontology at the animated documentary's heart (Rawson 1987: 19). In turn, and through that creative interpretation, the viewer perceives the terms and content of a particular documentary moment and space. The viewer simultaneously recognises an analogous representation of some documentary phenomena while also experiencing a particular emotional, aesthetic and/or corporeal sensation that is related to the animated representation's specific formal properties. For this reason, perception in an animated documentary context (not to mention many other visual art ones) arguably differs in essence from natural perception (Augustin et al. 2011). What is certainly needed, however, is more reception studies in order to better understand and explain the effects of animated documentary images on their viewers.

Persisting with the attempt to establish some defining parameters for the animated documentary mode, we might note that particular animated documentary works often encompass a diverse range of different forms and strategies. A provisional taxonomy of the latter might run something as follows:

- *Diverse techniques for creating the animated visuals*: from elementary sketches (*Six Weeks in June* [Stuart Hilton, 1996]), to clay figures (*War Story* [Peter Lord, 1989]), carved wooden figures (*L'image manquante* [Rithy Panh, 2013]), rotoscoping (*His Mother's Voice* [Dennis Tupicoff, 2008]), or pixelation and full CGI (*Walking with Dinosaurs* [Tim Haines and Jasper James, 1999]).
- *Unity of style versus a mixture of heterogeneous styles*: animated documentaries have used one consistent visual style throughout (*Walking with Dinosaurs*)

foundations and instead deliberately attempt to hoax viewers, as in the case of *The Blair Witch Project* (Daniel Myrick and Eduardo Sánchez, 1999). Elsewhere, *Ambush*, an episode of the long-running television series *ER* (1994–9), was broadcast live as if it were a form of reality TV, whereas in fact the programme consisted of pre-scripted scenes played by professional actors (Meakins 1998).

Journalistic or documentary comics represent another type of hybrid documentary (Lefèvre 2013). Graphic sequences have long been used to present nonfictional events, from the eleventh-century Bayeux Tapestry to *The Fifty-Three Stations of the Tōkaidō* (1833–4), the woodcut-print document of Utagawa Hiroshige's trip along the *Tōkaidō* road in Japan. Indeed, the late nineteenth century saw an explosion of graphic documentaries, both in illustrated journal and popular print form, and various forms of documentary comics, such as *Picture News* in the USA or *Les belles histoires de l'oncle Paul* in Belgium, were created throughout the twentieth century, before the recent documentary comics revival associated with figures such as Joe Sacco, Marjane Satrapi and Guy Delisle. In other words, the animated documentary, as a form of hybrid creative documentary practice, can be situated within a much broader historical and multimedia context or set of contexts than simply those immediately associated with moving image history and culture.

Trying to Grasp the Core of the Animated Documentary

While animated documentary film has blossomed in the last thirty years, this kind of animation has in fact been practised since the earliest days of cinema (Honess Roe 2013: 5–13). Winsor McCay's *The Sinking of the* Lusitania (1918), a twelve-minute live action/animation hybrid about the sinking of the *Lusitania* by a German submarine in 1915, presents itself as 'a historical record of the crime that shocked Humanity', forgetting to mention that the ship was carrying armaments for the British military. The film's real aim becomes clear at its end: its propagandistic intertitles seek to provoke an emotional American audience response against a perceived German enemy. After McCay, a diverse range of later films have also combined animation production techniques with documentary conventions, codes, contents and truth claims. *Hadashi no Gen* (Mori Masaki, 1983), adapted from a manga series of the same title, depicts the bombing of Hiroshima. Though the film does not explicitly claim to be autobiographical, its narrative is partly based on (while also taking some dramatic licence with) the personal experiences of the source manga's creator, Keiji Nakazawa. In contrast, a short film like Sylvie Bringas and Orly Yadin's *Silence* (1998) includes the explicit claim at its outset that: 'This is my story. I was born in Germany'. The film then relates the real-life experiences (including acts of imagination) of a persecuted Jewish

Hondius's photograph *Bus* (2000), for instance, shows black people dozing in a bus: viewers may easily take it as a typical reportage snapshot. In fact, the camera angle Hondius shot from was only possible thanks to a highly elaborate *mise en scène*, which included sawing an actual bus into two halves: a seemingly 'documentary' scene was in fact completely artificially created. This recalls Flaherty's use of a halved igloo to film the Inuit in *Nanook of the North* (Burton and Thompson 2002: 79). Similarly, Joan Fontcuberta and Pere Formiguera's black-and-white photographs in their exhibition *Fauna Secreta* (1999) were presented as the long-lost archives of a fictive German zoologist, Dr Peter Ameisenhaufen: but the images are in fact faked ones of constructed animals. While the majority of visitors to *Fauna Secreta* understood it as a satire, some appeared to believe Fontcuberta and Formiguera's deliberate fiction (Coleman 1991). Indeed, many seemingly 'journalistic' photographs have been tampered with by their creators. In certain twentieth-century totalitarian regimes, for instance, official photos were often doctored: fallen-from-grace former comrades were removed from the scene as if they had never existed (King 1997). Today, altered photographs are circulating widely in news media because technologies such as Photoshop offer photographers an easy way to change the appearance of what was originally in front of their lens.

Turning to the written press, the 'New Journalism', 'true fiction' and 'faction' movements have all constituted attempts to introduce narrative and stylistic techniques typical of fiction (for example, predominance of scene description/evocation over narrative summary, extended realistic dialogues, description of everyday gestures, and variable focalisation) into journalistic reporting of real-world events (see Wolfe 1973; Eason 1982; Keeble and Wheeler 2007). Notable examples of such practices include Truman Capote's *In Cold Blood* (1966) and Tom Wolfe's *The Electric Kool-Aid Acid Test* (1968). Literary writers, Ryan (2006) explains, can blend real-life figures with a partly fictional story (for example, Sandra Gulland's *The Many Lives and Secret Sorrows of Josephine B.* [1995]), or can invent fictions on the basis of real-life photographs (W. G. Sebald's *Die Ausgewanderten* [1993], for instance), or construct a detailed biography of a completely fictional person (see Wolfgang Hildesheimer's *Marbot Eine Biographie* [1981]).

This last approach is also popular within the so-called mockumentary film movement (Roscoe and Hight 2001) or in docufictions (Rhodes and Springer 2005), that 'invite the viewer to welcome and embrace [the work's] aesthetic hybridity as a formal strategy meant not so much to dupe, mislead, or mock, but *to offer a different tactic that exists along a fact-fictional continuum*' (Landesman 2013). Woody Allen's *Zelig* (1983), for example, narrates the life of a human chameleon by cleverly integrating this fictional character in real newsreel footage. Sometimes, mockumentaries or docufictions do not foreground their fictional and of 'fiction' and 'fact', are neither easily nor consistently separable. Indeed, though documentary is still today widely associated with ideas of the factual and claims of truth, we might argue that no existing documentary film work provides an unmediated view of the world (Roscoe and Hight 2001: 8). However, as narratologist Marie-Laure Ryan (2006: 58) argues, highlighting and playing with the boundaries between fact and fiction can at least serve to heighten our awareness of what is still an epistemologically responsible distinction. This is certainly so in the case of animated documentaries, which in most cases represent 'factual' subject matter through the use of visibly artificial animation production techniques.

That said, it remains difficult to clearly trace the boundaries of the animated documentary as a category. This is because individual animated documentary films come in quite different shapes and forms, and they possess a complex range of differences and similarities regarding what they assume to be the respective roles of the film creator and the film viewer – not to mention what they assume the status of the depicted documentary images and events will be in the viewer's mind. This essay will, therefore, first of all situate the animated documentary within the broader context of hybrid creative practices that deliberately mix fact and fiction. It will then attempt to further delineate the fluid concept of animated documentary. Finally, it will propose several formal categories of animated documentary based on the well-known general modes of documentary cinema formulated by the documentary historian and theorist Bill Nichols (2001).

THE 'HYBRID DOCUMENTARY' CULTURE

Before focusing on animated documentary as a specific cinematic concept and form of practice, it is first important to sketch the larger artistic context of hybrid documentary approaches that combine formal and narrative strategies associated with the respective realms of both fiction and fact. Such approaches can be found in various creative traditions and media: painting, photography, journalism, literature, comics and, of course, live-action film and television. Illustrative examples of hybrid fact/fiction creative traditions in visual art include, for example, the Romantic School's so-called 'historical' paintings (Wind 1938; Verschaffel 1987), Japanese Second World War documentary painting (Tsuruya 2006) and Soviet socialist realism (Brown 1998). Each of these painting movements took liberties in representing historical reality according to their respective worldviews and propagandistic aims.

Even in the domain of photography, a visual medium widely associated with ideas of journalistic endeavour since the late nineteenth century, many artists have played with the boundaries between fact and fiction. Juul

CHAPTER 1

From Contextualisation to Categorisation of Animated Documentaries
Pascal Lefèvre

The field of animated documentary production and reception is difficult to delineate, because it is heterogeneous and fuzzy-edged. The typical example is defined as a combination of some kind of animation technique (drawing, puppet-based, CGI and so on) with some prototypical codes and conventions of the documentary (including the traditional claim of veracity). As Annabelle Honess Roe (2013: 1) puts it, animated documentary is thus often seen as something like the cinematic equivalent of an odd couple, 'a marriage of opposites, made complicated by different ways of seeing the world'. The use of traditional formal characteristics of documentary cinema, however, does not necessarily imply that a given film's proffered content is real. For instance, *The Order Electrus* (Floris Kaayk, 2005) may present many obvious features (such as a voice-over explaining animal behaviour) of a classical David Attenborough nature documentary, but the work's so-called 'filmed reality' is partly fabricated. While the locations are real, the film's insects are in fact animated objects made of parts used in the manufacture of electronic equipment. It is precisely the explicit insistence on documentary status (through photorealistic sequences and presentational mimicry of the classic television nature documentary) combined with a highly constructed 'reality' that makes *The Order Electrus* such a fascinating and humorous experience.

In fact, many *non*-animated documentaries are also to some degree fabricated as well. So-called television 'wildlife' documentaries, for example, typically imply that real animals have been filmed in their natural habitat, but in fact, nature scenes are sometimes set up in a studio in order to achieve better filming quality (Mendick and Malnick 2011). Turning to the origins of cinema documentary, in the pioneering *Nanook of the North* (1922) director Robert J. Flaherty staged various events because he did not want to present his Inuit human subjects as they were at the time of the filming, but rather as he reasoned they *might* have been in a previous era (Burton and Thompson 2002: 79). Surveying many other such cases, Derek Paget (1998: 107) concludes that very often in documentary history, ideas of theory and practice,

Part 1

Past and Present

Rachel and Pepper for their unstinting support during the time when *Drawn for Life* has been in preparation. Perhaps most of all, however, we both thank the book's other eleven authors. We are indebted to them for generously sharing their time, work and ideas in the construction of one building block in the emerging edifice that is the study of animated documentary. It is our sincere hope that the collective efforts embedded in this publication will provide information and insight sufficient to sustain increased interest in animated documentary as a rich past, present and future field of artistic creativity and communicative innovation and impact.

Bibliography

Buchan, Suzanne (ed.) (2006), *Animated 'Worlds'*, Eastleigh: John Libbey.
DelGaudio, Sybil (1997), 'If truth be told, can 'toons tell it? Documentary and animation', *Film History*, 9: 2, pp. 189–99.
Honess Roe, Annabelle (2013), *Animated Documentary*, Basingstoke: Palgrave Macmillan.
Skoller, Jeffrey (2011), 'Introduction to the Special Issue "Making it (un)real: contemporary theories and practices in documentary animation"', *animation: an interdisciplinary journal*, 6: 3, pp. 207–14.
Strøm, Gunnar (2003), 'The animated documentary', *Animation Journal*, 11, pp. 46–63.
Ward, Paul (2011), 'Animating with facts: the performative process of documentary animation', *animation: an interdisciplinary journal*, 6: 3, pp. 293–305.

Finally, Sheila Sofian reflects on her pioneering, decades-long creative exploration of the possibilities inherent within animated documentary aesthetics and production processes. One of the foremost and most prolific of all contemporary animated documentarians, Sofian revisits and reconsiders her groundbreaking *oeuvre* from *Mangia!* (1985) to *Truth Has Fallen* (2013). Recounting each of the animated documentaries she has created over a thirty-year period, Sofian self-evaluates her evolving creative process and priorities in ways that illuminate many of the varied practical, aesthetic and ethical choices and opportunities that any documentary filmmaker engaging with animation could or should seriously consider. In doing so, she brings *Drawn from Life* full circle, echoing and bookending Lefèvre's introductory demonstration of the need for a volume such as the present one.

By definition, any anthology publication is an attempt to exemplify the potential of collaboration: ideas and individuals meet and work together in ways that enable them to transcend the sum of their isolated parts. In that spirit, we also need to extend our sincere thanks and gratitude to a range of people and institutions that, while not contributing essays within the following pages, nonetheless played vital parts in making our book a possibility. We thank Edinburgh College of Art, the University of Edinburgh, the Society for Animation Studies, the John C. Hench Division of Animation and Digital Arts in the School of Cinematic Arts of the University of Southern California and the Scottish Documentary Institute. All these institutions' generous material and/or in-kind support made our 2011 *Animated Realities* conference a reality animated by the enthusiasm and expertise of that event's forty contributing speakers. We also thank those individuals, without whom the need for a book such as this one would never have been made so palpably apparent to us. We also thank the Edinburgh International Film Festival for their contribution to the *Animated Realities* event. EIFF helped us curate a public film screening programme of animated documentaries for the 2011 Festival; their input thus helped involve a wider public audience in our deliberation and celebration of animated documentary film. We also express our gratitude to the many individual Edinburgh College of Art and University of Edinburgh staff and students who were instrumental in helping to organise and deliver the *Animated Realities* conference. Subsequent to that event, we also owe much to the administrative and editorial team of Edinburgh University Press (and most especially to Richard Strachan) for their assistance with this book over an extended period of editorial work.

On a yet more personal note, Nea Ehrlich would like to thank Sebastian, Elana and Avishai who, as always, helped her with and through it all. Nea also thanks the Van Leer Institute, Jerusalem, without whom her continued work on this project would not have been possible. Jonathan Murray thanks human memories of trauma and the workings of human memory as an overarching emotional and psychological phenomenon. In addition, Murray considers *Waltz with Bashir*'s individual illustration of the frequently vexed status of debates around animation's putative status as a documentary tool. He does so through brief examination of the film's construction of a controversial geopolitical event, the 1982 Lebanon War, and Folman's individual experience of that conflict. Murray weaves an account of *Waltz with Bashir*'s critical reception to date into his discussion. He thus illustrates the growing multidisciplinary scope of contemporary academic interest in Folman's film specifically and the field of animated documentary more generally.

Drawn from Life's concluding section, Practice-based Perspectives, brings together the creative experiences and reflections of a trio of internationally recognised animated documentarians. Together, their contributions help the reader to better understand the distinctive creative characteristics, opportunities and challenges associated with animated documentary filmmaking as artists encounter, understand and negotiate such things within concrete acts of making. Jonathan Hodgson shares an account of the development and production of his landmark 2011 film *The Trouble with Love and Sex*, the first major long-form animated documentary commission in British television history. Hodgson provides a fascinating applied perspective on many debates and issues that regularly surface within critical discussion of animated documentary. These include the genre's capacity to deal with socially taboo orders of subject matter and the distinctive ethical considerations that creating within an animated documentary format imparts to the working relationship between a filmmaker and their human subjects.

Samantha Moore echoes and extends Hodgson's consideration of ethical concerns within animated documentary practice. Drawing on her personal experience of practice-led animated documentary research work, Moore explores ways in which the ethical aspect of animated documentary production represents a creative opportunity as well as a moral obligation. This is because ethical questions can, as Moore's career shows, prompt artists to develop innovative forms of collaborative production process within their practice. Moore makes animated documentaries not simply about, but also *with*, particular human communities. She discusses her films *An Eyeful of Sound* (2010) and *Out of Sight* (2015) in this regard. Moore shows how the experience of making animated documentaries about people living with synaesthesia (*An Eyeful of Sound*) and prosopagnosia or phantom limb syndrome (*Out of Sight*) led her to develop production processes defined by a distinctively comprehensive degree of co-creative collaboration between documentary filmmakers and the individuals whose stories and experiences artists bring to the screen.

drawing's capacities as an activity that is simultaneously conceptual, corporeal and creative.

Andrew Warstat makes a compelling case for viewing the work of American filmmaker Lewis Klahr as an example of animated documentary practice. Warstat focuses on Klahr's 1994 film *Altair*, a work made using archival images culled from six late-1940s issues of *Cosmopolitan* magazine. In this, the film is representative of Klahr's signature production methods (cut-and-paste, stop frame animation) and materials (discarded physical ephemera associated with mid-twentieth-century American mass visual culture). Warstat's critical approach recalls that of Kraaikamp in several regards. Focusing on one film by one artist, he uncovers many of the creative and conceptual possibilities inherent within that individual's preferred method of animating. In Klahr's case, Warstat uses the work of Adorno and other members of the Frankfurt School in order to argue that this filmmaker's animated method and aesthetic result in a 'shuddering' form of moving image. The latter, Warstat proposes, is capable of cultivating enhanced critical engagement and awareness within film artists and audiences alike.

Lawrence Thomas Martinelli explores a trilogy of early twenty-first century animated documentaries by Swedish filmmaker Jonas Odell. Through sequential analysis of those films, Martinelli identifies and assesses key characteristics in the working methods and thematic preoccupations of an internationally prominent contemporary animated documentarian. These include Odell's employment of extended audio interviews with his documentary subjects as a basis from which to animate their personal experiences, not to mention the wider socio-political issues and phenomena those experiences speak of. In addition, Martinelli's analysis considers animation's capacity to create especially comprehensive and compelling depictions of subjective experience and identity, compared to live-action documentary filmmaking practices. The concept of re-enactment (key also to Paul Ward's contribution to this volume) looms large in Martinelli's interpretative account of Odell's *oeuvre*. Finally, Martinelli also pays painstaking close attention to various formal elements, such as colour palette, graphic layout and visual texture, of the films he discusses. In this way, he usefully draws attention to the importance of design choices as central meaning-making tools within animated documentary more generally.

Jonathan Murray's essay discusses possibly the most widely seen and debated of all contemporary animated documentary films, Israeli director Ari Folman's feature-length *Waltz with Bashir* (2008). Murray assesses some of the key authorial motivations behind Folman's decision to pursue his documentary project in animated form. He also explores animation's capacity, within the film in question, to depict and deconstruct both individual spectacle is frequently deployed within documentary filmmaking in the interests of 'expertise'. In this sense, CG simulations function to persuade the audience of the time and effort put into making the documentary and therefore act as an index of a given moving image work's veracity.

Finally in this section, Paul Wells offers a critical-autobiographical account, augmented by a consistently surprising and thought-provoking range of cross-disciplinary case study examples, of his active and path-breaking engagement in animated documentary theory and production since the early 1990s. As part of that project, Wells acknowledges and engages with the developing critical literature surrounding the concept and practice of animated documentary. Ultimately, however, he focuses less on questions of overarching taxonomy and more on the multiple ways in which animation can and does act as an enabling conduit for a range of visual and/or narrative arts, offering a wide-ranging creative toolbox that supports practitioners engaged in documentary work across a range of disciplines. Wells advances three central insights: the increasingly multidisciplinary nature of contemporary visual, literary and popular cultures; the notable aesthetic and ideological potentialities possessed by polyvocal, multidisciplinary and multi-register creative practices and strategies; and animated documentary's privileged position at the forefront of present-day re-theorisations of a range of foundational documentary concepts, such as the repository, the record and the archive.

While *Drawn from Life*'s first two sections propose wide-ranging historical and conceptual accounts of animated documentary, the third section, Films and Filmmakers, applies such critical awareness and insight within more focused case study work. This section's first two contributions explore notable contemporary examples of crossovers between animated documentary and fine art practice. Nanette Kraaikamp analyses a single animated film by the South African artist William Kentridge, *Felix in Exile* (1994), one of the individual entries within Kentridge's celebrated *Drawings for Projection* series of stop motion animated films. Kraaikamp discusses Kentridge's use of animated documentary in order to address his native country's troubled past, specifically, the era of Apartheid. She illuminates the ways in which Kentridge's preferred production and aesthetic choices enable him to present viewers with expressive accounts both of Apartheid's public history and of more private, individual and subjective memories and experiences of the former. In particular, Kraaikamp considers how and why Kentridge's pronounced personal investment in practices of drawing and a range of particular drawing mechanisms enable him to create distinctive, formally and conceptually complex images that explore concepts and experiences of time, history and memory. In doing so, she augments critical appreciation of an important late twentieth-century artist and contributes to broader understanding of position within a range of present-day popular journalistic texts. These range from daily news broadcasts made by providers such as the Taiwanese broadcaster Next Media Animation through to investigative short films produced by the UK's *Guardian* newspaper. Ehrlich advances a case for understanding animated documentary's increasing contemporary usage and perceived credibility by exploring the wider context of animation's use within news media. She reflects upon different modes of representation that many deem 'more real' and believable as legitimate documentation than traditionally privileged photographic and journalistic tools and strategies.

The contributions presented within the book's second section, Defining Terms and Contexts, explore a range of theoretical and conceptual frameworks that consider how individual animated documentaries are actually experienced by their audiences, not to mention the ways in which (and why) that experience might prove distinct in character and effect from those associated with other animated or live-action filmmaking traditions. Paul Ward focuses particularly on the concept of re-enactment, arguing that it raises varied questions about the nature of performance, agency, point of view and temporality within animated documentary. Ward grounds his theoretical speculations and conceptual distinctions in close readings of two animated documentaries, *Andersartig* (2011) and *The Children of the Holocaust* (2014), both of which depict individual childhood memories of living in Nazi-era Germany. He concludes that works such as these encourage audiences and critics alike to understand and engage with animated documentary as a filmmaking mode able to engage with intangible, often non-indexical (and therefore un-photographable) documentary phenomena.

Leon Gurevitch takes up the historical persistence of discourses of spectacle and the spectacular throughout moving image history. He discusses one specific type of contemporary animation symptomatic of that overarching phenomenon: computer-generated documentary simulations that function both as attractions and visual signifiers of expertise and authority. Gurevitch explores the increasing prominence of such images within a variety of documentary contexts since the digital revolution that began during the 1990s. He underscores the extent to which CG-animated documentary spectacles are today routinely encountered within a range of fields, many not readily associated in the popular mind with animated aesthetics, production technologies or histories: automotive, aerospace, military, scientific, architectural, engineering and construction industries, for example. Perhaps most importantly, Gurevitch argues that a signature characteristic of much present-day digital animated documentary spectacle relates to the self-legitimating claims it routinely makes for its own veracity and reliability. He explains that in the absence of live footage (or even in support of it), animated and simulated

Pascal Lefèvre, for example, provides a wide-ranging account of animated documentary cinema's evolution, one which relates that ongoing history to analogous developments in related fields including live-action documentary, painting, photography and New Journalism. Making reference to no fewer than twenty-eight key animated documentary works spanning the period between 1918 and 2013, Lefèvre not only introduces this volume – he also demonstrates the need for its existence. This is so because Lefèvre illustrates the extent to which the history of animated documentary represents a substantive, variegated, but also comparatively under-examined story within moving image scholarship. His essay highlights many of the critical and conceptual questions which that partially obscured history raises, laying out ten distinct sets of logistical, aesthetic and ideological issues that repeatedly manifest themselves across the history of animated documentary filmmaking. In doing so, he sets the scene for many of *Drawn from Life*'s later, more specifically focused chapters. Drawing on the work of feted live-action documentary theorist and historian Bill Nichols, Lefèvre considers the extent to which established film studies conceptual and analytical paradigms do – or do not – offer pre-existing tools that contemporary scholars can readily transpose to the study of animated documentary.

Mihaela Mihailova's work amplifies one of Lefèvre's main points, namely, the fact that animated documentary has always constituted an important (if overlooked) constituent part of moving image history more generally. She does so by examining the role and functions of the drawn image within early twentieth-century scientific and educational media texts (in this case, a range of 1920s educational animated short films). As Mihailova points out, while the importance of audio material has frequently been asserted within contemporary animated documentary discourse, one particular fascination exerted by extant films from the pre-1927 period relates to the fact that they necessarily drew on other formal strategies in order to establish animation's capacities as a documentary medium. Casting a new light on the activities of certain seminal names from animation history, such as Bray Productions and the Fleischer brothers, Mihailova demonstrates the contemporary resonances and applications of these works. She proposes and examines a range of foundational trends, methods and approaches that subsequently went on to shape animated documentary during the nine decades since the advent of sound.

Nea Ehrlich proposes that the present-day fascination with animated documentary stems largely from animated non-fiction's challenging of traditionally perceived differences between animation and photography as seminal modern and postmodern visual media. Ehrlich eschews the focus of many of *Drawn from Life*'s other essays on fine art and auteurist animated works. Instead, she develops her ideas through discussion of animation's central

In significant part, those concerns can be traced back to much animation's obviously constructed, and thus intrinsically self-reflexive, visual aesthetics. By actively forgoing any attempt at a visually transparent treatment of their documentary subject matter, many animated documentary films also perform a discursive move, tending to (directly or indirectly) question the supposed directness and believability of any work of documentary representation. In addition, we might also note animation's extensive capacity to visualise multiple aspects of reality and/or lived human experience, phenomena that might otherwise prove logistically difficult or impossible to depict onscreen using other film production methods. In this regard, it is thus perhaps unsurprising that, as many of the following essays demonstrate, animated documentary practices are assuming increasing prominence (and sometimes even pre-eminence) within myriad fields of contemporary visual, popular and technological cultures. From scientific and data visualisations, journalism, media and gaming studies through to music videos and military training exercises, the contemporary rise of animated documentary both drives and reflects the changing twenty-first-century sociocultural role and status of animation more generally. The subject of animated documentary offers both a fascinating contemporary visual cultural case study in its own right *and* a suggestive gateway through which we can engage with much larger ontological and epistemological questions that define the present cultural moment. While animation studies has traditionally been seen as a sub-set of film studies, *Drawn from Life* instead suggests that animated documentary images, and the ideas we build about and in response to them, need to be situated within a much more expansive, multidisciplinary set of theoretical and visual cultural contexts. The latter include contemporary fine art practice, art history, anthropology, psychology, politics, digital culture, media studies and STS (science, technology and society) studies.

Although *Drawn from Life* does not intend to advance an exhaustive typology and corpus of animated documentary practice, its individual chapters do cover a wide range of case study examples taken from different time periods, production techniques or histories and cultural contexts. As editors, we have therefore found it useful to organise our work by subdividing the book's contents into a series of themed sections. Of course, many of the essays possess affinities and share interests with certain of their counterparts in other sections of the work and could therefore have been relocated accordingly. Nonetheless we hope that the categorising strategy and schema we found helpful will also assist the book's reader in engaging effectively and enjoyably with its contents. The first section of essays, titled Past and Present, sets the scene for subsequent contributions by presenting animated documentary as both a long-established and contemporarily relevant moving image tradition.

As Suzanne Buchan notes, 'the fine-arts base of pre-digital animation [is] as varied as fine art production itself: sculpture, painting, drawing, graphics, illustration, collage and many other artistic media flow into animation filmmaking' (2006: vii). Furthermore, animation in the digital era has witnessed a notably fertile and unpredictable convergence between individual artistic creativity and more structural processes of technological evolution. The latter phenomenon continues to transform moving image production, dissemination and reception in ways difficult either to foresee or comprehensively fathom within the contemporary moment of their emergence. Elsewhere, 'documentary' as both theoretical object and/or distinctive history of cinematic production offers up a no less complicated or contested conceptual and creative terrain. Paul Ward, for example, has argued that the marked recent expansion of animated documentary production (not to mention the public profile and reach of some of that work) reflects, on the part of artists and audiences alike, 'an attempt to map what happens when two (apparently) opposed 'registers' meet [...] Documentary is associated with truth, representations of the real; animation is associated with flights of fancy and the imagination: how can these two ever be reconciled?' (2011: 294).

At the point in time when Ward posed his query, published scholarship on the topic of animated documentary was often admirable but relatively minimal in terms of collective amount (see, for example, DelGaudio 1997; Strøm 2003). The very same year, however, saw some stirrings of change, including the above-mentioned *Animated Realities* conference and an animated documentary-themed special issue of *animation: an interdisciplinary journal* (Skoller 2011). Shortly after, Annabelle Honess Roe's monograph *Animated Documentary* (2013) became the first book-length academic study of the subject. In contradistinction to broad-brush dismissals of animated documentary as an oxymoron, the early twenty-first century has witnessed a growing collective appreciation of the fact that many films of this kind serve to highlight and explore a range of central questions (perhaps most importantly of all, concerning relations between antinomic aesthetics of and aspirations towards artifice and authenticity). The unstable relations between discourses of fact and fiction, as well as between any notion of a pre-existing reality and its subsequent representation within discourse, are not only signature concerns of much animated documentary work; they are also defining preoccupations of twenty-first-century visual culture and realms of non-fiction more generally. *Drawn from Life*'s essays thus provide not simply an overview of the eclectic sources that inform animated documentary cinema's varied investigations of and engagement with factual data, phenomena and concepts of reality. They also by extension consider the cultural and ideological power of the image as an informational tool and signifier (or otherwise) within the contemporary moment.

growth of animation studies. The book's essays present interdisciplinary investigations into the aesthetic, practical, ethical, epistemological, philosophical, technological and political issues associated with animated documentary cinema. These include: competing theorisations and deconstructions of 'the real'; similarly energetic debates surrounding the identity of animation as a historically and aesthetically distinctive tradition of moving image practice; and an assessment of the impact of such critical debates and creative practices on contemporary visual culture more generally. As such, the book hopes to act as a useful reference point for future research conducted into both animated documentary specifically and broader questions of documentary, authenticity and authority as the latter manifest themselves across a wide range of post-photographic cultural practices and genres.

Drawn from Life developed from *Animated Realities*, a June 2011 conference co-organised by the editors and held in collaboration with Edinburgh College of Art, the Edinburgh International Film Festival and the University of Edinburgh. That conference brought together over forty international speakers drawn from a diverse range of scholarly and artistic disciplines. Such diversity seemed appropriate in the context of an event held to discuss and examine the emergent field of animated documentary, a hybrid audiovisual landscape that is characterised by blurred boundaries and unexplored territories. In both original conference and subsequent book alike we have found it important to bring film practitioners and theorists together, in order to create as deep and wide an understanding of the diverse issues raised by the topic of animated documentary. For those interested, basic video documentation of the proceedings of *Animated Realities* can be freely accessed online (in thirteen separate parts) by visiting a dedicated YouTube channel: https://www.youtube.com/user/AnimatedRealities. *Drawn from Life* is, however, not a straightforward volume of conference proceedings. Rather, it attempts to develop some of the main areas of collective critical and creative concern that emerged during *Animated Realities*. Moreover, the international roster of artists and theorists whose work is presented in the following pages also reflect on how the field of animated documentary, whether in creative practice or scholarly research, has further developed in the years since the conference took place.

To us, a publication such as this one seemed a useful endeavour because even the most basic starting points within the field – such as any given filmmaker's or theorist's preferred working definitions of, and proposed relations between, the respective concepts of 'animation' and 'documentary' – necessarily involve negotiation of a wide range of complex and variegated aesthetic and philosophical ideas and interrelations. For example, despite all involving the painstaking creation of motion, the kinds of animation production techniques encountered within animated documentary filmmaking are immensely diverse.

Editors' Introduction
Nea Ehrlich and Jonathan Murray

A collection of essays such as this begs – and hopefully responds to – a surfeit of pressing critical and creative questions. Animated documentary's expansion over the last two decades or so has not necessarily been accompanied by a settled creative or critical consensus regarding what exactly constitutes an animated documentary film, not least because the term 'animated documentary' almost sounds oxymoronic. This volume therefore considers if the use of animation, a medium conventionally associated with fiction, the fantastic and children's entertainment, can constitute a creatively and ethically viable documentary aesthetic. In various ways, its essays explore how animated imagery, which often assumes obviously artificial, non-indexical visual forms, can be used to create and communicate the qualities of believability, authenticity and factuality commonly ascribed to and expected from documentary artefacts. The writers contributing to this book also consider the varied kinds of subject matter animation might effectively document, and the extent to which animated documentary reflects and influences contemporary understandings and experiences of 'reality' and 'the real'. Tracing the historical roots of animated documentary and where its future directions might lead, *Drawn from Life* identifies a range of theoretical and practice-led bases from which animated documentary cinema can be productively understood and reimagined. The book draws its case studies from a varied sweep of films, filmmakers, historical eras, non-fiction cultural contexts (such as journalism, science, the military and education, to name a few), and audiovisual forms and techniques. The cumulative result, we hope, is a theoretically suggestive and historically comprehensive account of animated documentary's early cinema origins through to its contemporary manifestations in diverse arenas such as live-action cinema, video, digital art, scientific research and educational practice.

But *Drawn from Life* makes no claim to be the last or definitive word on its chosen subject. Rather, it seeks to raise new questions and open up fresh lines of investigation in relation to animated documentary. It does so by drawing attention to (not least by drawing substantially on) the ongoing international

Mihaela Mihailova

Postdoctoral Fellow and Assistant Professor in Film, Television and Media at the University of Michigan. Recent publications include articles in *animation: an interdisciplinary journal, Studies in Russian and Soviet Cinema, Post Script: Essays in Film and the Humanities* and *Kino Kultura*.

Samantha Moore

Senior lecturer, University of Wolverhampton. Animation director.

Jonathan Murray

Senior Lecturer in Film and Visual Culture, Edinburgh College of Art, University of Edinburgh. Author, *Discomfort and Joy: the Cinema of Bill Forsyth* (2011) and *The New Scottish Cinema* (2015).

Sheila M. Sofian

Professor, John C. Hench Division of Animation and Digital Arts, School of Cinematic Arts, University of Southern California. Guggenheim Fellow. Media Arts Fellow, Rockefeller Foundation. Pew Fellow. Jacob K. Javits Fellow.

Paul Ward

Professor of Animation Studies, Faculty of Media and Performance, Arts University Bournemouth.

Andrew Warstat

Lecturer in Art History and Media Theory at Manchester School of Art (Manchester Metropolitan University). Recent publications include 'Speeding to the Doldrums: Stalled Futures and the Disappearance of Tomorrow in *The Dead Astronaut*', in *J. G. Ballard: Landscapes of Tomorrow* (2016).

Paul Wells

Director, Animation Academy, Loughborough University. Chair, Association of British Animation Collections. Outstanding Contribution to Animation Studies, Animafest, Zagreb.

The Contributors

Nea Ehrlich
Lecturer, Department of the Arts, Ben Gurion University of the Negev. Polonsky Postdoctoral Fellow, Van Leer Institute, Jerusalem.

Leon Gurevitch
Associate Professor, Faculty of Architecture and Design, University of Wellington.

Jonathan Hodgson
Associate Professor of Animation Practice. Programme Leader BA (Hons) Animation
School of Art and Design, Middlesex University. BAFTA for Best Short Animation.

Nanette Kraaikamp
Visual artist and curator. Artistic director at Drawing Centre Diepenheim.

Pascal Lefèvre
Special Guest Professor in the Arts, LUCA School of Arts, campus Sint-Lukas Brussels.

Lawrence Thomas Martinelli
Chair of English at Communication and Performing Arts, University of Pisa. Director of DOCartoon, international animated documentary film festival. Author, *Il Documentario Animato* (2012).

Figures

2.1	Animation's penetrative gaze in *Communication: A Film Lesson in 'General Science'*	35
2.2	Minimalist representation of diminishing oxygen quantity as moving white stripes ensures clarity in *How we Breathe*	39
4.1a–c	The 'fading' school photo from *Andersartig*	76
4.2a	*The Children of the Holocaust*	79
4.2b	*The Children of the Holocaust*	80
5.1a–f	Stills from *The Sinking of the* Lusitania	93
5.2a–f	Stills from *Titanic*'s computer simulation scene	95–6
5.3a–c	Stills from *Loose Change*'s simulation sequences	101
5.4a–f	Stills of the simulations from Chevron's *Human Energy* commercial	103
7.1	William Kentridge, drawing from *Felix in Exile*	131
7.2	William Kentridge, drawing from *Felix in Exile*	132
7.3	William Kentridge, sequence of drawings from *Felix in Exile*	132
12.1	Still from *doubled up*	207
12.2	The collaborative process of visualising Dave's enormous phantom foot	212
12.3	Still from *An Eyeful of Sound*	213
12.4	Still image from *Out of Sight*	216
13.1	Still from *Mangia!*	223
13.2	Still from *Faith & Patience*	224
13.3	Still from *Survivors*	226
13.4	Still from *A Conversation with Haris*	230
13.5	Still from *Truth Has Fallen*	233

Carmi Cna'an's vision of a naked giantess who plucks him from a commandeered boat ferrying Israeli troops to the Lebanese front line; Ronny Dayag's experience of night swimming for hours, having miraculously escaped death in an ambush by Palestinian snipers; and a second-hand account of a man's breakdown-inducing encounter with a multitude of dead or dying Arabian stallions in the bombed-out Beirut Hippodrome.

But the full affective power and complexity of Folman's decision to animate *Waltz with Bashir* lies not simply in the practical scope he thus creates to visualise the sights and memories that he and his interviewees describe. As noted above, the introductory positioning of Rein-Buskila's experience helps to underscore many of the film's preferred thematic priorities. Consequently, many critics understand *Waltz with Bashir*'s use of animation as a vehicle designed to facilitate a much broader exploration of the nature of human memory per se. The purported result is a film 'as much about memory itself as it is about the retrieval of specific [individual] memories' (Landesman and Bendor 2011: 355; see also Hetrick 2010: 79; Yosef 2010: 311; Corbett 2016: 56). On a closely related note, many also argue that Folman's work is notable due to the intensity and acuity with which it poses pressing questions about moving images' capacity to write or rewrite received historical narratives within documentary film contexts. Jeanne-Marie Viljoen (2013: 69), for example, lauds *Waltz with Bashir* for 'establish[ing] a striking tension between experience and memory, in which the relationship of both to reality becomes less significant than what part of the [past] event can be brought into the scope of present experience'. Vitally, for Viljoen and many others, Folman's use of animation for documentary ends is an enabling precondition for such achievements.

Supporting evidence for critical contentions such as these abound within *Waltz with Bashir*'s opening scene and many other parts of the film. The film's preferred animated aesthetic articulates, with an immediacy and intensity that a conventional live-action documentary might struggle to match, the extent to which the mechanics of memory, and also our experience of these, collapse apparently stable physical, perceptual and psychological barriers between 'then' and 'now'. A live-action version of *Waltz with Bashir* would most probably preserve, by sheer force of formal necessity, some kind of clear dividing line between two orders of textual material. The first would be depicted (by Folman) and experienced (by Folman's viewer) as associated with the chronological present and/or the present tense of the film's narration, while the second would instead be ascribed to the chronological past and/or past tense. The numerous excerpts used from the director's talking head interviews in the early twenty-first century would fall into the former category; direct quotation of contemporaneous documentary footage of Sabra and Shatila and staged recreations of other events from Lebanon in 1982 would fall into the latter. The animated documentary form of Folman's actual film, however, grants that work the ability to put onscreen a range of logistically impossible and/or implausible spectacles of memory. The latter create, both individually and cumulatively, a different, far more disorientating and conceptually challenging effect. In this sense, Rein-Buskila's story constitutes the start, not the end, of something: although viewers never again see his recurring wartime nightmare after the film's first few minutes, animated re-enactments of other nightmares of the First Lebanon War are a signature recurrence. *Waltz with Bashir* visually reiterates the extent to which memory's workings dictate that the present is never completely free of the past's undead hand: 'the meditation the film wants to encourage regard[s] the simultaneity of past, present, and future' (Peaslee 2011: 230). Numerous sequences exemplify and explore that point through animated means. A traumatised forty-something Folman sees flares fired in early-1980s Lebanon light up the Israeli night sky twenty-five years on; car window reflections of a northern European winter landscape mutate into those of a thirty-year-old temperate Lebanese one, as the aftermath of Folman's first visit to Carmi Cna'an brings back previously repressed recollections of wartime experience.

Folman's use of animation in a documentary content also opens up other important creative avenues through which *Waltz with Bashir* explores and articulates its central ideas regarding memory's psychological workings and impact. Key in this regard, for example, is the question of character design. The lo-fi Flash aesthetic of Folman's film can be interpreted not simply as a budgetary choice or constraint, but also as a strikingly effective visual analogue for human experience of long-term, memory-induced trauma: 'though the level of kinetic detail has been limited . . . such constraints are in fact cashed out stylistically . . . the film's troubled bodies, heavy with dream and guilt, wad[e] through a lurid quagmire of deflected memory' (Stewart 2010: 58). Other critics argue that the limited degree of facial and bodily rendering of narrative protagonists dictated by the filmmakers' use of Flash also (or instead) creates a powerful and distinctive form of spectatorial identification with who and what is witnessed on screen. The latter is understood to constitute an empathetic-cum-ethical relationship substantially different from that which might be produced by a live-action version of the same documentary narrative: 'the human figures remain more simply drawn, so we can read the images as both them and us and what we have been and might become' (Schlunke 2011: 959).

Suggestive and substantive as such considerations are, they do not account for the full ambition and impact of the animated character design choices that Folman's film employs. As is by now widely known, seven of *Waltz with*

Bashir's nine major interviewees are drawn 'as themselves' and their own original interview commentary used on the film's final soundtrack. At their own request, however, the testimony of two protagonists (Rein-Buskila and Cna'an) is spoken by professional actors and Rein-Buskila and Cna'an's respective physical appearances on screen are radically altered by animated means (Dawson 2008: 94). However, the physical appearance of the seven realistically rendered protagonists could also be said to have been changed significantly, and in a way that further underscores *Waltz with Bashir*'s exploration of memory's nature and effects. When Folman shows a photograph of his teenage self to Ronny Dayag, *both* men fail to recognise the human subject in the image. In part, that failure stems from the received sense that the teenaged and middle-aged iterations of a single person may, in certain ways, be seen as two different people. Certainly, such a distinction would quite conceivably have been underscored if Folman had resorted to live-action dramatised recreations in which much younger actors performed present-day interviewees' memories. However, this conventional sense of multiple identities contained within one individual life is substantially and productively complicated by several deliberate animated character design choices. David Polonsky, *Waltz with Bashir*'s art director, notes, for example, that the film's animated reproductions of Folman and his former Lebanon War comrades were carefully stylised in order to minimise the scale of differences in physical appearance that would have been visible in a naturalistic attempt to represent both the men's teenage and middle-aged selves. Polonsky explains that he and Folman were interested in 'mak[ing] some of the guys in the present look younger . . . so that the character is believable as the same person' (Zanetti 2008) whose early-1980s experiences of armed conflict are witnessed in the film's memory scenes. As well as serving pragmatic ends, this decision also carries a profound emotional and intellectual impact. At certain points in the narrative, nineteen-year-olds appear aged in advance by their immersion within traumatic historical events that they can barely comprehend. Elsewhere, a lifetime wedded to guilt-ridden memory etches childlike vulnerability into the seams of much older men's visages. As a direct result, the narrative tense viewers experience during much of *Waltz with Bashir* becomes hard to categorise with surety or simplicity. Like the animated exteriors and real-life interiors of the men whose stories Folman's film shares, that tense becomes a complex hybrid of past and present elements. Protagonists' animated appearances may be experienced by the viewer as physically impossible but emotionally real – or, perhaps, as emotionally real precisely because physically impossible.

Waltz with Bashir's use of animation within a documentary context creates other important ontological possibilities and insights as well. Prominent among these is the film's conscious interrogation of received concepts of cinematic documentary and historiography. For Katrina Schlunke, *Waltz with Bashir* instantiates:

> a documentary form that through its style of animation allows us to glimpse the structure of the 'reality' in progress ... drawn forms remind us that the documentary is always a re-presentation, requiring the reproduction of forms of storytelling (narrative, revelation, correction) that produce 'reality,' ... and if [that is] so, what is the status of those carefully framed shots of realism found in other documentary forms? (2011: 953)

Indeed, it is Schlunke's question that the film's scene depicting Folman's first meeting with Carmi Cna'an seems deliberately designed to probe. 'Draw as much as you like ... it's fine so long as you draw, but don't film': Cna'an's injunction to the filmmaker crystallises a familiar set of beliefs surrounding the relationship between ideals of historical truth and particular cinematic forms and representational traditions. Cna'an distinguishes between the pen and the lens as differentially permissible historical recording and evidence-creating devices, especially where particularly sensitive documentary subject matter is concerned. In his line of thought, the live-action lens represents a form of access to the 'truth' of history that is unimpeachable – and also sometimes unacceptable because of that very fact. In other words, the assumedly direct and unmediated veracity of live-action documentary images is too painful to bear because too real to contest. The pen, by contrast, recreates subjectively rather than representing objectively. What results in *Waltz with Bashir*, so Cna'an's reasoning goes, is less an inescapable and comprehensive confrontation with the historical real and more a safer – because psychologically and aesthetically subjective – transfiguration or traducing of the same.

Such conventional taxonomical distinctions and value judgements are present not simply within *Waltz with Bashir* and extant critical response to it. They also appear within evolving debate and discussion around the wider notion of animated documentary per se (see, for example, Yosef 2010: 321). For example, Steven Aoun's assessment of animation's effect within Folman's film specifically – '[chosen] aesthetic as projected coping "mechanism"' (2009: 150) – clearly echoes Sheila Sofian's more general ascription of distinctive modes of spectatorial engagement and experience to animated documentary as a filmmaking mode:

> The audience reacts to animated documentary in a much different way than traditional live-action documentary ... iconographic images impact upon the viewer in a way in which live action cannot. The images are personal and 'friendly'. We are willing to receive animated images without putting up any barriers, opening ourselves up for a powerful and potentially emotional

experience. The simplicity of the images relieves some of the harshness of the topic being described. (2005: 10)

Waltz with Bashir simultaneously illustrates *and* complicates Sofian's contention. On one hand, the film's animated form allows it to put on screen horrified and horrifying human testimony that no camera was present to record in 1982, and which only the most (in both senses) bloody-minded live-action filmmaker would attempt to recreate quarter of a century later. But on the other, a recurring keynote of much contemporaneous response to *Waltz with Bashir*'s original theatrical release involved an argument that, with certain kinds of documentary subject matter, animated images might conceivably prove more disturbing (Ide 2008) or arresting (Fainaru 2008) than conventionally filmed equivalents. Dan Fainaru, for instance, proposed that 'replacing actual footage with animated images lends . . . a uniqueness that might have been lost otherwise, given the enormous amount of similar footage generated daily' (ibid.). Alternatively (and closer to Sofian's position), Katrina Schlunke argues that, rather than transcending the purportedly affectless quality of much live-action reportage of catastrophe, *Waltz with Bashir*'s animated imagery both compels and supports the viewer to self-critique the ethical limits and consequences of routine forms of (dis)engagement with live-action journalism of this kind. 'The affective force' of Folman's film:

> lies in reminding us what we might have seen and dismissed and now are seeing again as if (but not really) for the first time – the first time when this story, that footage will last in our memories, having first been seen and dismissed as one tiny part of a news cycle. (Schlunke 2011: 953)

Thus, one major topic that existing discussion of *Waltz with Bashir* identifies as a possible priority for scholarship on animated documentary per se is interpersonal in nature. It relates to the enhanced (or maybe just alternative) structures of emotional and ethical relation that animation's presence within a documentary context can foster between a filmmaker and their human subject(s), and between a finished film and its viewing audience.

However, *Waltz with Bashir* does more than just suggest animated documentary's potential to reimagine received forms of human relationship to officially sanctioned, public records of past and present-day people and processes. Folman's film also demonstrates animated documentary's capacity to transform the parameters of the public record itself. As noted above, the process of making *Waltz with Bashir* was, for Folman, one of augmenting and/or restoring his individual memory of the 1982 Lebanon War. But his finished work also arguably aims to rectify some of the larger-scale absences in hegemonic historical accounts of that event. This is so, moreover, in ways perhaps only – or, at very least, most fully – open to an animated aesthetic and mode of documentary production. The historical lacunae that the director at one point during the film terms 'the truth not stored in my system' can be retrospectively recovered within an animated documentary, even where particular evidence and events were not recorded contemporaneously in live-action film or other available media. The technology of live-action cinema suggests that the limits of any moving-image historical record will in some senses always prove finite: images and sounds of a given place and time recorded for posterity only by the camera that happened to be present there and then. In sharp contrast, however, Folman's animated documentary approach creates the possibility of an historical repository defined by more flexible epistemological boundaries. *Waltz with Bashir* suggests the possibility that for as long after a given event as human testimony and memory of it can be generated and recorded, attendant audiovisual historiographies may be expanded and reimagined accordingly.

In this way, *Waltz with Bashir* invites its viewer to take seriously Folman's contention that he 'do[es] not understand the difference in terms of truth or belief in drawn picture [i.e., animated documentary] and pixelized picture [i.e., live-action documentary] . . . who decides that pixel-image is more true or real than drawings?' (Ciarocchi 2008) The film simultaneously clarifies *and* complicates the established historical record of the Sabra and Shatila massacres. On one hand, more Israeli experience of that catastrophe is provided than was recorded by contemporaneous news media. But on the other, different elements of the new testimonial data that Folman's film generates conflict with each other. This is due to individual protagonists' inability or refusal to remember accurately and comprehensively. The consequent sense of paradox proves a productive one, however. *Waltz with Bashir* teaches its viewer that live-action footage of a given historical event can – however emotionally and/or ethically distressing those documentary images may initially seem in their apparently unmediated 'reality' – frequently provide a significant form of ontological comfort. Before an audience is 'what really happened' preserved in celluloid or digital file format, and thus relatively safe from subsequent contradiction or caveat. In contrast, Folman's animated documentary images work to underline the unreal and fantastical quality of *all* memorialising acts. This is so whether the latter are small-scale and subjective (a personal recollection of something) or systematic and public (the official historiography of public inquiries, television journalism or academic historiography). In this sense, *Waltz with Bashir* as animated documentary suggests, the more there is of history, the less easy it becomes to construct and cleave to a single definitive historical account of the 'truth' of any given past person, event or process.

Yet as well as being intensely valuable in nature, this latter point also opens Folman's film up to the possibility of sceptical critique as well as celebration.

Michael Koresky (2008), for instance, usefully articulates a now relatively settled aspect of the critical consensus around *Waltz with Bashir*. Koresky argues that Folman's work uses a 'new form' of documentary filmmaking 'to investigate the terrible persistence, not to mention unreliability, of memory and perception, and how personal and political deceptions often go hand in hand'. What remains contentious, however, is the extent to which *Waltz with Bashir*'s illustration of those ideas ought to be understood as primarily conscious, controlled and ideologically progressive in nature. Is it possible that one way in which the film draws attention to the problems that Koresky describes is by falling prey to them? In promotional interviews, Folman has frequently advanced a bullish (and, in many ways already noted above, convincing) ideation of animated documentary as a creative vehicle that facilitates the creation of new forms of historical record and historiographical approach. Questioned, for example, on the extent to which *Waltz with Bashir* develops a sufficiently rigorous and comprehensive documentary account of the logistical and ideological contexts that allowed the Sabra and Shatila massacres to take place, the director has protested:

> But that's really old news ... I didn't dig into it, because I didn't want to spend four years of my life interviewing Israeli politicians ... Everything is known in Israel. I was interested in different things. I was interested in the memory of the massacre as seen by the common soldier, not as seen by a general. (Esther 2009)

But it is precisely this aspect of Folman's animated documentary process and finished product that has generated significant amounts of critical complaint in response. Granted, certain important voices have argued that 'the film's aversion to realism could in fact be interpreted as a criticism of the impossibility of understanding war in rational terms' (Burgin 2010: 72). A more frequent perception, however, is that Folman's intense and subjectively motivated concentration on the individual wartime experience of him and other low-ranking Israeli veterans constructs them as victims of history in ways that unwarrantedly sideline the experience of non-Israeli civilian victims (most obviously, the victims of Sabra and Shatila) of the First Lebanon War. Steven Aoun proposes what is perhaps the current majority critical view when he complains that '*Waltz with Bashir* offers its limited perspective as the only reality worth investigating and representing ... the suffering of Palestinians is displaced in the process' (2009: 152; see also Yosef 2010: 322; Morag 2013: 100; Rastegar 2013: 63; Kraemer 2015: 65–6). On one hand, Folman's work – and, by extension, the possibilities of animated documentary as an emergent filmmaking mode – have been widely welcomed for their putative abilities in certain regards (including revelatory recovery of private memory and recuperation of private trauma). But on the other, the same things have also been more harshly scrutinised in others (including prescriptive definitions of the public ethical responsibilities of the professional documentarian).

In trying to navigate this notably complex aspect of a notably complex animated documentary film, a return to *Waltz with Bashir*'s introductory depiction of Rein-Buskila's nightmare again proves helpful. Rein-Buskila's exceptional personal sensitivity marks him out as an intensely – if paradoxically – sympathetic figure: an armed combatant who never killed another human being. 'They knew', Rein-Buskila claims, that 'I couldn't shoot a person. They said to me, "Go ahead and shoot the dogs"'. In this specific regard, *Waltz with Bashir* takes conspicuous pains to construct Rein-Buskila as a representative Israeli figure within the film's diegesis. Whether Folman personally killed anyone during his tour of duty in Lebanon is never clarified; Carmi Cna'an asserts doubt as to whether he ever actually shot anyone; Ronny Dayag's enduring guilt stems from *failing* to kill Palestinian opponents in defence of his comrades. Similarly, Israeli military casualties are witnessed more often during *Waltz with Bashir* than Lebanese civilian ones are. Two especially striking and surrealistic animated images within the film crystallise Folman's apparently preferred ideation of himself and his interviewees: unwilling and uncomprehending historical actors who can be retrospectively recuperated as victims precisely because they are ex-combatants with blood-free hands. At one point, a young soldier magically transforms his rifle into a functioning electric guitar. Elsewhere, in the set piece sequence that gives *Waltz with Bashir* its title, Shmuel Frenkel dances crazily through a free-fire zone. His gun sprays bullets harmlessly into the air while Palestinian snipers systematically pick off his ambushed Israeli army colleagues.

This reiterated microcosmic sense of individual Israelis being involved, yet not fully implicated in, the horrors of the First Lebanon War prepares the way for *Waltz with Bashir*'s climactic, and arguably self-exonerating, depiction of the Sabra and Shatila massacres. These events become understood within Folman's film as the fundamental moral responsibility of someone else, whether the Lebanese Christian Phalangist militia or individuals far higher up the Israeli military chain of command than Folman and his comrades. Despite the film's notable formal and intellectual achievements in many other regards, one can see how, in the words of one unconvinced observer, *Waltz with Bashir* may be deemed problematic to the extent that it 'psychologises a complex political event. . . convey[ing] a disturbingly skewed account of the First Lebanon War . . . even the atrocities against the Palestinian refugees are all about Folman and his apparent psychological suffering' (Rothschild 2008). Nowhere is this suspicion more apparent than in the evolving – but always audiovisually partial (Stewart 2010: 62; Rastegar 2013: 72;

Kraemer 2015: 65–6) – animated depiction of the mourning Palestinian women in the three memory sequences that locate Folman in the vicinity of Sabra and Shatila and convey that event's psychological impact on him.

Crucial here are certain subtle differences between the three scenes in question. In all of them, the teenage Folman emerges from the sea before stumbling into the streets of Beirut and into the path of the bereaved female survivors of the atrocity. In the first two depictions of these events, the camera follows Folman as the women come upon him (and the viewer) unexpectedly. Their faces are visible but their voices inaudible, obscured by the swelling orchestral strings that dominate the film's soundtrack at these points. In the climatic final depiction, however, once the full horror of Sabra and Shatila and the logistics of the massacres' execution have been presented as fully recovered by Folman, an act of reverse symmetry occurs. The camera follows from behind the tide of women flooding out from the refugee camps and encounters a bewildered teenage Folman standing in the city streets. On this occasion, although the women's voices can at last be heard, their words remain untranslated via subtitles and their faces are now unseen. Though Palestinian civilian suffering can hardly be said to be denied, the shifting audiovisual form of these three key sequences is symptomatic of a questionable trade-off that is attached to *Waltz with Bashir*'s conceptual and historiographical priorities. Exhaustive exploratory depiction of Folman and his comrades' traumatic re-visitation or recuperation of memory precludes any expanded consideration of the stories of indigenous, physical, Lebanese victims rather than their invading, psychological, Israeli counterparts. Caught up within, rather than sufficiently privileged by, the terms of Folman's animated documentary journey of self-discovery, the Palestinian women ultimately 'do not function as subjects in their own right' (Kraemer 2015: 66). Instead, they periodically and ritually intrude on the consciousness of filmmaker and viewer alike in a consistently circumscribed fashion. At some points they are image; at others, sound; but they are never both at once.

In this sense, *Waltz with Bashir*'s final major creative and ethical decision, an abrupt and unexpected cut to contemporaneous live-action news footage of both the living and dead victims of Sabra and Shatila during the film's final moments, speaks of several important considerations at once. Firstly, there is Folman's entirely laudable and understandable desire not for, as he puts matters, 'anyone to leave the theater thinking "This is a very cool animated movie with great drawings and music". I wanted people to understand this really happened ... It puts the whole film into proportion and perspective' (Erikson 2008). Secondly, however, the intensely emotive eleventh-hour formal shift to live action also perhaps puts *Waltz with Bashir* 'into proportion and perspective' in ways that are not intended by its maker. This fact in turn raises persistent questions that require further exploration in relation to critical understanding of the possibilities – and possible limitations – associated with animated documentary as a rapidly expanding mode of contemporary moving image practice.

Given the scale of such questions and their potential applications, it is fitting that no single dominant answer has yet emerged to them. For some, *Waltz with Bashir* ultimately foregrounds the alleged limitations of animated documentary as an epistemological strategy for apprehending 'reality' as conventionally conceived and discussed. Nicholas Hetrick argues that 'it is not until the [live-action] end of the film . . . that . . . we connect the recollections we have heard and witnessed throughout the course of the film with substantial human suffering' (2010: 89; see also Morag 2013: 103). Alternatively, others propose that what *Waltz with Bashir*'s belated embrace of live action really illustrates is less the limitations of animated documentary and more the obstacles posed for animated documentarians by most viewers' relative unfamiliarity with films of this kind. From this perspective, *Waltz with Bashir*'s last-minute divestment of its preferred animated form:

> is more about calling . . . viewers to awareness of their propensity to be shocked by the filmed image in a way that they are not by an animated image of the same cruelty . . . the awareness of this reaction is also an awareness of the degree to which we unreflectively place the [live-action] camera in the vaunted position of a recorder of the 'real'. (Peaslee 2011: 232)

Another possibility again, however, is to see *Waltz with Bashir* as an educative and accomplished exemplification of a nuanced – because non-hierarchical – artistic attempt to distinguish between the respective documentary properties and potentials of live-action and animated moving image modes and registers. Katrina Schlunke, for example, sees the animated images and narrative that comprise the vast majority of the film's running time as a fundamentally enabling preparation for productive spectatorial engagement with the live-action archival footage witnessed at the film's climax:

> a kind of practice in how to remember so we can see and remember what we see at the end . . . forgetting is undone through this juxtaposition of unsettling animation that questions what is real with the very real captured images of the dead . . . showing us how memory and the truth of documentary are produced. (2011: 950)

Whatever the case, two things *do* seem unquestionable. *Waltz with Bashir* will continue to be a critically fascinating and contentious animated documentary work for the foreseeable future. This is so because to consider Ari Folman's film at any meaningful length is also to explore the diverse formal, ontological and ideological properties and potentials associated with animated documentary images' ongoing proliferation in the early twenty-first century.

BIBLIOGRAPHY

Aoun, Steven (2009), '*Waltz with Bashir*: review', *Metro: Media & Education Magazine*, 163, pp. 148–52.
Ashuri, Tamar (2010), 'I witness: re-presenting trauma in and by cinema', *The Communication Review*, 13: 3, pp. 171–92.
Burgin, Alice (2010), 'Guilt, history and memory: another perspective on *Waltz with Bashir*', *Metro: Media & Education Magazine*, 164, pp. 70–4.
Cheng, Cheryl (2009), 'Interview: Ari Folman', in *Video Business*, 11 May 2009, p. 15.
Ciarocchi, Justine (2008), 'Interview with Ari Folman', *ScreenCrave*, 10 December, <http://screencrave.com/2008-12-10/interview-ari-folman/> (last accessed 4 January 2016).
Corbett, Kevin J. (2016), 'Beyond Po-Mo: the 'auto-fiction' documentary', *Journal of Popular Film and Television*, 44: 1, pp. 51–9.
Dawson, Nick (2008), 'Drawing from memory', *Filmmaker – The Magazine of Independent Film*, Fall, pp. 92–5, 127.
Erikson, Steve (2008), 'Ari Folman finds freedom in animation', *Studio Daily*, 18 December 2008, <http://www.studiodaily.com/filmandvideo/currentissue/10304.html> (last accessed 10 January 2017).
Esther, John (2009), '*Waltz with Bashir*: an interview with Ari Folman', *Cineaste*, 34: 2, Spring, p. 67.
Fainaru, Dan (2008), '*Waltz with Bashir*: review', *Screen Daily*, 15 May, <http://www.screendaily.com/ScreenDailyArticle.aspx?intStoryID=38809> (last accessed 30 April 2017).
Formenti, Cristina (2014), 'The sincerest form of docudrama: reframing the animated documentary', *Studies in Documentary Film*, 8: 2, pp. 103–15.
Hetrick, Nicholas (2010), 'Ari Folman's *Waltz with Bashir* and the limits of abstract tragedy', *Image and Narrative: Online Magazine of the Visual Narrative*, 11: 2, pp. 78–91.
Honess Roe, Annabelle (2013), *Animated Documentary*, Basingstoke: Palgrave Macmillan.
Ide, Wendy (2008), '*Waltz with Bashir*: review', *The Times*, 15 May, <https://www.thetimes.co.uk/article/waltz-with-bashir-wqzplr2nv3j> (last accessed 29 April 2017).
Koresky, Michael (2008), 'In living memory', *Reverse Shot*, 21 December, <http://www.reverseshot.com/article/waltz_bashir> (last accessed 10 January 2017).
Kraemer, Joseph A. (2015), '*Waltz with Bashir* (2008): trauma and representation in the animated documentary', *Journal of Film and Video*, 67: 3/4 (Fall/Winter), pp. 57–68.
Landesman, Ohad and Roy Bendor (2011), 'Animated recollection and spectatorial experience in *Waltz with Bashir*', *animation: an interdisciplinary journal*, 6: 3, pp. 353–70.
Llewellyn, Timothy (2013), 'Reporting Sabra and Shatila', in Caroline Rooney and Rita Sakr (eds), *The Ethics of Representation in Literature, Art and Journalism: Transnational Responses to the Siege of Beirut*, New York: Routledge, pp. 163–75.
Morag, Raya (2013), *Waltzing with Bashir: Perpetrator Trauma and Cinema*, London: I. B. Tauris.
Naylor, R. T. (1983), 'From bloodbath to whitewash: Sabra-Shatila and the Kahan Commission Report', *Arab Studies Quarterly*, 5: 4, pp. 337–61.
Peaslee, Robert Moses (2011), '"It's fine as long as you draw, but don't film": *Waltz with Bashir* and the postmodern function of animated documentary', *Visual Communication Quarterly*, 18: 4, pp. 223–35.

Rastegar, Kamran (2013), '"Sawnaru Waynkum?" Human rights and social trauma in *Waltz with Bashir*', *College Literature: A Journal of Critical Literary Studies*, 40: 3, Summer, pp. 60–80.

Rothschild, Nathalie (2008), 'Post-Zionist stress disorder', *Jewcy*, 2 December, <http://www.jewcy.com/post/postzionist_stress_disorder_waltz_bashir_reviewed> (last accessed 10 January 2017).

Schlunke, Katrina (2011), 'Animated documentary and the scene of death: experiencing *Waltz with Bashir*', *South Atlantic Quarterly*, 110: 4, Fall, pp. 949–62.

Shahid, Leila (2002), 'The Sabra and Shatila massacres: eye-witness reports', *Journal of Palestine Studies*, 32: 1, pp. 36–58.

Sofian, Sheila (2005), 'The truth in pictures', *Frames Per Second*, March, pp. 7–10.

Stewart, Garrett (2010), 'Screen memory in *Waltz with Bashir*', *Film Quarterly*, 63: 3, Spring, pp. 58–62.

Viljoen, Jeanne-Marie (2013), 'Representing the 'unrepresentable': the unpredictable life of memory and experience in *Waltz with Bashir*', *Scrutiny2*, 18: 2, pp. 66–80.

Waltz with Bashir, film, directed by Ari Folman. Israel/France/Germany/USA/Finland/Switzerland/Belgium/Australia: Bridgit Folman Film Gang, Les Films d'Ici and Razor Film Produktion GmbH, 2008.

Yosef, Raz (2010), 'War fantasies: memory, trauma and ethics in Ari Folman's *Waltz with Bashir*', *Journal of Modern Jewish Studies*, 9: 3, pp. 311–26.

Zanetti, Olly (2008), 'Interview with David Polonsky', n.d., <http://www.littlewhitelies.co.uk/interviews/david-polonsky> (last accessed 18 November 2008).

Part 4

Practice-based Perspectives

CHAPTER 11

Making The Trouble with Love and Sex
Jonathan Hodgson

INTRODUCTION: THE TROUBLE WITH *THE TROUBLE WITH LOVE AND SEX*

SUSAN

So what do I do, I can't explain why I'm feeling the way I am. How can I explain, how can I explain why I'm, quote, 'frigid'? Christ!
 Ok what am I going to, I don't know, I really don't know, I, I don't have an answer. Maybe I should take some pills, maybe I should take some drugs, maybe I should, you know, get some sex books! Maybe . . . I don't know!

IAIN

Well maybe, I don't know! (Beattie and Hodgson 2011)

The above quote from documentary interview footage used in the production of my and producer/director Zac Beattie's animated documentary *The Trouble with Love and Sex* (2011), a project commissioned as part of BBC2's Wonderland series, is indicative of a question that greatly preoccupied us as filmmakers during the making of the work. How do you go about creating an animated documentary using material as emotionally challenging (and thus, potentially off-putting) as this without alienating the mass audience that a BBC commission gives you the opportunity to engage with? *The Trouble* was about real people using the services of Relate, a British relationship counselling organisation, and was to be the first full-length animated documentary broadcast on British TV. Contributors had agreed to share extremely painful personal information; by using animation to preserve their anonymity, it was hoped they might feel less self-conscious about expressing their feelings. An initial rough cut was derived from video footage of counselling sessions, interviews and video diaries: that material was powerful, moving and, at times, very dark. However, I was concerned that, once introduced into the film-in-progress, animation might fail to deliver the same emotional intensity as the live-action footage we had recorded. This had the potential to be doubly problematic, in that (as noted above) the project's use of animation was one major factor in securing contributors' participation and consent in the first place. This essay will therefore provide a reflective account of the ways in which I and my collaborators adapted challenging documentary interview content, reworking it as animation, and thus developing distraught, angry and badly behaved real-life voices into sympathetic animated characters populating an accessible and stimulating film for a mass audience (see also Beattie 2011).

Origins and Initial Evolution

In February 2009, I received an email from Nag Vladermersky, Director of the London International Animation Festival, saying that Zac Beattie, a documentary producer/director, was looking for an animation director for an animated documentary he was developing for the BBC. I expressed interest and Zac and I arranged to meet in order to discuss the project. Zac was interested in making a film about relationship therapy, but the only other things he could confirm at that stage was that the film was going to be about 50 minutes long and would be fully animated. It is hard to explain to a non-animator how exciting that last sentence sounded. Privately, however, I felt bemused by how easily a non-animator had secured a commission to make a long-form animation, while experienced animators such as me struggled to fund even a short. But when I learnt more about Zac's background (he won a BAFTA for his 2005 television film *Make Me Normal*) and met him in person, I came to feel that collaborating would be a rewarding experience. Over the next couple of weeks we had several conversations. Zac confirmed that he was taking forward the idea of relationship counselling as the basis for the envisaged animated documentary and was in the process of approaching Relate. He also subsequently confirmed, however, that the BBC insisted that an unspecified number of animation directors besides me should also have the opportunity to pitch for the project.

In spite of the inevitable competitive aspect, pitching can be a very interesting and creatively productive stage in the preproduction of a film. It encourages you to do your very best work and can help to give shape and direction to a project at a very early stage. It was agreed that, as part of my pitch for *The Trouble*, I would produce a short moving test sequence interpreting a dialogue-driven, live-action sequence from the BBC archives. I agreed to produce a twenty-second sequence with five to seven seconds fully animated. The remainder of the running time would comprise a series of still images indicating my suggested graphic treatment of the archival material I was working with. I deliberately set low expectations of what I could deliver in a short timeframe while actually intending to deliver a fully animated test. The archive material I was animating in response to was from a fly-on-the-wall, live-action documentary series called *The Family* (2008). This featured a husband and wife sarcastically bickering about their mutually hazy memories of their first date. I took a strong dislike to both characters (they came across like spoilt teenagers), and the animated test sequence I produced therefore had a satirical edge to it, portraying both protagonists as unpleasant caricatures. The narrative location presented in my test was very much middle England suburbia, but I limited the colour palette to a range of pinks, reds and blacks, in order to give the sequence an unnatural look that was intended as an ironic play on the idea of looking at the world through rose-tinted glasses. The sequence took three weeks to complete, and Jonathan Bairstow, a producer at Sherbet (the independent animation production company who represent me), was now sufficiently committed to the project to invest enough funds for a small production team to work on the pitch.

Jonathan, Zac and I subsequently met with Nick Mirsky, the executive producer of the BBC's Wonderland strand. Although their response to the test sequence I had produced was broadly positive, they had some reservations regarding what they felt was the caricaturing, visual and otherwise, of the characters from *The Family* excerpt. The latter looked (in their words) too 'grotesque and gothic'. Zac and Nick emphasised how important it was that any commissioned film showed sensitivity and sympathy to contributors going through a very difficult stage in their lives, and who would have shown considerable courage in agreeing to share their private troubles with the general public. It was essential, they argued, to produce an animated work that exhibited due consideration towards our documentary subjects, did not alienate a viewing audience, and thus helped the latter to empathise with the formers' troubles as depicted onscreen. This, for me, was the biggest lesson from the initial test and pitch period, and it was clearly something very central to Zac's filmmaking philosophy. He and the BBC asked if I would be prepared to do one further pitch. Although this was the first time I had ever been asked to do two pitches as part of a commissioning process, I felt I had no choice but to say 'yes'.

I was therefore given another clip from a different archival documentary (which I never found out the name of) featuring a rather conservative, middle-aged couple discussing their marital problems. This time I took a very different approach to the design and characterisation of the animated test sequence that I produced in response: the characters needed to be appealing. This was quite a tall order for me, given that much of my work to that point in time concentrated on bringing out people's worst points. My film *Nightclub* (1983), for example, was based on sketchbook drawings of the clientele of Liverpool drinking clubs and was directly inspired by the art of German expressionists such as George Grosz and Otto Dix. Similarly, *Camouflage* (2002) was based on interviews with people who were the children of people with schizophrenia; my depictions of the harrowing experiences interviewees described were deliberately designed to feel nightmarish and unsettling. I therefore imagined how I might represent the couple in empathetic (as well as interpretative) terms: as if they were members of my own family, people who I instinctively wanted to protect and not offend, even if I simultaneously wanted to offer honest and unsparing commentary on their emotional state and actions. The new moving test accordingly had more benign characterisation and a broader, more naturalistic colour palette. The couple was given a more realistic visual treatment, carefully designed to have no obviously unpleasant physical characteristics. However, I was aware that this visual treatment might be in danger of appearing too cosy and conservative: it did not fulfil my usual desire to surprise and unsettle the audience. The conversation in the clip centred on the woman's frustration with her husband's reluctance to engage with her sexual fantasies, so for shock value I added a short sequence featuring a naked woman astride a giant flying penis, intended as a bawdy response to the idea of a woman uninhibitedly embracing her libido.

The second pitch convinced Beattie and Mirsky that I was the right animation director for their envisaged project. However, there was still room for improvement. Zac and Nick now felt that the second test's gentle characterisation and conventional styling, was perhaps a little too polite. In my effort to compromise my usual habit of ridiculing people, the new material lacked some of the excitement and inventiveness of the first test sequence. Gradually, however, we seemed to be getting closer to a visual treatment that would chime with Zac's vision for *The Trouble with Love and Sex*.

INFLUENCES AND REFERENCE POINTS

Given the now-understood importance of finding an agreed visual modus operandi for the film, one capable of sustaining an audience's attention for the envisaged near-hour-long running time, we began to look for useful lessons and ideas within existing animated documentary work. We did not want to replicate other directors' methodology, but felt it important to understand why certain animated documentary films had the power to move us, and also to identify problem areas that we should steer clear of. At this stage, we were not fully sure of what these areas might be. We wanted, however, to identify creative approaches within an animated documentary context to issues of characterisation, art direction, sound design and cinematography that had (in our view) succeeded or failed to create an empathetically and emotionally immersive viewing experience. Several filmmakers immediately came to mind, and we studied their work in an attempt to inform our own creative process.

For example, Oscar-winning Chris Landreth's film *The Spine* (2009) felt like a prime example of what we wanted to avoid at all costs. This film offers a nightmarish depiction of ordinary people with common problems. Attending group therapy, a literally spineless husband passively endures constant verbal attacks from his morbidly obese wife. Landreth is, of course, an animation artist of enormous creative imagination, and characters in his films often show physical manifestations of their psychological problems. Because his experimental approach to CG animation is essentially photorealistic, his representations of hideously tortured humanity are often the stuff of nightmares. But far from responding sympathetically to his subjects, I felt physically repulsed by them (and this was clearly what Landreth wanted me to feel). Zac and I agreed that *The Spine*'s grotesque characterisation and overacted performances created a psychological barrier preventing the kind of audience identification with, and empathy for, protagonists that we wanted to cultivate within our own film.

Elsewhere, Ari Folman's feature-length animated documentary *Waltz with Bashir* (2008) is a pivotal work exploring the phenomenon of collective amnesia with regard to traumatic events. Folman developed a semi-realistic animated style (inspired by, among others, contemporary comic artist Joe Sacco) that incorporated dynamic and spacious elements reminiscent of big-budget Hollywood blockbusters such as Francis Ford Coppola's *Apocalypse Now* (1979). Impressive as Folman's meticulously stylised quest for lost memories is, we felt that the film did not fully master the ambitious technical challenge of animating a visual style perhaps better suited to the still image. This was particularly apparent in scenes containing long conversations, where slick graphic treatment of the character design is often undermined by animation which at times feels clumsy and mannered. We felt that Marjane Satrapi's much simpler designs for her and Vincent Paronnaud's film *Persepolis* (2007) translated much more easily into animation, although in this case, the character design felt too closely associated with children's series animation, which we felt would be an inappropriate style to convey the serious content of our film.

Aardman Animation's *Creature Comforts* series (1989; 2003–5) was another important point of reference. The verbatim theatre of these short films brilliantly marries character with voiceover, but it would not have been appropriate to have our contributors bare their souls whilst masquerading as penguins or armadillos. Delving deeper into Aardman's back catalogue, we were more inspired by the straightforward, stripped-down approach of the *Lip Synch* series (1989–90), and in particular, Peter Lord's *Going Equipped* (1990), which features a stark portrayal of a young ex-offender describing how he was lured into a life of crime. The protagonist sits alone in what looks like an interview room, giving a monologue illustrated with occasional flashbacks to his earlier life. The deliberate simplicity of this film (nothing in the animation process interfered with the clarity of what was being said) meant that Lord's method felt much closer to what we were hoping to achieve with our own animation. We concluded that we should avoid an overly ornate visual style. If the character design was too detailed, the audience could be distracted by protagonists' appearance and concentrate less on what was being said.

Beginning Pre-production

The next stage of production involved finding and filming documentary contributors brave enough to share intimate details of their lives, the raw material for our film. While Zac tackled this aspect of the project, I put together an animation production team. At first, Zac's seemingly obsessive attention to the detail of proposed character design had taken me aback, but gradually it started to make sense, and also to influence my own working methods. I began to give greater consideration to how combinations of small physical details can sometimes make a huge difference to the way an animated character is perceived by an audience. The *Trouble with Love and Sex* film would be venturing into new territory, not just within our own respective bodies of work, but also in the genre of documentary animation. It therefore made complete sense to consider every aspect of the project in fine detail and from multiple angles. I felt it was vital, for instance, that we assembled the right combination of animators for the project. All applicants were therefore asked to produce a short animated test, something that I had never done before.

The main quality I looked for in my animator-collaborators was an ability to create very naturalistic character animation with equally subtle body language. Finding people who could achieve this was not easy, however. Most experienced animators follow Walt Disney's '12 Principles of Animation', and tend to stylise and exaggerate animated protagonists' physical poses and movement with squash and stretch. The animation in *The Trouble* would need to be far more understated: the audience had to be able to read the suppressed emotions, vulnerability and minute changes of mood experienced by the film's documentary subjects. For instance, when a middle-aged man cries in front of another man he may well feel a complex combination of pain, relief and desperate embarrassment. He will thus try hard to appear composed, precisely in order to conceal the fact that he has lost control of his emotions. For the prospective animators' test, therefore, I created a series of full-artwork keyframes (drawings that identified the envisaged start and end points of animated movement within given short sequences of the film-in-progress) based on the characters I had designed for the second pitch meeting discussed above. These keyframes were then put onto a timeline with a soundtrack taken from the BBC documentary around which the second test sequence discussed above had been built. Prospective animators were asked to animate as much of the resulting animatic (a series of still images revealed over time rather like a slideshow, but with synched sound) as possible. Interestingly (but perhaps unsurprisingly), it was younger animators, some straight out of art college, who came closest to what I was looking for. Many seasoned professionals who we considered seemed unable to shake off the more amplified approach to characterisation that they had become used to working with. In the end, we picked five key animators: Bishoy Gendi, Malcolm Mole, Martin Oliver, Joseph Pelling and Chrisoph Steger. Due to budget restrictions, that quintet would be assisted by student interns, most of whom were selected from the students on my BA Animation degree course at Middlesex University.

By midsummer 2009, Zac had shot all the footage he needed and was assembling a rough cut edit. Initially, it looked like we might be able to start animation work by early autumn, but this was subsequently put on hold until after Christmas, due to the work commitments of Zac's editor, Joe Carey. This was worrying because we were at risk of losing our carefully assembled production team to other productions. On the other hand, the delay also gave me more time to design the characters and the world that they would live in. This was just as well, because by September of that year we were still a long way from resolving the final look of the film. Zac and I agreed that the film should have a quintessentially English suburban setting: a familiar, plausible location that felt appropriate for the various characters and that did not distract or confuse the audience. We decided to create a fictitious southern English town and have all the animated characters live there. In reality, our documentary contributors came from different towns, but the animated version of their lives showed them arriving at the same Relate office and even passing each other's homes. Specifically, I took the leafy avenues of Letchworth Garden City as my main inspiration and chose to use a muted and faded colour palette inspired by the watercolour paintings of American outsider artist Henry Darger. I showed Darger's work to Zac, who loved Darger's combination of predominantly muted colours with small areas of very strong primary colour, helping to direct the eye towards important details.

Designing Characters

Meanwhile, the process of finding the right animated characters was haphazard and fraught. As I developed the character designs I kept in mind the need to avoid stereotypes and caricatures of the types of person we were depicting, searching instead for archetypes that were easy to recognise from each demographic group (for example, upper-middle-class people from Surrey). In my research, I tried to identify visual clues such as hairstyles, dress code and body language that would make each social group that our characters belonged to easily identifiable, but without being too clichéd or, conversely, too eccentric and strange. Our creative team felt a big responsibility to our documentary contributors, all of whom had generously agreed to reveal things that many people would choose to keep secret. It was thus important to represent our protagonists as normal, likeable people, developing sympathetic and believable visual and emotional depictions with which they would feel comfortable and that our eventual audience would find easy to empathise with.

As part of his work sourcing documentary interviewees, Zac had chosen two couples and a single man as our film's subjects: Susan and Iain, an upper-middle-class, fifty-something couple from Surrey; Ian and Mandy, a lower-middle-class, thirty-something couple from Essex; and Dave, a working-class single man from West London. The two couples were happy for their real first names to be used, but the single man preferred to have his changed. It is important to remember that our use of animation was key to contributors' involvement in the project: none would have been prepared to take part in our film had it been a live-action documentary. Animation did not simply reduce our interviewees' fears of being identified on national television; it also provided them with a paradoxical form of camouflage, something they could be hidden behind in one sense while simultaneously freeing them to reveal themselves (through candid discussion of their relationship problems) in another.

At this stage in the production process, I made a firm decision to not look at the live-action footage of contributors, as I was keen to develop animated characters who possessed their own unique identity. It was an interesting creative challenge to invent characters based on contributors' voices alone, rather than be influenced by how the latter looked and behaved in front of a camera. Initial character design sketches were loosely based on people I knew. I photographed friends and colleagues who were similar in age to our contributors and who (to me) looked interesting and reasonably attractive, and then created designs based on these photos. Guided also by Zac's descriptions of the contributors' physical characteristics, social backgrounds and psychological constitutions, my challenge was to create characters that fitted into recognisable British socioeconomic and regional archetypes without literally exposing the real person hidden behind an avatar.

This proved to be one of *The Trouble*'s most difficult preproduction stages. I made numerous attempts to find the right 'look' for each character, and there seemed to be a direct correlation between the time it took to get a given character's animated appearance right and how deep-seated their relationship problems were. The challenges that some contributors faced in their personal lives were related to overarching psychological problems rather than more day-to-day complications of normal life. Zac was concerned that we needed to give sustained thought to how characters dealing with psychological problems could be made to look more visually appealing for our eventual audience. Every day, I emailed the latest character designs to Zac; the following morning, a lengthy late-night missive would be waiting in my inbox with a long list of revisions.

Zac had very strong feelings about what each character should look like, but I did not always find it easy to interpret his thoughts. Certainly, the characters in his imagination were not simply based on contributors' actual appearance; he was also trying to predict how an audience might respond to different physical types and was looking to me to design characters that would send out a suitably nuanced, sympathetic but also interrogative message to our audience. We spent a lot of time perfecting the look of Dave, for example, because of concerns that some viewers might perceive a man in his forties who had never had a successful relationship as 'creepy'. Zac was keen that I make each character reasonably attractive, physically speaking, but also keep them believable as ordinary people. I started off by trying to visualise Susan and Iain, whose marriage clearly had substantial problems that neither partner was dealing with well: bitterness, anger and cringingly unpleasant arguments were all present in the live-action footage. Although their story was fascinating, it was quite hard to like them as people. Thus, Susan and Iain's character designs had not only to match their key psychological traits, but also to compensate for what I and an eventual television audience might perceive as their personal shortcomings.

It became clear that none of my character design drawings based on photographs of personal acquaintances were quite hitting the mark. I therefore started to sketch from life: drawing in the street, in cafes, and on the London Tube. In addition, many of Zac's reference points in our ongoing discussions about character design were film stars and celebrities. I therefore broadened my visual scope to reference film and TV personalities, models and random faces from the media and internet, thus creating new characters that were rather like 'photofit' combinations of many different people. Over time I amassed a library of faces that were, for the most part, wrong. But this material at least helped Zac to identify the types of character design that he did not want. After numerous failed attempts, I felt it might speed up the process if I saw some video footage of the contributors after all. This proved extremely helpful: once I knew what Susan and Iain actually looked like, it became much easier to develop characters that, to my eye, appeared physically and socially similar but also different enough to be unrecognisable when viewed onscreen.

Once Susan and Iain's design had been approved, I moved onto the Essex couple, Mandy and Ian. Of all the film's contributors, they were the easiest to visualise, partly because their relationship problems were less intractable than Susan and Iain's. Because their dialogue was accordingly more diplomatic, it felt as though Mandy and Ian's visual appearance did not need to play such a crucial role in giving them audience appeal. Even so, it took quite a while to dovetail their looks. Zac had a skill for summing people up with a few helpfully succinct keywords. For example, his comment that Mandy and Ian should 'look a bit more Bluewater' (a reference to a large shopping and retail destination situated on the south side of the Thames Estuary) gave me a much clearer context for my character design, steering me away from an earlier more bohemian look. When he added that 'they need to be the film's Posh and Becks', meaning that the characters needed a touch more glamour, I was able to resolve the characters very quickly.

The last contributor, Dave, was the hardest to get right. He was a complex character: from the video clips I saw, handsome, engaging, seemingly kind and gentle, a bit of a dreamer and a great storyteller. This made Dave's single status hard to understand, but his story soon revealed problems that were psychological as well as romantic relationship-based: cripplingly low self-esteem caused by childhood abuse. Zac worried that some viewers might not immediately empathise with a man in his early forties who had never had a proper relationship. It was therefore essential that Dave's character design pre-empted any such problems. This goal was a lot easier said than done: it took several weeks and dozens of attempts to finally design a character that Zac felt comfortable with. This was a frustrating period of pre-production: I felt we were becoming far too analytical and, as a result, my drawings were looking stiff and over-worked. I therefore went back to a more spontaneous process of drawing people on the Tube: the constant turnover of passengers forced me to work quickly and the shaking and rattling of the train carriage prevented me from making the drawings too tight. One drawing in particular, almost a scribble, stood out: an image of a man with sad eyes and a smile with lips that turned down at the edges, giving him a friendly, but rather apprehensive, appearance. I showed this drawing to Zac and he loved it. It was a huge relief to have found the final piece in the puzzle, although it still took some time to refine Dave's final character design into the fully suitable and appropriate embodiment of physically attractive vulnerability.

ANIMATING IMAGES

With character designs finally signed off, we could start to approach our animated characters as, in certain senses, the stars of the film. With the exception of Dave, none of our real-life contributors was particularly photogenic. We began to suspect that reinventing them as slightly better-looking animated characters might make it easier for the audience to engage, unencumbered by instinctive reactions to real-life physical appearance, with what protagonists were saying about relationship issues. By early March 2010, we were ready to start the animatic. In this film's case, the animatic's spine was a soundtrack compiled from a variety of recorded sources. While most of our sound had come from video footage of Relate counselling sessions, Zac had also interviewed our protagonists in different locations. In addition, he had lent them video cameras with which to make video diaries kept during their time in therapy. Lastly, temporary music had also been added to certain sections of the recordings in order to act as a placeholder emphasis of emotion. But when Zac and his editor were working on the rough cut they found the video footage of the contributors distracting, making it difficult to imagine the film as animation. As a solution, they replaced the video footage with crude thumbnail sketches of the various scenes. In spite of their primitive execution, these drawings proved incredibly helpful because they functioned well as an initial (albeit rough) animatic. The first time I saw a full edit, I was immediately engaged by the film's three interweaving narratives. Moreover, the melding of sound from disparate sources seemed to strengthen and compress each storyline.

I subsequently worked on the animatic with Laurie J. Proud, a fellow animation director at independent production company Sherbet. Laurie originally trained as a storyboard artist and has an encyclopaedic knowledge of film language. It is hard to overestimate the importance of the role storyboard artists play on large-scale animation productions. Like film editors, they often influence a finished film's eventual shape more than the work's director. I created pencil layouts of the characters in situ for each scene and gave them to Laurie, who would redraw them in Flash, adding additional poses, angles and camera moves wherever necessary. He worked incredibly quickly, producing up to three minutes of footage a day. Every evening, Laurie would email a Flash movie of the day's work to be added to the timeline next day. Every Friday, Zac Beattie and Nick Mirsky came over to Sherbet and, together with me and Jonathan Bairstow, would spend several hours reviewing the work-in-progress. Although these meetings often resulted in large sections of the animatic having to be reworked, I found Zac and Nick's objectivity, insight and experience as live-action documentarians very enlightening, and I had to agree with their opinions in most instances. By the end of April 2010, the animatic was getting close to completion and we called in the animators.

Having spent months developing character designs and locations, we knew it was equally important to pay similar attention to the treatment of the animation process in order to achieve maximum audience engagement and empathy. When considering how best to communicate *The Trouble*'s socially and emotionally challenging thematic material, subtlety and restraint seemed to be the best creative approach. However, this type of aesthetic is not always employed in animated films. Having worked professionally as an animator for many years I have experienced again and again a general public expectation that animation should, by definition, amuse and/or astonish through sensation, showmanship and visually thrilling imagery. Because much mainstream feature animation accordingly does just that, the experience of watching animation can often feel like attending a particularly noisy firework display: the viewer is required to stand well back in order to take in the whole spectacle.

This is precisely the opposite to the kind of relationship that we wanted an audience to have with our film. Given the markedly intimate nature of *The Trouble*'s subject matter, we wanted our viewers to concentrate on fine detail, both emotionally and visually speaking: the subtleties and nuances of body language that are often overlooked in favour of more expansive, cartoon-like gestures. I was inspired in this specific regard by the minimalist animation of Don Hertzfeldt's more recent films, such as *Everything Will Be OK* (2006). In this film, Hertzfeldt's sometimes virtually inanimate stickmen manage to communicate a depth of feeling and meaning that is often lacking in many more flamboyantly animated characters. By simplifying and underplaying the acting of our animated protagonists in a comparable way, we hoped to construct a quiet and uncomplicated approach to the animation of *The Trouble with Love and Sex* that would help draw the audience into the work.

Our animators thus commenced work employing a 'less is more' approach, only animating that which needed to be animated and mainly concentrating on facial movements. As the first scenes rolled out, we felt that the characters undoubtedly had emotional credibility (and thus, were capable of provoking empathy), but were also concerned that a fifty-minute-long animated film comprising wall-to-wall talking heads might not sustain an audience's interest. From time to time, we felt, conversations needed to be punctuated in some way. *The Trouble*'s production budget was much higher than most of the live-action films produced for BBC2's Wonderland documentary strand, but was still only two-thirds of Sherbet's normal bottom line. This meant that we needed to employ markedly economical animation production techniques. The relative visual simplicity of our consequent treatment of the counselling scenes, which made up about 80 per cent of the finished film, helped to convey emotional tone and nuance by providing ample opportunities for subtle depiction of body language and movement. Just as importantly, it also enabled us to spend a larger proportion of our budget on the other 20 per cent of the film, which needed to be more complex and dynamic in animated terms. In a series of short punctuating sections between counselling scenes, we exploited animation's capacity to shift seamlessly through space, time and from one location to another. We used flashbacks to blur the temporal boundaries between past and present and fantasy sequences to shift between the real and imagined, thus allowing us to create multidimensional accounts of the contributors' respective stories. Early on in the film, for example, there is a scene that introduces Dave. In this sequence we used dynamic tracking shots to take the audience on a journey through the fictitious animated town that formed our narrative setting, transporting the viewer from one story location to the next and also helping to place the characters in a recognisable and credible diegetic world.

CONCLUSION

At the start of *The Trouble with Love and Sex*'s production, I was concerned that viewers might not register the understated nuances of animated body language with the same instinctive recognition that live-action images could facilitate. But at the finished film's press launch, I was startled by how much viewers laughed during the film's first ten minutes. True, this introductory section is lighter in tone than the work's later parts, but had we inadvertently created a situation comedy? Then, as the film reached the point where Dave shared the details of his father's abuse, the audience suddenly went quiet. Perhaps those who had brought along preconceived ideas about how emotionally complex narrative and thematic content might normally be delivered in animation had been wrong-footed, or perhaps they simply had not known what to expect in the first place. Certainly, any concerns that the film would fail to emotionally engage the audience were unfounded. Public response was extremely positive, including supportive press reviews in the *Daily Telegraph*, *The Independent* and *The Guardian*, among other publications (see, for example, Dowling 2011; Radford 2011). Many people admitted to shedding a tear during certain sections and felt genuine empathy with the film's characters, suggesting that viewers felt more connected with contributors' stories specifically because (rather than despite the fact that) these narratives were unfolding through the medium of animation. It seemed that viewer laughter was predicated on feelings of recognition rather derision or incomprehension: the most common anecdotal response I got to our work was: 'That felt exactly like our relationship!'

Over the two years between my first meeting with Zac Beattie to *The Trouble with Love and Sex*'s May 2011 British broadcast premiere on BBC2, I learned a great deal about how animation can used as a tool for communicating difficult and emotional content within documentary narrative works. First and foremost, I was able to put aside my serious doubts at the project's outset as to whether animated documentary characters could really convey powerful, but at times extremely subtle, emotions as efficiently as conventional live-action equivalents. The most astonishing revelation for me was that hiding real people behind animated characters actually allowed audiences to focus more fully on what those people were saying, rather than being distracted by the contributors' appearance. As one reviewer put it: 'It's self-evident that this [animated] approach deprived us of our ability to judge by appearances. But did that make it more difficult for us to exactly interpret the nuances of meaning ... or did it oblige us to listen without prejudice?' (Sutcliffe 2011) I also gained enormous insight into another director's working methods. It is often very illuminating to work in association with another creator: when a joint effort really gels, some mysterious alchemy means that combined creative inputs can add up to more than the sum of their individual parts. Zac's fastidious approach to planning and development seemed at first almost obsessive, but I quickly understood the value in analysing subject matter from every angle and trying to second-guess every possible audience response to characters and content. From the way our animated protagonists' conversations were edited and juxtaposed through to the style and colour of the clothes they were wearing, Zac left nothing to chance and was able to maximise the impact of our film's every second. My own directorial approach tends to be more spontaneous and impulsive, allowing a certain degree of randomness and unpredictability to enter the production processes and embracing happy accidents that can add something intangible to the texture of a finished film. Zac and I each had to make creative compromises during the making of our film, but I am convinced that by combining our differing approaches to documentary filmmaking we succeeded in delivering a stronger and more original work than would have been possible had we not had the opportunity to work together. While I would never abandon my own idiosyncratic working methods, the insights gained from working on *The Trouble with Love and Sex* will inform my approach to research and development in subsequent animated documentary productions.

BIBLIOGRAPHY

Beattie, Zac (2011), 'Wonderland: *The Trouble With Love And Sex*', BBC TV Blog, 11 May, <http://www.bbc.co.uk/blogs/tv/2011/05/wonderland-trouble-with-love-and-sex.shtml> (last accessed 18 October 2016).

Camouflage, film, directed by Jonathan Hodgson. UK: Sherbet, Channel 4 and Arts Council of England, 2002.

Dowling, Tim (2011), 'TV review: Wonderland: *The Trouble With Love and Sex*', *The Guardian*, 11 May, <https://www.theguardian.com/tv-and-radio/2011/may/11/trouble-with-love-and-sex?INTCMP=SRCH> (last accessed 18 October 2016).

Everything Will Be OK, film, directed by Don Hertzfeldt. USA: Bitter Films, 2006.

Going Equipped, film, directed by Peter Lord. UK: Aardman Animations and Channel 4, 1990.

Nightclub, film, directed by Jonathan Hodgson. UK: Merseyside Arts and Royal College of Art, 1983.

Persepolis, film, directed by Vincent Paronnaud and Marjane Satrapi. France/USA: France 3 Cinéma, The Kennedy/Marshall Company and French Connection Animations, 2007.

Radford, Ceri (2011), 'What couples really say to each other in therapy', *The Telegraph*, 11 May, <http://www.telegraph.co.uk/culture/tvandradio/8507659/What-couples-really-say-to-each-other-in-therapy-Wonderland-BBC-Two-review.html> (last accessed 1 June 2018).

The Spine, film, directed by Chris Landreth. Canada: Copperheart Entertainment and National Film Board of Canada, 2009.

Sutcliffe, Tom (2011), 'Last night's TV: Wonderland: *The Trouble with Love and Sex*', *The Independent*, 11 May, <http://www.independent.co.uk/arts-entertainment/tv/reviews/last-nights-tv-wonderland-the-trouble-with-love-and-sexbbc224-hours-in-aampechannel-4-2282574.html> (last accessed 18 October 2016).

The Trouble with Love and Sex, film, directed by Zac Beattie and Jonathan Hodgson. UK: Sherbet and BBC, 2011.

Waltz with Bashir, film, directed by Ari Folman. Israel/France/Germany/USA/Finland/Switzerland/Belgium/Australia: Bridgit Folman Film Gang, Les Films d'Ici and Razor Film Produktion GmbH, 2008.

CHAPTER 12

'Does this look right?' Working Inside the Collaborative Frame
Samantha Moore

INTRODUCTION

As artists we often start a project with a list of self-interrogatory questions. For example: Why use animation for this work? Why make animation in the documentary genre? What is it specifically that only animation can document? In the process of trying to answer this last question, I have in my creative practice looked at one of the things that animation can passably attempt to document: the subjective processes that unfold inside someone else's head. In order to represent such subject matter, one might imagine that collaboration could be necessary. Therefore, I have been thinking about the idea of 'the collaborative frame' within an animated documentary context. What is it? Why would we need one? How would we use it and produce film work within it?

The works this chapter discusses in terms of the collaborative frame are films that Paul Wells (1998: 122) describes as being in the 'penetrative' mode: 'penetration', he argues, 'is essentially a revelatory tool, used to reveal conditions or principles which are hidden or beyond the comprehension of the viewer'. On a closely related note, Annabelle Honess Roe describes animated documentary used in this way as 'evoking' (2013: 25) a particular state of mind precisely in order to express the 'world in here' (ibid.: 106). Working with this critical context in mind the films discussed in this chapter all attempt to use animation as a vehicle to communicate the internal experience of their human documentary subjects rather than that of the filmmaker themselves. The films deal with different kinds of internal experiences, but all endeavour to achieve a collaborative approach to their documentary gathering, authentication and communication of their subjects' experiences: from being an artist with Down's syndrome to having synaesthesia.

In my filmmaking practice the collaborative nature of what goes on inside the frame, and how to develop a methodology which supports that collaboration, is something that increasingly interests me. On one level, my work in nonfiction animation has always included aspects of collaboration with the

Figure 12.1 Still from *doubled up* (2004)

film's human subjects by simple necessity. For example, *doubled up* (2004), a film about multiple births, was autobiographical and included rotoscoped images of my twin sons, as well as images made by them, their voices, and the voice of Jane Denton, head of the Multiple Births Foundation at Queen Charlotte's Hospital, London (Figure 12.1). The images (paintings, collages and mark-making) that my sons had made were included in the film's visuals in order to underscore the verbal contribution my children made to the work's soundtracvk, and also to include them and their images in the film's pictorial layering. This was so not least because the film itself was about the layers of roles and identity present within the artistic process. However, it was not until I made my film *An Eyeful of Sound* (2010) that I really began to address what it meant to explicitly collaborate with human subjects on the outcome of a nonfiction animated film in its entirety, not just on an aural contribution to the film's soundtrack.

What is the Problem?

Much animation is primarily defined by its visuals, relying far less on the aural: as Brian Wells (2011: 15) argues, if you watch a silent animated film it is immediately clear which general order of cinematic form you are looking at. Documentary, however, relies more heavily on the spoken word; as Bill Nichols points out (1991: 20), it is hard to watch a silent live-action documentary and still grasp the work's intended message and meaning because elements like context and content are mainly communicated through the soundtrack. Animated documentary as a developing film subgenre has tended to default to a production and aesthetic model that is irrevocably led by sound (the 'animated interview', as Gunnar Strøm [2005: 15] terms it), thus relegating the visual to a constrained role, merely offering illustrative service to the communication of aural material. In his examination of the ways in which comics work, Scott McCloud calls this hierarchical arrangement a 'word-specific combination' (1994: 153), wherein pictures illustrate elements of a text but do not add up to a complete language contribution to that text.

In addition to the above consideration, we also need to remember that the process of mediating between a lived experience and a moving image representation of it is a form of translation. Walter Benjamin (1923) argues that the two main concepts which govern the necessarily imperfect and inevitably transformational process of translation are 'fidelity' and 'licence'. These terms are helpful to appropriate for consideration of the translation of a subjective perception into moving image form. If such a translation displays too much fidelity, if it is too rigidly faithful to its original, it can demolish the latter's meaning entirely: for example, by tautologically visualising the contents of the soundtrack in a given animated documentary at the cost of viewer understanding of the wider possible meanings of that aural material. Conversely if too much license is taken within a translation of this kind and the image departs too radically from the intrinsic characteristics of its documentary source then the delicate chimerical balance of translation, the 'documentary guarantee' (Takahashi 2011:231), is disrupted and the film struggles to maintain its claim to constitute a recognisable representation of some aspect of reality.

When making nonfiction animation that specifically represents another person's internal experience, the image itself can therefore become a problematic area. After all, the filmmaker engaged in such a documentary project typically attempts to represent frequently non-visual experiences such as emotional and/or physical feeling and sensation, sensory perceptions, or lack thereof. When making a film of this nature, do you replicate a live-action documentary talking head-style visual aesthetic? If so, then why bother to animate your work at all? Do you attempt to visualise linguistic metaphors, even though these may themselves be inadequate verbal substitutes for your human documentary subjects' somatic experiences and the formers' attempts to describe and share the latter with you and your eventual audience? Do you choose to visually illustrate exactly what your subjects happened to say on the given day that you interviewed them? If so, are you really representing what those subjects meant? Such questions relate to the phenomenon that Benjamin (1923) terms the *'intentio'* in the context of translation: namely, the translator (or, in this essay's case, the animated documentary filmmaker's) attempt to conceive and execute their creative intervention 'not as reproduction', but rather, as a discourse that acts '[in] harmony' with the original material that is translated.

Animated documentary can be a potent cinematic genre and tool when filmmakers aim to develop present a 'subjective' (Wells 1997: 40) or 'evocative' (Honess Roe 2013: 25) documentary mode, often within an autobiographical or biographical context. Animated documentary can also be a convincing creative solution when making what Honess-Roe (ibid.: 23) calls a 'mimetic substitution' for footage of someone or something that would be impossible to capture in any way other than by re-making and re-presenting it at some point and/or in some place after its original historical occurrence. But when an indexical soundtrack within which a human documentary subject describes aspects of their subjective experience is combined with a referential animated image track, then the role of the filmmaker in choosing what to present to (and privilege for) their audience can become dangerously blurred. Bill Nichols's argument that 'the distinctive formulation of the camera's (and filmmaker's) presence as absence, so common to classic narrative, poses problems of a peculiar nature in documentary' (1991: 89) is amplified in the case of much animated documentary work. This is so because what might be termed a 'double absence' arguably characterises such films: not only the filmmaker but also the film's human subject is simultaneously present in, yet absent from, the frame. How, therefore, can the viewer know whether or not the animated imagery they see is mediated beyond all recognition from whatever was the human documentary subject's original intent at the point(s) in time when they were being interviewed by the filmmaker? Kees Driessen (2007) points out that animated documentary offers the filmmaker the opportunity to add 'extra information about reality' to the frame. Given, however, the above-described possible drawbacks and/or qualifications to that opportunity, it seems worthwhile to explore further some of the processes related to this information's origins and the creative processes by which it is created and/or collected.

WHAT DO I MEAN BY A COLLABORATIVE FRAME?

The term 'collaboration' is a meaningful one for a great deal of contemporary filmmaking. Perhaps most familiarly and visibly, the collaborative ideal resonates in the context of crowd funding (as used, for example, to finance Franny Armstrong's feature documentary *The Age of Stupid* [2009]). It is also worth noting, however, that certain contemporary films have also, or instead, used collaborative methods and mechanisms in order to generate plot and ideas (as in, for example, Samuel Torssonen's Finnish *Star Wreck* series [1992–2005]). In this latter context, the idea of collaboration is intrinsic to the narrative and audiovisual content of the frame. Extrapolating this idea to the context of animated documentary film practice, the type of film that the intrinsic collaborative approach would be most useful to is 'the subjective'. By this I mean films in which the documentary material in question is explicitly respected and represented as intrinsic to that person's perspective as a unique individual (in other words, something that can only be properly apprehended, in filmmaker Shira Avni's words, 'from the inside' [National Film Board of Canada 2009]). Therefore, what I refer to as 'the collaborative frame' that operates within animated documentary filmmaking of this kind is the antithesis of Strøm's above-noted 'animated interview' model, in which an indexical documentary soundtrack is recorded by the filmmaker with their interviewees, but is then taken away by the filmmaker in order to be animated by them alone without further reference to the 'subject' of the work. In contrast, the collaborative methodology that I have developed in order to make my films is a model adapted from ethnographer Luke Eric Lassiter (2005)'s 'collaborative ethnography', taking some of Lassiter's key ideas – such as *transparency*, *collaboration* and *dialogue* – as concepts that can be usefully adapted to and applied within an animated documentary filmmaking context. It is worth briefly explaining the terms of that adaptation-cum-application before proceeding further.

Lassiter's privileging of the principle of transparency resonates within my own filmmaking practice because, when developing the collaborative methodology that now structures it, I realised that it is imperative that my films' 'collaborative consultants' (that is, their human documentary subjects) have a clear understanding of a given film project's goals and scope, and also of their contributory role within these. Firstly, animation is very often a convoluted technical process and, therefore, non-animators generally possess only an incomplete understanding of what animation processes can and do involve. Additionally, the deliberately dialogic nature of my collaborative methodology means that collaborative consultants come to play a much more active role in the animated filmmaking process than they may initially realise. Secondly, it is important that lines of communication are open between all the parties concerned in the production of a given film and that it is clear to all from the outset that ethical guidelines are being followed. In the case of my doctoral study, this was ensured via a mutually signed ethics agreement (provided by the University of Loughborough). Having an agreement of some kind is an important part of establishing trust and lines of communication between filmmaker and collaborators, and can be helpful to both parties in spelling out the parameters of a project.

Lassiter points out (2005: 16) that collaboration is inherent within all ethnography. To a certain extent, the same is true of filmmaking. More specifically, in my own filmmaking practice collaboration is central, not incidental, to the creation of individual film works. My preferred definition of a collaborative frame for the filmmaking process is one within which the collaborative consultants of my documentary interviews also have an opportunity to help devise the animated images that we produce in response to our cumulative conversations. By drawing a given film's animated imagery themselves and/or having a given film's animated imagery based on either their own drawings or verbal descriptions of visual imagery, my collaborators take part in the incremental revision of a given animated documentary project's material through dialogue. In turn, that idea and material process of dialogue forms the final component to the adapted collaborative filmmaking model that I develop from Lassiter's ethnographic work. Dialogue refers to the range of opportunities I provide for a given film's human subjects to feedback, comment on and discuss the various ways in which that film's visual imagery is developed.

For my PhD study (Moore 2015), I used the above-described collaborative methodology with a group of people with phantom limb syndrome (that is, the continued perception of sensations, including pain, in a limb that has previously been amputated). The dialogic process led to unexpected discoveries both for the facilitator (me as the filmmaker) and their collaborative consultants (the subjects of my film work). For example, using a semi-structured interview model (Wengraf 2001: 5), and following a discussion of V. S. Ramachandran's work regarding remapping sensory input (see, for instance, Ramachandran and Altschuler 2009), one of my collaborative consultants, Dave, discovered that he had the ability to enlarge his phantom foot until it encapsulated his entire body. This was an experience that Dave had never had before, and it resulted entirely from the discourse between us during our first semi-structured interview (a roughly two-hour discussion that represented the start of our collaborative process). The subsequent process of animating Dave's novel experience was done via email discussion. Dave tweaked and improved upon my initial visual suggestions until we had a version that he felt adequately represented his particular experience (Figure 12.2).

Turning attention now to other filmmakers who produce work in a similar fashion, animator Shira Avni has worked on collaborative animation within the Down's syndrome community since 2001. She has described how working in this way allows both a voice and a substantive sense of creative empowerment to be given to an often-ignored community. Avni says (Avni et al. 2011) of her 2009 film *Tying Your Own Shoes* that it: 'provides a forum for [a] group of artists with Down syndrome to portray themselves as they wish to be seen, through their own voices and artwork, rather than through the usual filters – family, caregivers, teachers, or the medical community'. Similarly, Tim Webb has described how his 1992 animated documentary

Figure 12.2 The collaborative process of visualising Dave's enormous phantom foot

short *A is for Autism* (which is subtitled 'A Collaboration') was commissioned by British broadcaster Channel 4 largely on the basis of its collaborative approach to the production of the work itself. But, he says:

> Finding artists and other collaborators who wanted to be involved was quite difficult to start with due to [the difficulty of] finding professionals and societies willing to help and support the project's aims . . . This resulted in the decision to have one true animation collaborator, Daniel Sellers [the nine-year-old boy who contributed many drawings and detailed animation sequences of trains to the film]. (Webb 2011)

Returning to my own practice, my 2010 film *An Eyeful of Sound* involved collaborating with people with audiovisual synaesthesia. A range of people with this condition were interviewed about their synaesthetic responses, and played sounds and asked to describe, draw and identify the exact colours of their synaesthetic reactions to those sonic stimuli. This practice used a Munsell color chart (that is, the colour ordering system first developed by Albert H. Munsell in the very early twentieth century, which specifies colours based on three distinct dimensions: hue, value [that is, lightness] and chroma [that is, colour purity]). The methodology was developed in collaboration with consulting cognitive neuroscientist Jamie Ward (Ward 2008: 129). As the process of animating our sample of synaesthetes' reactions progressed (through an alternating production/discussion of still images, animated images, composited frames and the final edit) they had the opportunity to alter, inform and ultimately veto the proposed animated documentary representation of their experience (Figure 12.3).

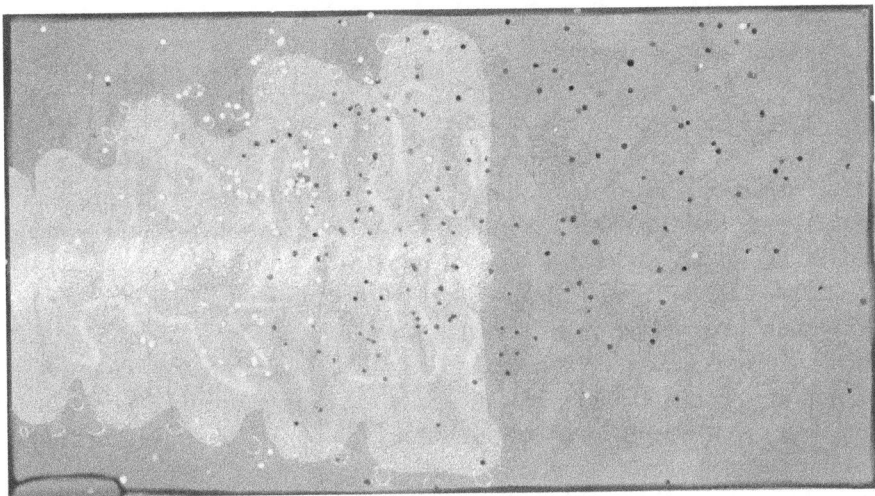

Figure 12.3 Still from *An Eyeful of Sound* (2010), depicting a consensually agreed animated visual depiction of consulting collaborator Tessa's synaesthetic reaction to the sound of a harp scale

An Eyeful of Sound was the trigger for my interest in a sustained investigation and testing of the collaborative frame methodology's serviceability via a course of doctoral study. My PhD dissertation (Moore 2015) deliberately worked with individuals living with unusual non-visual perceptual brain states; either prosopagnosia, the developmental or acquired brain state where a person cannot retain recognition of faces (more commonly known as 'face blindness'), or with phantom limb syndrome. There are two types of prosopagnosia: acquired and congenital. Acquired is usually the result of a traumatic brain event and their prosopagnosia can be extreme in its manifestation. Congenital, or developmental, prosopagnosia is experienced from birth and tends to be milder, so a person may not even be aware they have it (although they will not be able to recognise faces as easily as their neurotypical peers). Congenital prosopagnosia is thought to be much more common than initially thought (Duchaine and Nakayama, 2006), although very severe cases of this type are extremely rare. Phantom limb syndrome refers to kinaesthetic sensations of limbs after they have been amputated. This induces very specific and vivid perception that the missing limb is still there, and sometimes severe accompanying pain. Documentation of the existence of phantom limb syndrome goes back to the sixteenth century (Ramachandran, 1998: 22), although, in common with other internally experienced brain states (synaesthesia, for example), the condition was not taken seriously for a great length of time after its existence was first reported. These brain states seemed like especially interesting and challenging ones to document through animation because visual referents for the symptoms and sensations that sufferers describe are often conspicuous by their absence.

WHY WOULD YOU USE A COLLABORATIVE FRAME?

On a basic level, the use of a collaborative frame methodology in filmmaking practice attempts to collapse some of the hierarchies inherent in classically conceived documentary production processes. Robert Coles (1998: 83) quotes, for example, one documentary photographer's guilt regarding the potentially exploitative power balance they understood to be inherent to their creative role and identity: 'we do our "documentary work", and we get recognition, and we build our lives up, our careers – and they [the human subjects of our documentary photographs], there's nothing in it for them.' Similarly, the maker of a documentary film, animated or otherwise, can record an interview with their human subject (and/or re-purpose existing audio), take that material away and subsequently use it in whatever way best suits their concept of the work-in-progress without any further consultation with the subject. Sociologist Gary Alan Fine terms this the 'slash and burn' (1999: 533) approach to documentary practice. But by filmmakers using a collaborative frame, the collaborative consultant represented has the opportunity to contribute to the work beyond provision of their audio testimony, entering into a dialogic process with the filmmaker and shifting from a passive ('subject') to active ('collaborative consultant') role within the creative process.

Another key reason for filmmakers to use a collaborative frame methodology involves the latter's capacity to assist in process of externally visualising documentary phenomena that are, either in large part or in whole, internally experienced by human beings. The films this essay examines, for example, all either portray a different human *perspective* on the world (Avni's *Tying Your Own Shoes*) or a different human *perception* of the world (Webb's *A is for Autism*, my own *An Eyeful of Sound* and *Out of Sight* [2015] PhD project). Those perspectives or perceptions change the ways in which these films' human subjects are cognisant of the world around them. Animation's visual plasticity as a visual medium, and, paradoxically, its long association with imagination and the fantastic, can be exploited within the documentary genre to make visually explicit a range of different forms of idiopathic processing. *A is for Autism*, for example, uses metamorphosis between images to delicately point to central character Daniel's obsessive drawings of a train from the same angle. *Tying Your Own Shoes* used extensive workshopping processes to allow the subject-cum-artists involved to animate distillations of their recollections and impressions of their lives. In *An Eyeful of Sound*, the animation was used more straightforwardly, since it was employed precisely to present a visualisation of what people with synaesthesia see and the rest of us do not. My collaborative consultants' synaesthetic reactions were an externally imperceptible (yet tangible) sensation that they could verify as easily as someone else might check the colour of their socks, since the synaesthetes only needed to re-experience a specific sound in order to have exactly the same perceptual response to it. As mentioned above, my doctoral research chose to study the brain states of phantom limb syndrome and prosopagnosia, and their characteristic lack of a visual component was chosen precisely in order to further analyse just how far the collaborative cycle methodology could be stretched within animated documentary filmmaking practice. Because phantom limb syndrome is a kinaesthetic sense and prosopagnosia involves a *lack* of visual referencing, the moving image work produced through collaborations with consultants who have these conditions became much more reliant on the former's analogical descriptions of the latter. Strøm's 'illustrated radio interview' animated documentary methodology might attempt to show a director's interpretative perception of their subject's words but, ultimately, unless subjects themselves are invited into the frame of creative making then any resultant film will remain a third-person reinterpretation uncomfortably reliant on the verbal articulacy of the person interviewed.

In my opinion, animated documentary work becomes more meaningful when any given film strikes a fully considered balance between telling and showing, by allowing the work's visual components to transcend the position of illustrative adjunct to an indexical soundtrack. In the various films this chapter references, for example, I argue that the fact that human subjects (that is, collaborative consultants) also made a significant contribution to the respective works' visual content enhances and strengthens those works' documentary claims to be authentic representations of the human experiences they variously depict. The collectively animated image is a negotiated and collaborative form of visual outcome (Figure 12.4). As such, its potential integrity as a respectful, accurate and authentic representation of the human experience or perspective that it attempts to depict is very often, in my opinion, at least as relevant and productive as the (often single-point) perspective of possible photographic equivalents. Of course, these two documentary image types are emphatically not mutually exclusive. My point here, however, is that over-emphasis and reliance on an ideal of photographic indexicality can represent a creative and ethical dead end for any documentary film attempt at accurate communication of phenomena that cannot readily be physically observed and recorded on film (such as, within my own practice, audiovisual synaesthesia and other brain states).

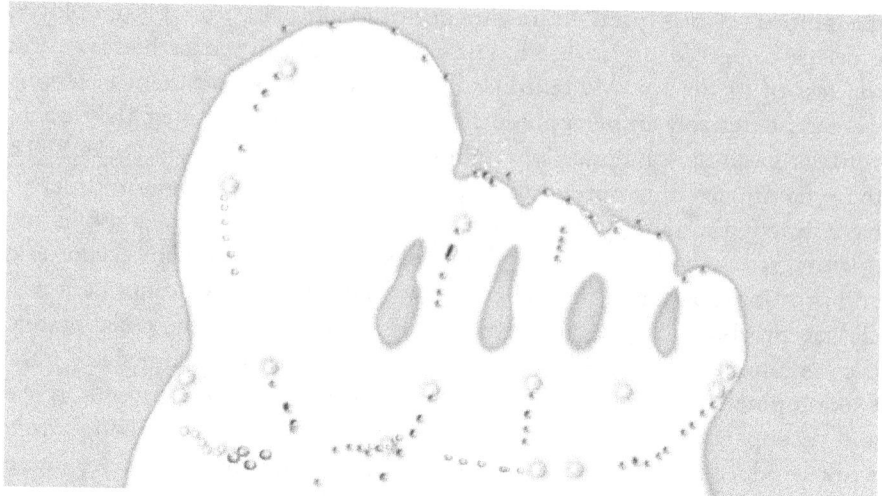

Figure 12.4 Still image from *Out of Sight* of Stephen's fizzy foot: an analogical visual description of the 'bubbles' inside his phantom limb

HOW CAN WE WORK WITHIN THE COLLABORATIVE FRAME?

As noted above, my doctoral creative practice explores how the perceptual brain states of prosopagnosia and phantom limb syndrome can be documented through animation. I attempted to examine, assess and elucidate my methodology for creating the collaborative frame, informed by my previous filmmaking work. This is what Lassiter (2005: 16) calls a move from 'incidental and conditional collaboration to the building of a more deliberate and explicit' collaborative practice. My research work encompassed a cycle of interviews, image-making, animation and feedback with six collaborative consultants over an extended period of time (three years). The entire process is too extensive to describe in detail here, but one of the crucial tasks in setting up a collaborative cycle was a transparent feedback process that included making collaborators aware of the depth and range of feedback I required from them. Lassiter (ibid.: 77) cites 'honesty about the fieldwork process' as being one of the cornerstones of collaborative ethnography, as well as 'ethical and moral responsibility to consultants ... accessible and dialogic writing ... collaborative reading, writing and co-interpretation of ethnographic texts with consultants'. My adaptation of Lassiter's methodology to frame-by-frame moving image practice brings its own set of interpretative challenges. Working within a collaborative frame has drawbacks. It is time-consuming (and therefore expensive). It requires a comprehensive understanding from collaborators on all sides of the processes involved and can be frustrating, since it relies on disparate opinions being balanced to make a whole. It can also mean a simplification of the animation production process. Shira Avni, for example, has spoken about the usual production pipeline of animation being hard to translate when working with non-professional animation artists. In *Tying Your Own Shoes* she worked without storyboard or animatic because those pre-production concepts and tools were hard to convey to the artists she was working with. Eventually the rhythm, style and pace of her collaborators' working methods dictated the ways in which her own and their material was gathered and made (National Film Board of Canada 2009; Avni et al. 2011).

Tim Webb also acknowledges, with regard to *A is for Autism*, the problem of collaborating in this way with a larger group of people: 'to have more than one animation collaboration would have resulted in missed deadlines' (Webb 2011). Webb's point is an interesting one because working collaboratively potentially opens the director up to a great many opinions, perspectives and directions that may be hard to accommodate into the production schedule for a broadcast production. Use of a semi-structured interview model could threaten to overwhelm an animated documentary filmmaker with data and possible avenues for investigation. There is also the issue that, if the collaborative consultant's role is moved from that of passive to active collaborator, there may be a concomitant shift in the filmmaker's role: from active 'director' to passive 'facilitator' during the collaborative cycle process. This may prove problematic when the active directorial role is reinstated by the filmmaker in order to reach the final edit of the film.

At this point, it may be helpful to differentiate between two interrelated (but distinct) concepts: the *document* (the collected data from which a film is made) and the *documentary* (the resulting film itself). My doctoral study *Out of Sight* was a series of animated documents made using the collaborative methodology. However, if that material were to be made into a completed short film, there would be a shift in the hierarchical structure of the production process. *Out of Sight*'s documents are made for the collaborative consultants, but any subsequent unitary documentary film is made for a broader outside audience. A final edit represents the decisive conclusion of the material: what to show and what to leave out has been unequivocally decided, even if done so in conversation with collaborators. Shira Avni has talked (Avni et al. 2011) about the dilemma of the final edit when faced with so much material to potentially include: should one cut for clarity (for a film's external audience) or for authenticity (for one's filmmaking participants)? Whatever the eventual decision made, this power remains with the named director. In that sense, collaboration dissolves at this point as the role of facilitator gives way to the more autocratic one of director. Even if (as with *An Eyeful of Sound* and *Tying Your Own Shoes*) collaborators have substantial input and final veto over the material to be included within the finished film, a range of fundamental creative choices (to do with filmic structure, clarity and context) still rest with the director.

CONCLUSION

A collaborative methodology in documentary animation presents several problems to prospective proponents of that practice. The already convoluted animation production process is extended further with the introduction of a dialogic 'collaborative cycle' methodology, which can make the production process protracted and expensive. Additionally, the very process of collaboration is predicated on all participants being equally invested in, and affected by, a given film project's successful conclusion. Collaboration, both as principle and practice, assumes an equal interest in such: but this is unlikely to be precisely the case in any given real-life instance. Finally, while Walter Benjamin's 'translation' model has been suggested as a productive to employ within the process of turning individual somatic experience into a screen-bound extrinsic version, the final cinematic result may always still constitute an imperfect interpretative rendering of an individually unique human experience.

But despite these drawbacks, the collaborative frame process can be a fascinating and useful exercise in communication for all involved. In an April 2012 email about one animation clip, *Out of Sight* collaborator Stephen said that:

> I find this project very interesting, and one reason it is interesting is that it is to some extent quite mysterious. Phantom sensations are mysterious in themselves, and communicating them is not an easy thing to do ... apart from talking to you, I never really attempt to describe it to anyone, assuming most people would have only the tiniest interest!

Animation as a vehicle for documentary translation possesses qualities which can prove useful in developing rapport. For example, animation is for many people associated with childhood and thus seen as unthreatening. It is also slow and iterative in its production process, which allows for dialogue between filmmaking collaborators to develop and mature. Lastly, it is not confrontational or intrusive in its production methods. These qualities may make it advantageous to the developing of long-term collaborative relationships within documentary filmmaking contexts.

Of course, the collaborative cycle may always be a marginal documentary methodology because of the involved and protracted production commitment that it necessitates. Lassiter's methodology (which, as noted above, my cinematic equivalent was adapted from) has not had a wide impact on the field of ethnography. His perspective on why his collaborative model has not been better received within his own discipline is that it is too disruptive of academic hierarchy because there is an abridgement of academic complexity for the sake of greater shared understanding by prospective collaborators:

> Perhaps collaborative ethnographies linger at the margins because they do not engender the same kind of authority, prestige, and recognition as the texts we explicitly write for our academic colleagues; or perhaps they remain at the margins because our interlocutors' constructions of culture differ too profoundly from the academy's instructions of culture. (Lassiter 2005: 13)

The collaborative cycle methodology opens new ways of working and broadens the scope of the contemporary animated documentary field, which may have become too formulaic and constrained in its structure due to an over-reliance on the aural as documentary source and guarantor of documentary authority. While my own doctoral studies are now concluded, the wider application of their main conceptual and practice-based formulations is not. I continue to wrestle with a collaborative frame methodology; most recently in the production of *Loop* (2016), an Animate Projects commission supported by the Wellcome Trust and made working in collaboration with microbiologist Serge Mostowy at Imperial College London. Here the collaborative cycle was used to express each research scientist's perspective of the central scientific concern of the lab: septin cages and how they assemble. I do not claim to have achieved the definitive version of this methodology; however, I think that if animated documentary is going to prove meaningful and sustainable we need to look more carefully at its potential to make unique contributions within nonfiction filmmaking contexts. My suggestion here is that the collaborative frame, both as a guiding concept and as a materially executed form of creative practice, may represent one useful place from which to engage in that process.

Acknowledgements

In researching this aspect of making animated documentaries I am indebted to film makers Shira Avni and Tim Webb, both of whom have been generous in sharing insights into how they have gone about grappling with the issues I am discussing here.

Bibliography

A is for Autism, film, directed by Tim Webb. UK: Fine Take Productions and Channel 4, 1992.
The Age of Stupid, film, directed by Franny Armstrong. UK: Spanner Films, 2009.
An Eyeful of Sound, film, directed by Samantha Moore. Canada/Netherlands/UK: Sapiens Productions and Wellcome Trust, 2010.

Avni, Shira, Ann Fudge Schormans, Adele Iannantuono, Petra Tolley and Chris Tolley (2011), '*Tying Your Own Shoes*: one film, four perspectives', *Journal on Developmental Disabilities*, 17: 1, <http://www.oadd.org/docs/41009_JoDD_17-1_83-92_Avni_et_al.pdf> (last accessed 21 October 2016).

Benjamin, Walter (1923), 'The task of the translator', <http://www.ricorso.net/rx/library/criticism/guest/Benjamin_W/Benjamin_W1.htm> (last accessed 21 October 2016).

Coles, Robert (1998), *Doing Documentary Work*, Oxford: Oxford University Press.

doubled up, film, directed by Samantha Moore. UK: Animate!, Finetake, Arts Council of England and Channel 4, 2004.

Driessen, Kees (2007), 'More than just talking mice', *IDFA Magazine*, <www.idfa.nl/.../More%20than%20just%20talking%20mice%20(Paul%20Fierlinger).pdf> (last accessed 27 April 2011).

Duchaine, Bradley C. and Ken Nakayama (2006), 'Developmental prosopagnosia: a window to content-specific face processing', *Current Opinion in Neurobiology*, 16: 2, pp. 166–73.

Fine, Gary Alan (1999), 'Field labor and ethnographic reality', *Journal of Contemporary Ethnography*, 28: 5, pp. 532–39.

Honess Roe, Annabelle (2013), *Animated Documentary*, London: Palgrave Macmillan.

Lassiter, Luke Eric (2005), *The Chicago Guide to Collaborative Ethnography*, Chicago: University of Chicago Press.

Loop, film, directed by Samantha Moore. UK: Animate Projects and the Wellcome Trust, 2016.

McCloud, Scott (1994), *Understanding Comics*, New York: William Morrow Paperbacks.

Moore, Samantha (2015), *Out of Sight: Using Animation to Document Perceptual Brain States*, unpublished PhD dissertation, Loughborough University.

National Film Board of Canada (2009), *Tying Your Own Shoes*, <http://www3.nfb.ca/sg/100590.pdf> (last accessed 21 October 2016).

Nichols, Bill (1991), *Representing Reality*, Bloomington: Indiana University Press.

Ramachandran, V. S. (1998), *Phantoms in the Brain*, 3rd edn, London: Fourth Estate.

Ramachandran, V. S. and Eric L. Altschuler (2009), 'The use of visual feedback, in particular mirror visual feedback', *Brain*, 132: 7, pp. 1693–710.

Star Wreck, film series, directed by Samuel Torssonen et al. Finland: ST Films et al., 1992–2005.

Strøm, Gunnar (2005), 'How Swede it is . . . ', *fps Magazine*, March, <http://www.fpsmagazine.com/mag/2005/03/fps200503lo.pdf > (last accessed 21 October 2016).

Takahashi, Tess (2011), 'Experiments in documentary animation: anxious borders, speculative media', *animation: an interdisciplinary journal*, 6: 3, pp. 231–45.

Tying Your Own Shoes, film, directed by Shira Avni. Canada: National Film Board of Canada, 2009.

Ward, Jamie (2008), *The Frog Who Croaked Blue: Synaesthesia and the Mixing of the Senses*, London: Routledge.

Webb, Tim (2011), Personal email communication with the author

Wells, Brian (2011), 'Frame of reference: toward a definition of animation', *Animation Practice, Process & Production*, 1: 1, pp. 11–32.

Wells, Paul (1997), 'The beautiful village and the true village: a consideration of animation and the documentary aesthetic', in Paul Wells (ed.), *Art and Animation*, London: Academy Editions, pp. 40–5.

Wells, Paul (1998), *Understanding Animation*, London: Routledge.

Wengraf, Tom (2001), *Qualitative Research Interviewing: Biographic Narrative and Semi-Structured Methods*, London: SAGE.

CHAPTER 13

Creative Challenges in the Production of Documentary Animation

Sheila M. Sofian

INTRODUCTION

A question raised by the use of animation in documentary filmmaking is: Does the use of animation reveal the filmmaking process in a more overt fashion than live-action methods? Customarily in the production of traditional live-action documentaries, the filmmaker does not reveal the crew behind the camera. Often, the interviewer asking the questions is not shown or heard, and the viewer is not privy to whatever footage is left unused on the cutting room floor. The filmmaking process is somewhat undetectable and self-effacing in these instances. However, in the production of an animated documentary it is obvious that the animator is entirely responsible for creating the image that is displayed on the screen. There is no illusion of 'reality'. However, this lack of apparent realism is sometimes confused with a lack of truth.

It has been widely argued that all documentaries are required to introduce evidence on screen in order to make their viewpoints rationalised and known. Some animated documentaries, including my own, provide evidentiary documentation in the form of a documentary audio track. The use of animation in documentary assumes that the viewer does not require photographic evidence, and the animation does not attempt to use the image to represent reality. Animation therefore challenges the audience's perception of 'documentary'. Live action may often be perceived as being a more impartial documentary mode, a 'pure' unadulterated recording of reality as it unfolded, when in fact the very nature of the filmmaking process ultimately allows the filmmaker to manipulate what audiences perceive as reality and shape it according to the filmmaker's agenda. One could argue, therefore, that the use of animation is in some ways more transparent, more 'honest' than the use of live action in that it does not conceal the filmmaker's control over the media. Since the filmmaker's hand is plainly visible, the viewer is presented with an obvious construct: there is no disguising the filmmaker's manipulation of the imagery. Animator Orly Yadin makes this same point when she states: 'The honesty of animation lies in the fact that the filmmaker is completely upfront about [their] intervention with the subject and if we believe the film to be true it is because we believe the intention was true' (Yadin 2003).

Animation can portray a wide variety of realistic and unrealistic scenarios. As *Waltz with Bashir* (2008) director Ari Folman states, animation gave him the creative freedom to move from one dimension to another while constructing his autobiographical documentary narrative: 'from reality to dreams to subconscious issues to hallucinations to drug influences to war, which is probably the most surreal thing on earth' (NPR 2008). This statement illustrates some of the possibilities present in animation's use in documentary filmmaking contexts: the animator is limited only by his or her imagination. This chapter describes my own animation works and experience, focusing on the creative process and varied choices that a documentary filmmaker engaging with animation must consider.

It is true that an animator has the ability to shape each and every frame of a film in order to guide the audience in whatever direction the filmmaker desires. Perhaps animation therefore amplifies the filmmaker's connection with their audience. In my case, I draw the images I visualise in my mind, thus forcing the viewer to observe scenes in the same way as I do. As such, animation can be an extremely visceral and expressive visual medium. This manipulation is also possible in live action, but perhaps the connection between maker and viewer in live action is less direct than it is in animation. Because live-action documentary cinematography consists of the language of real-world imagery, it is not required to shape the images to the same extent as animation does. The use of animation allows the filmmaker to expose their audience to a more personalized subjective viewpoint. Whether analogue or computer-generated, animated imagery is constructed from scratch as the filmmaker envisions it. This fact could be seen as an advantage. All filmmaking is manipulative to some degree. All films, whether animated or live action, have some form of authorial agenda. It is important to clarify that it has not been my goal within my animated documentary filmmaking to attempt to create an 'impartial' film. As a filmmaker, I am interested in the creative reasons to choose animation over live action in documentary filmmaking. To my mind, the main reasons are as follows: to elicit greater empathy with the film's subject; to effectively illustrate the subject's point of view; to add additional information about a given film's documentary subject matter through use of animation. These and other uses of animation for documentary purposes will be discussed through an analysis of my own animated documentary works since the 1980s.

Figure 13.1   Still from *Mangia!* (1985)

PERSONAL PERSPECTIVES

I began my studies in animation at the Rhode Island School of Design (RISD), where I majored in Film/Video/Animation. My first attempt at creating a short nonfiction animation was the production of my senior film, *Mangia!* (1985) (Figure 13.1). *Mangia!* was a five-minute film based on my own experience as an American student living with an Italian family, a light-hearted animation centred around the dinner table. I did not think of this film as a documentary, due to the fact that I did not record documentary audio interviews. Instead, I scripted the film's dialogue based on my real-life experiences and then recorded the voices of the actual individuals involved (the Italian family I lived with), who were then represented as animated characters in the film. I have since come to think of this film as a form of documentary, due to the tradition of re-enactment in live-action documentary productions, which, arguably, is not so very different from animated visualisations of past events.

As was the case in *Mangia!*, animation is often used in documentary when there is no photographic record of an event that a filmmaker wishes to document in some way. Animation is also frequently used in order to depict personal perspectives of an event being documented. In an effort to recreate, based on my own recollections, the experience of living with an Italian family, I used painting-on-glass animation. I feel this specific medium has a particular ability to capture the concept of 'memory', due to its use of painted transitions and watery dissolves. Painting-on-glass animation involves the photographing of individual paintings on glass or Plexiglas. In my case, paintings were made using tempera paint mixed with glycerine in order to keep the paint wet while animating. After the painting has been rendered, a photograph of it is taken. The painting is then modified in order to create the film's next frame and re-photographed. Each previous frame of original artwork is destroyed in the creation of the next frame throughout the animation process. As a result, the painted images melt into one another and thus resemble fading memories.

I staged *Mangia!* from the first-person perspective of the film's central protagonist (myself), often showing the characters interacting with the camera. All of the scenes in the film were based on experiences that had originally occurred in real life. I interpreted these moments as I remembered them. I exaggerated scenes that had particularly impacted on me, such as the dinner table conversation, the making of ravioli, and the continuous offering of food. During the film's mealtime sequences, images of food fill the screen and the layered sound crescendos as overlapping dialogue and the clatter of dinner plates and glasses combine to create a lively atmosphere. My hope was that, through this combination of layered images and sound, *Mangia!*'s audience could share in my experience and understand the warmth and kind gestures I experienced as a foreigner in Italy.

In 1990, while a graduate student in the Experimental Animation Program at the California Institute of the Arts (CalArts), I directed, produced and animated *Faith & Patience* (Figure 13.2), an animated documentary about a four-year-old girl, Patience, who was adjusting to the arrival of her newborn sister, Faith. *Faith & Patience* consists of an unscripted audio interview in which Patience describes her connection with her *Transformer* doll, a connection that appears to parallel her relationship with her newborn sister. A portion of the film was shot in live action, which I then used as

Figure 13.2 Still from *Faith & Patience*

the basis for rotoscoping. Rotoscoping is a technique in which live-action photography is traced (in *Faith & Patience*'s case, on paper) frame-by-frame in order to imitate realistic motion. This technique allows the animator to imitate live-action photography, resulting in an accurate representation of a character's physical expressions and mannerisms. The filmmaker can extract the specific portion of the original photographic image that they choose to highlight, and remove unwanted backgrounds and details that are often unavoidably present in live-action images. Some animated documentary filmmakers prefer the use of rotoscoping in order to provide a more faithful depiction of an original interview. In the case of *Faith & Patience*, I chose this technique in order to capture the more subtle behavioural nuances of the main character, Patience.

As a filmmaker, I was intrigued by the idea that Patience's world would dramatically change with the introduction of a new sister into her life. My documentary goal was to capture the manner in which Patience coped with this change. Through a combination of sweet gestures towards her 'Robot Baby' doll (a *Transformer* toy), including burping and diaper changing, Patience seems to be adapting to the idea of a new baby in the family. However, when asked who Robot Baby's mother is her adamant response is: 'No one!' Patience does not want to be given the title of 'Robot Mommy', and at the end of the film she admits that she prefers to be the youngest child.

I think that in the case of *Faith & Patience*, use of animation allows the audience to perceive the film's documentary moments in a natural and intimate manner (and, perhaps, in some way from a child's more fanciful perspective). Use of live action instead would potentially have created a more detached, clinical viewing experience. As an animator, I had the ability to select specific parts of the originally recorded live-action frame to illustrate and remove extraneous content from. In addition, the filmic design, technique and staging of the film's animation and the live-action footage I used as a basis for that animation (camera angle, point of view, distance of camera from recorded subject) all play a role in how the audience perceives scenes within the work. The film's final sequence utilises xerography (photocopied frames printed on paper from a live-action shoot). I took these xeroxed frames, animated abstract lines and shapes on top of each one, and then re-photographed them in sequence. The result is a combination of reality-based live action and fanciful, abstract animation. All of these factors combine to create a childlike vernacular that softens the manner in which the audience interprets *Faith & Patience*. My documentary use of animation therefore enabled me to form an additional layer of meaning within this film work.

EMPATHY, ANONYMITY AND SIMPLIFICATION

After completing *Mangia!* and *Faith & Patience*, I then decided to resurrect an unfinished live-action documentary that I had begun years earlier while still a student at RISD and rework it as an animated film, titled *Survivors* (1997) (Figure 13.3). The subject matter was domestic violence: while working as a volunteer at a women's shelter I had interviewed and filmed victims of domestic violence and the counsellors who worked with them. Later I recorded additional interviews in Philadelphia. Similarly to *Mangia!*, use of animation in this case enabled the portrayal of events that were not filmed at the time of their occurrence. However, my decision to animate in this instance also introduced certain further advantages to using animation in nonfiction contexts. Because the majority of the people I interviewed preferred to remain anonymous, I had shot my live-action interviews in silhouette. This presented something of a dilemma: visually speaking, the resultant images were uninteresting and did nothing to illustrate the interviewees' testimony effectively. Years later, however, when I paired the audio interviews with animation I was free to interpret the survivors' stories in an expressive manner. Animation protected the identity of my human subjects while also allowing me to make visual additions to the information contained in the interviews with them. For instance, when an interviewee described a particular situation, I could imagine and illustrate what that scene had looked like from her point of view. When facts and statistics related to the subject of domestic violence were discussed by professionals working in the field, I could visualise these in

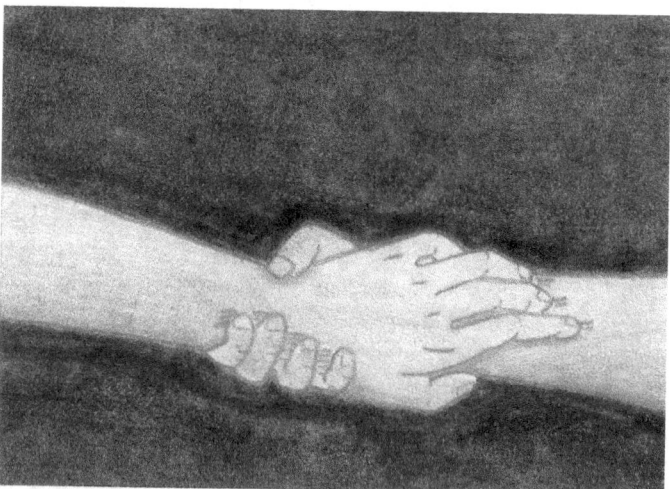

Figure 13.3 Still from *Survivors*

a manner that would hopefully increase the audience's understanding of the material. Throughout the film I utilised very slow and meditative transitions, trying to both respect and heighten the thoughtfulness of the interviewees' dialogue and creating a visual pause that encouraged the viewer to fully listen to the audio material and therefore comprehend its meaning without having to deal with the distraction of extraneous visual information.

Due to the labour-intensive nature of drawn animation, *Survivors* was in production for four years. I created over 10,000 drawings for this film, a fact that presented several creative challenges. Throughout the production process, I was concerned both with maintaining the consistency of the artwork while also preventing potential repetitiveness of the visuals. It was important to me that I continue to find new ways to illustrate the interviewees' interview material. I often found myself initially storyboarding new sequences in a manner similar to scenes already completed. I worried that this repetitive use of a particular visual style would become monotonous and prevent the film's audience from listening to its human subjects' stories as a fresh and important experience. I therefore continuously challenged myself to find new ways to present the information and would often serially rework my visual approach, striving for solutions that were unlike other images I already created. It was important to me to keep the audience engaged and to try to avoid any possible disconnect from the film's interview material.

Another strategy I employed was to not explicitly identify and distinguish each separate individual interviewed in *Survivors* from all the other interviewees. I did not illustrate each interviewee's voice with a specific consistent character design, and did not identify the person speaking with a title card. Not only did this strategy maintain the anonymity of the speakers, it also gave each scene a more universal context, rather than exclusively associating a particular line of dialogue with a particular person. Much of the film consisted of first-person point-of-view shots, visual metaphors, or nonspecific characters representing women in the situations interviewees described. In addition, the entire film consisted of a series of vignettes strung together only by the overarching subject matter of domestic violence. It was difficult to know if these strategies would be successful or if the audience would find the finished film too disjointed. After interviewing the subjects in *Survivors*, I transcribed all of the audio and then organised selected outtakes into chapters, which ultimately served as the basis of the film's twelve-part structure: Introduction; First time; Profiles; Physical abuse; Society's response; Mental abuse/Self-esteem; Control; Affection; Denial; Change; Leaving; and Epilogue.

There were several important lessons that I learned from the production and exhibition of *Survivors*. It was interesting to note the manner in (and extent to) which the use of animated imagery within the film connected with different people. For instance, there is one scene in which the speaker describes how her pastor told her that: 'God does not want people to be divorced. You must stay together and make it work. If you both believe in God, and you both go to church, you can make it work.' At this moment, a man and woman appear on screen facing each other. A cross materialises between them: its 'arms' stretch out and push the couple towards each other. After being crushed, the couple become entangled together in rope; the female member of the couple struggles, but cannot escape. This scene has resonated strongly with some viewers who connected with its religious material and metaphoric animated imagery. Since animation facilitates visualisations of documentary narrative content or metaphors, visual incorporation and interpretation of documentary information (in this specific case, my interviewee's story about her pastor's advice) adds meaning and has powerful spectatorial effects.

Another scene from *Survivors* that has affected audiences in particularly powerful and consistent ways occurs during a moment in which a counsellor, Brian Hanstock, describes how abusers will throw or break objects as a way to use these in order to intimidate someone. If they throw or break something, the clear message is: 'I can do this to you'. During the scene in question, a mug materialises. Cracks begin to appear and cover the mug; pieces of it fly apart. Such destruction of property is a form of abuse that many people have experienced: it is a 'threat' and not overt abuse. The image of the mug breaking into pieces, along with the audio explaining how this threat is a very real one, brings home to viewers the realisation that this type of behaviour is abusive.

I was surprised at how strongly viewers empathised with the people interviewed in *Survivors*. Several audience members have admitted to me after screenings of the film that its use of animation prevented them from judging the person speaking based on their appearance, since I did not reveal interviewees' images on camera. As a result, viewers identified with speakers in a more empathetic and open manner. In my opinion, when viewing a live-action interview with someone, you are partly distracted by that person's physical image and make judgements based on their appearance. With the use of animation set to an audio interview, the viewer is instead more immersed in the contents of the testimony and pays much closer attention to the testimony's substance because the physical appearance of the person testifying is not present to influence the viewer's opinions. In other words, if a viewer has a personal bias based on physical appearance, it will not manifest itself when the speaker's appearance has been simplified, through use of animation, to a more iconic representation of the human form.

Because we have a conditioned response to iconographic images, my opinion is that animation can utilise this tendency in order to encourage an unobstructed viewer response to the documentary material that is being depicted and communicated. As Scott McCloud states (1994: 30) in his graphic novel *Understanding Comics*:

> Cartoon [is] a form of amplification through simplification. When we abstract an image though cartooning we're not so much eliminating details as we are focusing on specific details. By stripping down an image to its essential meaning, an artist can amplify that meaning in a way that realistic art can't ... the more cartoony a face is, the more people it could be said to describe.

Survivors had a greater impact on audiences than I could have anticipated. I believe that the film's use of animation allowed for an easier audience consumption of a difficult documentary subject. The simplicity of the animated image does appear to relieve some of the harshness of the subject matter encountered and explored in many documentary films. I like to say that the use of animation for documentary purposes is akin to Mary Poppins's 'spoonful of sugar to help the medicine go down'. Not only does iconic imagery make difficult material more palatable, it also allows an enhanced level of identification as barriers between subject and viewer are diminished.

The use of animation in documentary also has the ability to illustrate and simplify complex ideas that might be more difficult to demonstrate in live action. Animator Paul Fierlinger states: 'With animation we can do more than describe reality, we can feed in secondary information ... we can compress stories in a meaningful way' (Sherer 2011). An example from *Survivors* that illustrates this point is a sequence where counsellor Brian Hanstock states that some men have very rigid ideas of what a man's role is and what a woman's role is. Viewers see an image of a woman taking notes, which morphs into an image of a woman carrying shopping bags, which then morphs to an image of a woman carrying a baby and holding on to a young child. Although the visual content of these images are not described in Hanstock's testimony, they offer explicatory examples of the roles in which society is used to seeing women. In another scene, Hanstock explains how the media has a big impact on how men view women. At this point, viewers see animated images of a scantily clad female (a deliberate reference to the US marital sitcom *I Dream of Jeannie* [1965–70]), a close-up of male and female lips kissing, a woman proffering a plate of food towards the camera, a man pulling a woman towards him and kissing her, a man surrounded by bikini-clad women, and a close-up of a woman's feet as she undresses. None of these images are specifically mentioned by Hanstock, and yet their presence through animation offers the viewer guiding and corroborating examples of how the media can influence our perception of women, thus further illustrating the point that Hanstock is heard making.

Another unexpected audience response to *Survivors* was that I was held more responsible for the film's factual content than a live-action filmmaker might have been. In the film, I interview Dr Sandra Folzer, an expert in the field of domestic violence. She explains that:

> Women at either end of the educational status are more vulnerable to abuse. So if a woman has a lot of education, like I have a PhD, I'm more vulnerable than somebody who doesn't have as much education. So it's either women who are uneducated or very educated who are highly vulnerable.

Some audience members took issue with this statement and insisted on supporting references to prove the information's accuracy. When I shared this experience with live-action documentary filmmakers, they told me they are rarely challenged on information provided by experts interviewed in their films. I believe that may be due to the fact that in most live-action films we are presented with a photographic image of the expert on camera, along with a title card detailing their name and credentials. Although my interviewee was an expert in their field, the audience was not given that information in the manner described immediately above, and they were also not provided with a photographed face to associate with Folzer's statement. I, therefore, was the film's de facto 'expert' in some viewers' eyes, and it was my responsibility to defend the factual correctness of the information the film provided.

PERSONALISATION VS PERSUASION

In 2001, I made *A Conversation with Haris* (Figure 13.4), a six-minute, painting-on-glass animation based on an interview with Haris Alec, an eleven-year-old

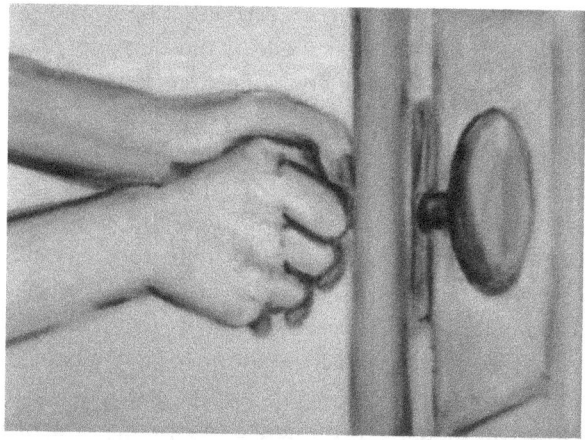

Figure 13.4 Still from *A Conversation with Haris*

Bosnian refugee living in the United States. As Haris describes his experiences during the war in Bosnia, his testimony is illustrated with painting-on-glass animation that depicts images representing his point of view. This film is both the most lauded *and* the most criticised work I have made. It was criticised for a perceived lack of objectivity, the use of 'leading' questions, and (for some observers) the supposedly manipulative use of a child's voice. This fact points back to important general issues and debates related to the subject of animated documentary cinema. Some viewers complain that animated documentaries are manipulative. They argue that the animator controls how the viewer interprets the documentary subject matter a given film depicts (although the same argument could be made about live-action documentaries). As a result of the perceived manipulation of images by the animator working in a documentary context, animation is sometimes regarded as propaganda, a reductive and imbalanced depiction of the animator's agenda. This hostile view may also be a result of animation's historical use within propaganda films. Furthermore, since animation is often viewed as a medium for children, it could be perceived an attempt to persuade or educate the impressionable and vulnerable.

I was surprised and shocked by these responses to *A Conversation with Haris*. This was the first time I had tackled a subject matter explicitly perceived as political. My intention was to make a film about peace: Can you forgive your enemy? Can you live together in peace after an atrocity? I was fascinated by Haris's experience and I was interested in his opinions. However, many people saw this film as an attempt to further a particular agenda. As a result, I now have a better understanding of how an audience's viewing experience can be shaped by their own already-existing opinions of the documentary subject matter a given film explores. When working with politically charged material, it is difficult to represent the protagonists' points of view without the added baggage of the audience's preconceived opinions influencing their own interpretation of the film. True, this is not unique to animation: but the use of animation to depict intimate experiences within a documentary narrative may challenge the audience's own personal viewpoint on the subject matter represented onscreen.

I originally intended *A Conversation with Haris* to be a much different film, one dealing with the experience of immigration to the United States. The plan was to interview Haris's parents about their struggle to make a new life for themselves and their son in the US after emigrating from Bosnia. Ultimately, however, I was logistically unable to conduct these interviews due to a language barrier: the parents spoke almost no English. It was at this point I discovered that Haris, although he had only lived in the US for six months, already had a strong grasp of the English language.

In my opinion, Haris's age contributed to his unfiltered honesty as a documentary interviewee. When asked what they would do if they could meet the person who murdered their relative, an adult may not have responded by saying, 'I would put them in jail'. When asked if he could become friends with a Serbian child, Haris replies, 'Maybe, because they are not responsible for the war'. *A Conversation with Haris* closes with Haris stating: 'Land isn't worth people'. These seemingly naïve, simple and honest statements carry universal truths that are rarely spoken by adults. Some critics have suggested that the film would have been more balanced if I had also interviewed a Serbian child. In my opinion, this juxtaposition would have done a great disservice to Haris and his own narrative. My goal as a filmmaker was to tell Haris's story. *A Conversation with Haris* is a simple portrait of a young boy who has experienced the tragedy of war. The film does not attempt to shed light on the Balkan conflict or the politics of the region.

Conclusion: *Truth Has Fallen*

As an animator, I am extremely interested in the relationship between sound and image. The use of literal or abstract animated imagery allows the animator to influence their viewer's comprehension of the subject matter that a given film depicts. The challenge I face as a filmmaker is to engage my viewer visually without distracting them from the content of the audio interview(s) around which many of my animated documentary works have been based. It is important to strike the right tone with the choice of cinematic technique, image and quality of the animation. If the image is too rich or beautiful, it can potentially distract from the audio: the filmmaker's choice of literal, abstract or metaphorical imagery directly affects how viewers understand the interview material that they hear. I liken it to two instruments harmonising: both the image and the sound need to work together to be successful. If one competes with the other, the combination becomes distracting and ineffective.

My most recent film is *Truth Has Fallen* (2013) (Figure 13.5), a one-hour documentary about three people convicted of murder and later proven innocent in a court of law. The film examines their cases and sheds light on weaknesses in the United States justice system. *Truth Has Fallen* combines audio documentary interviews, painting-on-glass animation and Errol Morris-style live-action re-enactments. Along with the personal stories of those wrongfully convicted, *Truth Has Fallen* exposes the causes of wrongful convictions more generally, such as the inaccuracy of eyewitness identification, the unreliability of 'snitch' testimony, forced confessions, inadequate resources for public defence attorneys, and the limitations of DNA evidence. Moral and

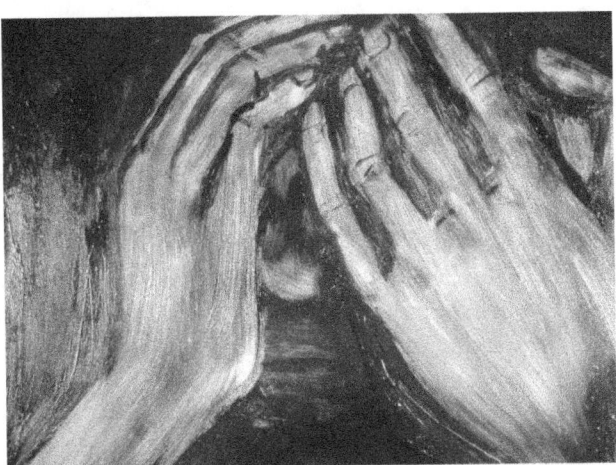

Figure 13.5 Still from *Truth Has Fallen*

legal issues regarding the death penalty are also examined. Experts advocate for relatively simple changes in the US justice system in order to reduce the rate of wrongful convictions. Potential changes include videotaped confessions and improved 'sequential' methods of eyewitness identification.

When I planned *Truth Has Fallen*, I decided to utilise animation when the wrongly convicted individuals were speaking and live action when 'experts' were interviewed. As a result, the wrongfully convicted characters would, hopefully, elicit more sympathy, whereas the scenes involving experts' testimony could be viewed with more detachment and acceptance of authority. *Truth Has Fallen* represents new territory for me as a filmmaker. I was concerned that audiences would be distracted by the combined use of animation and live action. I attempted to soften the transitions using layered animated textures, matching the animation to the live-action images when cutting between the two, and colour balancing the animation and live-action footage. Ten years in the making and employing more than 20,000 individual paintings, *Truth Has Fallen* represents my most ambitious work to date.

As a filmmaker, I hope to continue to push the boundaries of animation and documentary, exploring the effect of visual images on documentary narrative, and learning to enhance the viewer's experience of the personal interview mode that most of my films to date adopt. This hybrid form of filmmaking has great potential, and I will continue to work with subject matter involving human rights and social issues that I feel is important in contemporary society. Hopefully, the use of animation will impact on audiences and bring a greater understanding to personal stories that could be difficult to relate to in other mediums.

To conclude, there is great potential for animation in documentary. The medium of animation can elicit empathy, impact on audiences, illustrate documentary material unavailable on film, visualise concepts difficult to comprehend, demonstrate alternative points of view, and simplify and provide additional information through visual stylisation. The many advantages of animation discussed here may help to explain the growing use of animation in documentary films, which has become more prevalent in recent years. The success of the feature-length animated documentaries *Persepolis* (Vincent Paronnaud and Marjane Satrapi, 2007) and *Waltz with Bashir* has opened new doors for documentary animators. Mainstream live-action documentaries such as *Man on Wire* (James Marsh, 2008) have also embraced the use of animation. Documentary filmmakers such as Errol Morris, Morgan Spurlock and Michael Moore have frequently integrated animation into their films. Media-savvy audiences understand that animation is just one more tool documentary filmmakers can use to illustrate their stories. Most people familiar with media understand that all filmmaking is subjective, and the 'truthfulness' or accuracy of any given film is less dependent on its production medium and more dependent on the filmmaker's representation of the subject matter that film depicts.

Bibliography

A Conversation with Haris, film, directed by Sheila M. Sofian. USA: Sofafilms, 2001.
Faith & Patience, film, directed by Sheila M. Sofian. USA: CalArts, 1990.
McCloud, Scott (1994), *Understanding Comics: The Invisible Art*, New York: William Morrow.
Mangia!, film, directed by Sheila Sofian. USA: Rhode Island School of Design, 1985.
NPR (2008), 'Filmmaker reflects on 'Waltz With Bashir' reception', *npr.org*, 26 December, <http://www.npr.org/templates/story/story.php?storyId=98723606> (last accessed 23 October 2016).
Sherer, Daniela (2011), 'The legacy and future of anima-doc: Paul and Sandra Fierlinger's workshop at DocAviv 2011', 18 May, <http://www.midnighteast.com/mag/?p=12474> (last accessed 23 October 2016).
Survivors, film, directed by Sheila M. Sofian. USA: 1997.
Truth Has Fallen, film, directed by Sheila M. Sofian. USA: 2013.
Yadin, Orly (2003), 'But is it documentary?', <http://www.yadinproductions.com/but_is_it_documentary.htm> (last accessed 23 October 2016).

Index

Note: references to documentaries are followed by director and date; page references to images are in *italics*.

9/11 attacks, 100

A is for Autism (Webb, 1992), 26, 211–12, 214, 217
Aardman Animation, 195–6
Adorno, Theodor, 8, 144, 147–8, 150
  and machinery, 151–3
  and shuddering image, 152–4
Adventures of Prince Achmed, The (Reiniger, 1926), 145
aesthetic comportment, 151–3
Aesthetic Theory (Adorno), 151–2
aestheticisation, 108, 112–13, 117–19, 123
Age of Stupid, The (Armstrong, 2009), 209
Alberro, Alex, 50
Alec, Haris, 230–2
Allen, Woody, 17
Alphen, Ernst van, 136
Altair (Klahr, 1994), 8, 145–7, 149, 153
Ameisenhaufen, Peter, 17
American College of Surgeons (ACS), 34
Andersartig (Stein-Schomburg, 2011), 6, 75–7, 78, 80, 82
anima (soul), 40
Animated Introduction to Cancer Biology (Cancerquest, 2013), 48
Animated Realities conference, 2, 3, 10
Aoun, Steven, 180–1, 183
apartheid, 7, 129, 130
Arcades Project (Benjamin), 147
archive, 7, 111, 113–15, 117, 118–19, 120, 121, 123
Armstrong, Franny, 209
atavism, 70, 73–5
attraction, 6, 41, 73, 85–6, 87, 89, 90
Ausgewanderten, Die (Sebald), 17

Avatar (Cameron, 2009), 58
avatars, 25, 158
Avni, Shira, 210, 211, 217

Baader-Meinhof group, 165, 168
Babbage, Charles, 97–8
Bairstow, Jonathan, 193, 201–2
Barnouw, Erik, 21
Bateson, Gregory, 73
Bayeux Tapestry, 18
Beattie, Zac, 191, 192, 193, 194, 196, 197, 204
  and animation, 201–2
  and characters, 198, 199–200
believability, 1, 4, 50, 62
Belles histoires de l'oncle Paul, Les (comic), 18
Bendor, Roy, 173, 176
Benjamin, Walter, 84, 130, 140–1
  Arcades Project, 147
  and language, 137–8
  and translation, 208–9, 218
  'Work of Art in the Age of Mechanical Reproduction, The', 150
Bennett, Bruce, 93
Berger, John, 135–6
Bissonnette, Sylvie, 43
Blair Witch Project, The (Myrick/Sánchez, 1999), 18
bodily identification, 55–6
Bollacker, Kurt D., 118–19, 120
Bosnia, 230–1
Brain, Robert, 87
Bray, John Randolph, 40, 45n2
Bray Pictures Corporation, 40
Bray Studios, 5, 33, 38
Bridson, Robert, 91

Brooks, Richard, 108
Broomfield, Nick, 107
Brussel Winter (Wellens, 2009), 23
Buchan, Suzanne, 3
Bus (photo, Hondius), 17

Caldwell, John, 86
Cameron, James, 93–4
Camouflage (Hodgson, 2002), 194
Capino, Jose B., 55–6
Capote, Truman, 17, 108–9, 110
Carey, Joe, 197
categorisation, 21–7, 69, 143–4
CG-animation *see* computer graphics
character design, 178–9, 193–4, 195–7, 198–201, 227
Children of the Holocaust, The (Fettle Animation, 2014), 6, 78–80, 82
Cholodenko, Alan, 107
cinema-vérité, 22
Clough, Brian, 114
Cna'an, Carmi, 174, 177, 178, 179, 180, 184
Colbert Report, The (TV show), 53
Coles, Robert, 111, 214
collaborative frame, 206–7, 209–19
comics, 18, 169, 208
Communication: A Film Lesson in 'General Science' (unknown, 1927), 33, 34–5
computer graphics, 6–7, 25, 59, 78, 87–8, 97–9
Congo, 115
consumerism, 147
contemporaneity, 50–2, 61–3
Conversation with Haris, A (Sofian, 2001), 230–2
Corner, John, 80–1
Cosmopolitan (magazine), 8, 146, 149
Cosmos: A Personal Voyage (TV show), 42
Cosmos: A Spacetime Odyssey (TV show), 42
Crafton, Donald, 34
Crary, Jonathan, 56
Creature Comforts (Aardman, 1989; 2003–5), 195
Critical Theory, 147–8
Cubitt, Sean, 85, 88
Culture Industry, The (Adorno), 150
Curtis, Scott, 37
cut-out animation, 145, 153, 160

Daily Show, The (TV show), 53
Damned United, The (novel, Peace), 114
Darger, Henry, 197
data, 59, 87–8, 89–94, 118–19

Dayag, Ronny, 174, 177, 179, 184
Death of Stalinism in Bohemia, The (Svankmajer, 1991), 110
Decker, Christoph, 22–3
deGrasse Tyson, Neil, 42
DelGaudio, Sybil, 36, 91
Derrida, Jacques, 136, 138
DeVry, Herman, 33
dialogue, 210, 211
digital photography, 56–8, 84–5
digital technology, 50–1, 154–5
Disney, Walt, 45n2, 196
Disney studio, 40, 91, 110, 150
Do-it-yourself (Ledune, 2007), 20, 24, 27
Doane, Mary Ann, 32, 99–100
docufiction, 17–18
document, 143–5, 147, 217
'Documentary Uncertainty' (Steyerl), 154
DOK Leipzig Festival, 107
domestic violence, 226–8, 230
doubled up (Moore, 2004), 207
Down's syndrome, 211
drawing, 129–30, 131–9, 140, 141, 180, 201
Drawings for Projection (Kentridge), 7, 129–30, 133, 138
Driessen, Kees, 209

Eastman Kodak, 34
Edison, Thomas, 31
educational media, 5, 31–44
edutainment, 40–1
Ehrlich, Nea, 5–6
Einstein Theory of Relativity, The (Fleischer, 1923), 24, 33, 36, 38, 39–40, 41, 42
Eldritch, Tristan, 74
Electric Kool-Aid Acid Test, The (book, Wolfe), 17
Ellis, John, 73
enactment, 72
Engram Sepals (Klahr, 2000), 146
ER (TV show), 18
ethics, 9, 55, 210
ethnography, 210, 211, 218
Everything Will Be OK (Hertzfeldt, 2006), 202
evocation, 77–8, 206
expertise, 6–7, 85, 87, 89, 90–102
expository mode, 22, 23–4, 27, 28n1, 71
Eyeful of Sound, An (Moore, 2010), 9, 77–8, 207, 212–15, 217

factuality, 1, 15–18, 20
Fainaru, Dan, 181
Faith & Patience (Sofian, 1990), 224–5

Family, The (TV show), 193
fantasmatic, 69–70, 72, 73
Fauna Secreta (exhibition, 1999), 17
Felix in Exile (Kentridge, 1994), 7, 129–41
fiction, 15–18, 20
fidelity, 208
Fierlinger, Paul, 229
Fifty-Three Stations of the Tōkaidō, The (woodcut, Hiroshige), 18
Fine, Gary Alan, 214
Flaherty, Robert J., 15, 17
Flash animation, 176, 178, 201
Fleischer brothers, 5, 33, 41, 42
Folman, Ari, 8–9, 26, 27, 172, 173, 183
    and freedom, 222
    and Hodgson, 195
    and memory, 174–7, 181–2
    and style, 179
Folzer, Sandra, 230
Fontcuberta, Joan, 17
Fore, Steve, 72–3, 77
formats, 21
Formiguera, Pere, 17
Forty Hearts (Kuleshov, 1930), 32
Frankfurt School, 147–8
Frenkel, Shmuel, 174, 184

games, 21, 25
Gaycken, Oliver, 31
Gendi, Bishoy, 197
Gertie the Dinosaur (McCay, 1914), 42
Globalised Slavery: How Big Supermarkets are Selling Prawns in Supply Chain Fed by Slave Labour (*Guardian*, 2014), 54, 55
Glynne, Andy, 81–2
Going Equipped (Lord, 1990), 196
Grand Theft Auto (game), 25
Grandpa Looked Like William Powell (Levy, 2010), 112
Green Wave, The (Ahadi, 2010), 110
Grierson, John, 53, 70–1, 110–11
Groys, Boris, 51
Guantánamo Bay: The Hunger Strikes (*Guardian*, 2013), 54, 55
Guardian (newspaper), 6, 54–5
Gunning, Tom, 73, 85, 89
Gurevitch, Leon, 6–7

Hadashi no Gen (Masaki, 1983), 18
Hertzfeldt, Don, 202
Herzog, Werner, 107
Hetrick, Nicholas, 175–6, 186
Hiroshima, 18

history, 139–41, 144
Hobermann, James, 145
Hodgson, Jonathan, 9
Holocaust, 18–19, 78–80
Hondius, Juul, 16–17
Honess Roe, Annabelle, 15, 31, 69, 81, 84, 206
    Animated Documentary, 3
    and mimetic substitution, 78, 80, 209
    and re-enactment, 70, 73, 77, 82
Horkheimer, Max, 147–8
horror films, 152
How we Breathe (Bray, 1920), 33, 38, 39, 44
Human Energy (Chevron, 2008), 100, 102, *103*
Human Planet (TV show), 86
hybrid documentary, 16–18, 53

Ihde, Don, 97
In Cold Blood (Brooks, 1967), 108
In Cold Blood (Capote), 17, 108–9, 110
information, 58–9
Inner Life of the Cell, The (Liebler, 2006), 42–3
instructional films, 32–4, 37–9, 40, 42–4, 91, 110
interactivity, 21
International Documentary Festival, 107
interviews, 158–63, 164, 178–9
    and Sofian, 226–8
    and *The Trouble with Love and Sex*, 198, 201
Iraq, 57, 155
Ivanov-Vano, Ivan, 32, 40

Jag Varen Vinnare (I Was a Winner) (Odell, 2016), 158
Johannesburg – 2nd Greatest City after Paris (Kentridge, 1989), 130
Johns Hopkins Science Review, The (TV show), 91
journalism, 5–6, 17, 108; *see also* news
Jurassic Park (Spielberg, 1993), 86
justice system, 232–3

Kahana, Jonathan, 72
Kapel, Martin, 79
Kaye, Nick, 116, 117–19
Kentridge, William, 7, 129–41
Khmer Rouge, 20
Kielland disaster, 121–3
King, Rodney, 57
Kino-Nedelya (Vertov, 1918), 32
Klahr, Lewis, 8, 143, 145–7, 149, 153
Klee, Paul, 133

Koch, Gertrud, 148
Koresky, Michael, 183
Kovalyov, Igor, 110
Kraaikamp, Nanette, 7–8
Kracauer, Siegfried, 147, 148–9, 151
Kröcher, Norbert, 165–9
Kuleshov, Lev, 32
Kurz, Howard, 53

Lai, Jimmy, 53
Landesman, Ohad, 173, 176
Landreth, Chris, 27, 72, 163, 164, 195
Lange, Dorothea, 108
Larkin, Ryan, 23, 27
Lassiter, Luke Eric, 210, 211, 216, 218–19
Learned by Heart (Rimminen/Takala, 2007), 114–15, 116
Lebanon War *see* Waltz with Bashir
Lee, Hyunseok, 119
Lefèvre, Pascal, 5
Leijon, Anna-Greta, 165, 168, 169
Leone, Sergio, 169
Leslie, Esther, 150, 152
Leventhal, J. F., 37
Levi-Strauss, David, 112
Levy, David, 112
Liebler, John, 43
Lies (Odell, 2008), 158–9, 161–4
Life (TV show), 86
Life, Animated (Williams, 2016), 48
Lind, Maria, 51
Lip Synch (Aardman, 1989–90), 196
Loop (Moore, 2016), 219
Loose Change (Avery, 2005), 100, *101*
Lord, Peter, 196
Lusitania, HMS, 18, 91–3
Lye, Len, 111

McCay, Winsor, 18, 42, 91–2
McCloud, Scott, 208, 229
McElhatten, Mark, 145
machine vision, 59–60
Machinima, 25
McLaren, Norman, 106–7, 111, 120
Mad Men (TV show), 145
MAGI (Mathematical Applications Group Incorporated), 90
Magritte, René, 73
Man on Wire (Marsh, 2008), 234
Mangia! (Sofian, 1985), 10, 223–4
Manovich, Lev, 59, 84–5, 99, 103n1
Many Lives and Secret Sorrows of Josephine B., The (Gulland), 17

Marbot Eine Biographie (Hildesheimer), 17
Martinelli, Lawrence Thomas, 8
Marx, Karl, 149
Matisse, Henri, 135
Mechanics of the Brain, The (Pudovkin, 1926), 35–6, 40
medical film, 34–40
Memoirs of the Blind: The Self-Portrait and the Other Ruins (Derrida), 136
memory, 9, 75, 119
  and Kentridge, 129–30, 134–5, 136, 141
  and *Waltz with Bashir*, 173–8, 179, 181–5
Merrill, Guy, 154
Meunier, Jean-Pierre, 81
Mihailova, Mihaela, 5
mimetic, 56–8, 60–1, 138
  and substitution, 77–8, 80, 209
Mirsky, Nick, 193, 194, 201–2
mockumentary, 17–18, 20, 53
Mole, Malcolm, 197
Molotov Alva and his Search for the Creator (Gayeton, 2007), 25
Monceaux, Dan, 116, 117
Moore, Michael, 234
Moore, Samantha, 9, 77
Morris, Errol, 232, 234
Mosse, Richard, 115–16
Mostafaei, Mohammed, 54
movement, 39–40, 133–4, 148–9
Murray, Jonathan, 8–9
My Trip to Liberty City (Munroe, 2003), 25
Myhre, Aslak Sira, 121, 123

Nanook of the North (Flaherty, 1922), 15, 17
narrative, 85–6, 139–40
nature documentaries, 15
neoliberalism, 154
Never Like the First Time! (Odell, 2006), 22, 24, 158–61
Never Mind the Bollocks (album), 118
news, 49, 52–6
Next Media Animation (NMA), 6, 52, 53–4
Nichols, Bill, 5, 22–7, 28n1, 207–8, 209
  and re-enactment, 69–70, 71–3, 75, 78
Nightclub (Hodgson, 1983), 193–4
Norling, J. A., 37, 40
Norway, 121–3
Nowhere Line: Voices from Manus Island (Schrank, 2015), 48

objectivity, 107, 108, 116–17
observational mode, 22
Odell, Jonas, 8, 22, 158–71

oil industry, 121–3
Oliver, Martin, 197
'On the Concept of History' (Benjamin), 140–1
One Iranian Lawyer's Fight to Save Juveniles from Execution (*Guardian*, 2012), 54
One Mind (Lee, 2011), 119
Order Electrus, The (Kaayk, 2005), 15
Osborne, Peter, 50
Ostherr, Kirsten, 34, 44
Our Friend the Atom (Luske, 1957), 20, 23, 27
Out of Sight (Moore, 2015), 9, 214, *216*, 217, 218

Paget, Derek, 15–16
painting-on-glass animation, 223–4, 230–1
Parn, Priit, 110
Paronnaud, Vincent, 21, 47, 143, 195, 234
participatory mode, 22, 24–5
Pas de Deux (McLaren, 1967), 106
Passer Passer (Morton, 2013), 23
Peace, David, 114
Peaslee, Robert Moses, 174
Pedagogical Sketchbook (Klee), 133
Pelling, Joseph, 197
penetrative gaze, 34–6, 206
perception, 19, 116, 117, 135
performative mode, 22, 25–7
Persepolis (Satrapi/Paronnaud, 2007), 21, 47, 143, 195, 234
Pettifogger, The (Klahr, 2011), 145
phantom limb syndrome, 211, *212*, 213, 215, 216
photography, 16–17, 34, 47–8, 49
    and journalism, 108
    and Kracauer, 148–9
    and mimetic, 56–8, 60–1
    and Mosse, 115
    and news, 55
    and rotoscoping, 225
    see also digital photography
photorealism, 98
Picture News (magazine), 18
pitching, 192–3, 194
Planet Earth (TV show), 86
Plantinga, Carl, 21, 71
Pliny the Elder, 134
Podmore, Guy, 52
poetic mode, 22, 23
Polonsky, David, 179
pop culture, 145, 146, 166
pornography, 55–6
Posner, Miriam, 34

Powell, Colin, 57
Powers of Ten (Eames, 1977), 86
production techniques, 19
propaganda, 18, 50, 110, 115, 231
prosopagnosia, 213, 215, 216
Proud, Laurie J., 201
Pudovkin, Vsevolod, 35

Rancière, Jacques, 119–21, 122–3
re-enactment, 6, 8, 69, 70–5, 77–82
    and Odell, 161, 165, 166
reality, 1, 2, 4, 15, 47–8
    and digital technology, 154–5
recollection, 75, 82
reflexive mode, 22–3
Reid, Jamie, 118
Rein-Buskila, Boaz, 173–4, 175–6, 177, 178, 179, 184
Reiniger, Lotte, 145
Renov, Michael, 21–2, 32
reportage, 49
repositories, 116–17, 121, 123
Rimminen, Marjut, 114–15, 116
Ritchin, Fred, 57
Rogoff, Ruth, 78, 79
Rosenthal, Alan, 106
rotoscoping, 37, 45n2, 207, 225
running time, 20–1
Russia, 32
Ryan, Marie-Laure, 16
Ryan (Landreth, 2004), 20, 27, 72–3, 163, 164

Sabra massacre, 174–5, 176–8, 182, 184–5
Satrapi, Marjane, 18, 21, 47, 143, 195, 234
Schermer, Gerben, 107
Schlunke, Katrina, 180, 181, 186
science, 33–44, 90–1
screens, 60
Second World War, 75, 114–15; *see also* Holocaust
Seitler, Dana, 74–5
Serviss, Garrett P., 41
Seven Wise Dwarfs (Disney, 1941), 51
Sex Pistols, 118
Shatila massacre, 174–5, 176–8, 182, 184–5
Shift in Perception, A (Monceaux, 2006), 116, 117
Silence (Bringas/Yadin, 1998), 18–19
silent era, 24, 31–44
simulation, 85, 87–92, 94, 97–100, 102
Sinking of the Lusitania*, The* (McCay, 1918), 18, 24, 91–3, 94
sites, 114, 116–17, 121, 123

Smith, Terry, 50
Smithson, Robert, 116
Snow White (Disney, 1937), 51
Sobchack, Vivian, 55, 81
Sofian, Sheila, 10, 180–1
sound, 32, 207–8
South Africa, 7, 129, 130–2
special effects, 85
spectacle, 6–7, 85, 86, 88–98, 102
spectralisation, 75, 77
Spine, The (Landreth, 2009), 195
Spurlock, Morgan, 234
Star Wreck (Torssonen, 1992–2005), 209
Starevich, Vladislav, 40
Steger, Chrisoph, 197
Steyerl, Hito, 51, 154–5
  'Documentary Uncertainty', 154
Stiassny, Melanie, 74
stop-frame animation, 145–6
Story of Coal, The (unknown, 1920), 33, 36
style, 19–20, 38
  and *Andersartig*, 75
  and Folman, 178–9
  and Hodgson, 193–6
  and Odell, 122, 160–3, 165–71
Sukharebsky, Lazar, 32, 37
surveillance, 58
Survivors (Sofian, 1997), 226–30
synaesthesia, 77, 212–13, 214–15

Takala, Palvi, 114–15, 116
Telotte, Jay, 91
temporality, 80–1
Theory of Film (Kracauer), 148–9, 151
Titanic (Cameron, 1997), 93–4, *95*, *96*, 98, 99–100
TomoNews, 52, 53–4
tonality, 20
Torssonen, Samuel, 209
training films, 45n2, 110
translation, 208–9, 218
transparency, 210, 221–2
Treachery of Images, The (Magritte), 73
Trip to the Moon, A (Méliès, 1902), 41
Trouble with Love and Sex, The (Hodgson, 2011), 9, 24, 191–204

truth claims, 20
Truth Has Fallen (Sofian, 2013), 10, 232–3
Tussilago (Odell, 2010), 158–9, 165–70
Tying Your Own Shoes (Avni, 2009), 211, 214, 217

US justice system, 232–3

Van Drunen, Eric, 107
Van Riper, A. Bowdoin, 40
Vertov, Dziga, 32
Viel, Alain, 43
Viljoen, Jeanne-Marie, 177
Virilio, Paul, 59
virtualisation of culture, 60–1
vision, 32–3
visual effects, 85, 86–7, 90–2, 97
Vladermersky, Nag, 192
voice, 21, 23–4, 32, 198
voice-over, 32, 158, 160, 167–8

Waal, Edmund de, 113, 114
Walking (Larkin, 1968), 23
Walking with Dinosaurs (TV show), 78, 86
Walt Disney Studios/Walt Disney Corporation, 40, 91, 110, 150
Waltz with Bashir (Folman, 2008), 8–9, 20, 21, 26, 27, 47, 143, 172–87, 222
  and Hodgson, 195
  and live-action footage, 180–1, 182, 185–6
Ward, Jamie, 212
Ward, Paul, 3, 6, 32
Warstat, Andrew, 8
Webb, Tim, 26, 124n2, 211–12, 217
Wells, Brian, 207
Wells, Paul, 7, 34, 84, 98, 206
White, Hayden, 110, 116, 139, 140
Winston, Brian, 70–1
Wise, Norton, 87
witnessing, 81–2
Wolgemuth, Hildegard, 75

Yadin, Orly, 18, 222

Zelig (Allen, 1983), 17

EU representative:
Easy Access System Europe
Mustamäe tee 50, 10621 Tallinn, Estonia
Gpsr.requests@easproject.com